M000012963

"A. J. Swoboda is the kind of pastor, writer, and theologian today's church desperately needs. Capable and engaging, he has a bent toward vulnerability that is simply honest and beautifully human. And it's this human touch that makes *The Dusty Ones* a unique, well-rooted, and spiritually nourishing work. If you've experienced your own desert seasons or periods of wandering, this book is Swoboda's gift to you."

—**Seth Haines**, author of *Coming Clean: A Story of Faith*

"A. J. Swoboda is one of the most authentic, profound, and kind people I know. In *The Dusty Ones*, this pastor-theologian-friend tackles the topic of wandering, reminding us, for example, of the mistakes Israel made while journeying to the promised land. Yet, the wandering in *The Dusty Ones* is about more than physical years in the desert; it's about the wilderness and yearning of the heart. Reading *The Dusty Ones* is like talking to a friend who's wandering alongside us on this road of truth, which is "always bumpy, but always worthwhile." A. J. draws from St. Augustine, noting how we were made for God and that our hearts are restless until they find rest in him. And that's okay. After all, on the road of life, you will get dusty."

—**Cornelia Becker Seigneur**, author of *WriterMom Tales* and *West Linn* (Images of America series); founding director of Faith & Culture Writers Conference

"At a time when the Christian faith is all too easily reduced to a neatly designed journey to a glorious destination, A. J. Swoboda brings us back to the ancient theme of wandering. Drawing on the stories of biblical characters and historical figures, Swoboda reminds us that God has always walked alongside his people, even through life's more arduous terrain: God walks with wanderers and speaks to wandering hearts. A. J.'s words are like water in our own wilderness, reminding us that God is forging a deep work in our desert spaces. May we all have the courage to live as one of the dusty ones."

—**Jo Saxton**, chair of the board of 3D Movements; speaker and author

"In *The Dusty Ones*, pastor and seminary professor A. J. Swoboda wrestles with the paradox of faith: on the road toward perfection in Christ, we can only move forward by acknowledging how far we have to go. This book is a must read for anyone concerned by how far our personal and cultural wanderings have separated us from God. Kudos to Swoboda for addressing a difficult issue with honesty and grace."

—**Matthew Sleeth**, director of *Blessed Earth*; author of *24/6*

"A. J. is one of those writers you discover as if he were a new indie band that you can't shut up about. That's how I feel after reading his work. I connect with both his writing style and his message. And I want to tell everyone about it, and especially about *The Dusty Ones*. This notion of wandering has given words and hope to my own struggle as a 'professional pastor,' where it sometimes seems dangerous to not know where I'm at or where I'm going. Read this book on your journey toward Christ, and be encouraged that we're all just broken wanderers in search of Jesus."

—David Lomas, pastor of Reality San Francisco;
author of *The Truest Thing about You*

"My favorite line in the whole hymnal comes from that old standard 'Come Thou Fount': 'Prone to wander, Lord I feel it.' And oh, do I feel it, and so does my friend A. J. Swoboda. In *The Dusty Ones*, A. J. explores that inclination and, with his characteristic wit, charm, and insight, takes the reader through a personal journey of wandering along the pilgrim way of those who follow after Christ."

—R. Anderson Campbell, assistant professor of Christian studies
at George Fox University

"A. J. Swoboda uses timely illustrations to discuss a timeless biblical trope: wandering. Using topics ranging from Freud to farming, he tackles the richness and agony of the twenty-first-century Christian journey with refreshing transparency. Along the way, he invites followers of Jesus to join in the grand pilgrimage and reminds us of Tolkien's great truth that 'not all those who wander are lost.'"

—Leah Payne, professor of theology and cultural studies
at George Fox Evangelical Seminary

"I know A. J. Swoboda well. I know that his theology is historically grounded and profoundly biblical. I also know that, because of his gifts as a preacher, he has a rare ability to communicate that theology creatively and comprehensibly. This book is about the spiritual discipline of wandering, that mysterious counterpoint to the discipline of rootedness. As the evangelical community leans into a blossoming array of spiritual practices, it will look to books like this one."

—Dan Brunner, professor of church history
at George Fox Evangelical Seminary;
coauthor of *Introducing Evangelical Ecotheology*

THE
DUSTY
ONES

WHY WANDERING
DEEPENS YOUR FAITH

A. J. SWOBODA

BakerBooks

a division of Baker Publishing Group
Grand Rapids, Michigan

© 2016 by A. J. Swoboda

Published by Baker Books
a division of Baker Publishing Group
P.O. Box 6287, Grand Rapids, MI 49516-6287
www.bakerbooks.com

Printed in the United States of America

All rights reserved. No part of this publication may be reproduced, stored in a retrieval system, or transmitted in any form or by any means—for example, electronic, photocopy, recording—without the prior written permission of the publisher. The only exception is brief quotations in printed reviews.

Library of Congress Cataloging-in-Publication Data
Names: Swoboda, A. J., 1981–
Title: The dusty ones : why wandering deepens your faith / A. J. Swoboda.
Description: Grand Rapids, MI : Baker Books, 2016. | Includes bibliographical references.
Identifiers: LCCN 2015037189 | ISBN 9780801016974 (pbk.)
Subjects: LCSH: Spiritual life—Christianity. | Christian life. | Nomads—Miscellanea.
Classification: LCC BV4501.3 .S975 2016 | DDC 248.4/6—dc23 LC record available at http://
    lccn.loc.gov/2015037189

Unless otherwise noted, Scripture quotations are from the Holy Bible, New International Version®. NIV®. Copyright © 1973, 1978, 1984, 2011 by Biblica, Inc.™ Used by permission of Zondervan. All rights reserved worldwide. www.zondervan.com

Scripture quotations labeled ESV are from The Holy Bible, English Standard Version® (ESV®), copyright © 2001 by Crossway, a publishing ministry of Good News Publishers. Used by permission. All rights reserved. ESV Text Edition: 2011

Scripture quotations labeled KJV are from the King James Version of the Bible.

Scripture quotations labeled MSG are from The Message by Eugene H. Peterson, copyright © 1993, 1994, 1995, 2000, 2001, 2002. Used by permission of NavPress Publishing Group. All rights reserved.

Published in association with literary agent David Van Diest of D. C. Jacobson & Associates, an Author Management Company, www.dc-jacobson.com.

16 17 18 19 20 21 22   7 6 5 4 3 2 1

In keeping with biblical principles of creation stewardship, Baker Publishing Group advocates the responsible use of our natural resources. As a member of the Green Press Initiative, our company uses recycled paper when possible. The text paper of this book is composed in part of post-consumer waste.

For Mom.
When possible,
send the gazpacho recipe.
It's to die for.
With love,
Your son

CONTENTS

PREFACE

There is a story passed down about the Amish and the quilts they make. The Amish—a people who have over the centuries honed and mastered the art of quilt making—have a knack for creating by hand the most elaborate, intricate, beautiful, and seemingly perfect quilts one could possibly imagine. But one finds a surprise with each work of art. Although the quilts have an appearance of perfection to the glancing eye, the Amish intentionally do something unique to their quilts that even a machine would never think to do. That is, somewhere, if one examines long enough, a keen observer will find *one* blatant mistake hidden in the piece of art—a bad stitch, an off color, a loose end. Whatever the mistake may be, don't be confused: that mistake is intentional. The mistake is because of God. Whenever the Amish make a quilt, they always leave one mistake in the otherwise perfect work. The reason is simple: *only God is allowed to be perfect.*

In what's to come, I have a certain person in mind. E. B. White once said that a writer is fueled mostly by their "childish belief that everything he thinks about, everything that happens to him, is of general interest."[1] Writing is an arrogant business fueled by a class of people who assume we all care what they have to say. I admit my arrogance. In my own hubris, I guess, I've come to believe there are a few out there who need to hear what I have to say about wandering. I don't write because I've somehow arrived or have attained perfection. Rather, I write because wandering toward God is done better with others.

This book is written *by* a wanderer *for* wanderers. To be sure, a book about Christian wandering isn't a book for everyone, particularly for people who think they've already managed to iron out every little wrinkle in their picture-perfect faith. I'm aware there remain religious folk who see such a state of perfection as their current state of being. I don't share in that kind of arrogance. Candidly, those who assume they've already arrived at the shores of glory should return this book— it will disappoint them greatly. Get a refund. It will do you no good. Because the intended audience of this book remains quite specific indeed: people who still have some major ironing to do.

By stating this at the onset, I'm admitting that this book isn't a book for just *anyone*. As I survey the scene, there remain countless kinds of audiences that a writer like myself may feel at liberty to address: I could speak to libertarians, or mothers, or people with glaucoma. And certainly each of these audiences will bring to their reading a unique set of questions and sensibilities and experiences that must be attended to. I once read of a Christian missionary who, showing up by horseback to a town, would first visit the local library. There, he would look around to see what books the locals had been checking out. He knew he could bring answers *only* if he knew the townspeople's questions. That's the writer's task, as tedious as it may be. For writers with their wits about them learn early on to anticipate such questions, sensibilities, and experiences in the formation of their writing. Writers mustn't solely busy themselves with what they themselves bring to the book; rather, they must give surplus attention to what the *readers* bring to the book. Writers must learn how to read their audience before they can offer them a single word.

In what follows, I've attempted to do just that. In short, an author, when she or he sets out to write, does best to pay keen attention to identifying the very particular person. Certainly, a good many overly ambitious writers hamstring themselves at the onset by writing a book to some vague, generalized audience in their minds—a book for *anyone* and *everyone* and *all* in between. Still, I have yet to find that to be an advantageous means of getting ideas across. And this doesn't even begin to account for the fact that few (if any) writers have in their bones a message that everyone wants, or needs, to hear. I have in mind that specific person who deeply desires to know God and embody the ways of Jesus, and who passionately seeks to breathe the life of God's Spirit but finds themselves losing their way from time to time. If that's you, let's be friends for the next few chapters. Let's wander together.

I write with the wanderer in mind. Why? I *was* a wanderer. I *am* a wanderer. Until glory, I *will continue being* a wanderer. I'm still pressing on. Perhaps you are in the same boat. George Bernard Shaw once joked that the statistics on death were staggering—one hundred out of one hundred will die. I think there is ample evidence to suggest that the same statistics are at work among people and their wandering along the geography of faith. If we aren't wandering now, we will be soon; if we are wandering now, we probably will be tomorrow as well. And to our surprise, the Bible, a book for wanderers, anticipates all the questions we may bring to it.

The Bible has the most general audience in mind ever: *everyone, of every time, everywhere*. That's ambitious, isn't it? Unlike any merely human literary invention, the Bible is the only book in history, I'd argue, that actually addresses the exact needs of its readers with perfect clarity across time, space, and culture. For in all history, no book has had the ability to speak to as many audiences in as many times and places as the Bible. An admission: I've got little if anything by way of experience or advice to address the libertarian, or mother, or person with glaucoma, let alone the subniche market of libertarian mothers with glaucoma. But the Bible speaks to them all. Why? Because *all* wander.

The Bible is a book for wanderers who are willing to acknowledge that they wander. While I think everyone wanders, only the brave are willing to admit it. The Bible is a wanderer's textbook—it is filled with them, and it always has them in mind. My hope is that this book will illuminate that for my reader. The truth remains that the way of

Jesus, the pursuit of God, and the life of God's Spirit are far more often a bumpy dirt road than a paved highway. Discipleship is dusty. This is, one would think, why we find that the earliest Christians self-identified as "the way," not "the arrived." Over the bumps and through the woods—and there will be lots of them—they journeyed toward God and his kingdom through the pain and death and persecution it would awaken. As God would have it, it is even in the getting lost that happens from time to time that one learns something beautiful and true and good. Jesus came to seek and save the lost, good news for the lot of us. I once read that the late novelist Walker Percy had said that the most important difference between people is between those for whom life is a quest and those for whom it is not.[2] This is for the quester, the seeker, the sojourner, and the wanderer; basically, anyone still doing the *er*—those along "the way." You are just the wanderer God has always had in mind.

And all those "mistakes" on the quilt of our lives are really just part of the fabric of God's grace and perfection.

Remember, wanderer: only God is allowed to be perfect.

Acknowledgments

This book is dedicated to my loving mother, Robyn Lee Wilkerson. As a new parent, I am slowly beginning to wrap my head around why it was that you always wept at my off-key choir recitals, came and watched my plays multiple times during their two-week runs, and put even my worst artistic creations on our fridge with great pride. I get it now. Also, I'm beginning to comprehend the nuanced difficulties of parental life. Thank you for the love you showered upon me—despite the difficulties you faced, and even when I never saw or thanked you for it. I will eternally be proud to call myself your son.

My wife, Quinn, read this manuscript. More than that, she breathed a life into it no one else could. I love you, Swoboda. Also, my four-year-old boy Elliot perpetually asked to wrestle with me throughout the writing of this text as I sat at the wooden table in our living room. Although he's never won any of our matches, I can foresee the day when he will. Take it easy, boy, I'm becoming a fragile old man.

My church, Theophilus, gave me a pulpit, time, and space to write and iron these ideas out, all without firing me. Thanks for that. I hope and pray that these words bring hope and life to you as we learn to wander together the dusty road of discipleship with Jesus.

To the blogger (whose name escapes me to this day) whom I met at the Faith & Culture Writers Conference at Warner Pacific College in Portland who cried with joy as she reflected with me over the five bloggers she gets to write for. You reminded me why I write. Kudos to you for being a person of integrity.

The baristas at Dapper and Wise Coffee on Division and 32nd let me hang out a lot even when I didn't buy anything. Thanks Grahm, Rachel, Morgan, and Seth. You make a good joe, friends.

I must acknowledge Chad Allen and Terry Glaspey, who both rightly rejected my first book proposals at their respective publishing houses. A no is hard. But a no is often necessary. A no makes you go inside and ask big questions. Chad and Terry said no, but they found a way to believe in me at the same time—a hard balance indeed. It was in their nos that I learned to press in and grow as a writer; and for that I am eternally grateful. Rejection, one discovers, is often God's way of giving us a rain check. Also, Bob Hosack and James Korsmo at Baker Books are gifts from God. Thanks for sharing your skills to make this project a reality.

I also wish to acknowledge the voices of the saints who have wandered before me. Every year I read the writings of one of these saints. This year, I poured myself into the writings of St. Augustine of the fourth century. Augustine, I read everything you wrote and kept finding myself struggling through the same things you did. It feels like we are friends now. I wish you wrote more, even though some of your stuff got kind of weird. I guess I'll have time to ask you about those things later on.

Father, Son, Spirit—you are the death of my death. I am hidden in you. And all the glory is yours.

Wandering and Lamaze

This is what the Lord says about this people: "They greatly love to wander."

Jeremiah 14:10

This book is about *wandering*.

It wouldn't be fair to say I make my final approach to the topic of wandering out of nowhere or free of baggage. I've checked some heavy bags for the flight. Indeed, I bring myself with a cargo load of luggage from my own story that's sure to affect the way I reflect upon it. For one, I approach the topic of wandering as a preacher. Preaching is my trade, my vocation, and my life's passion. Preaching is also my paycheck—it puts food on my family's table. But my preaching isn't entirely driven by economic forces alone. I preach because I am a Christian. And as a Christian who has done a considerable amount of wandering, I can't shut up about the topic. Standing there week after week in front of the people of God with an open Bible, I've come to

1

observe that every follower of Jesus does a good deal of wandering from Sunday to Sunday.

Preaching is a powerful yet mysterious act akin—in the ancient words of Jeremiah the prophet—to having fire in the bones (Jer. 20:9). Preaching is what I do even if at times I don't fully comprehend it. "I don't understand preaching," once quipped the famed preacher Ian Pitt Watson, "but I believe in it deeply."[1] The same goes for wandering: I don't get it, but I really believe in it. As a preacher, I preach the centrality of wandering as the pathway to Christian maturity. There is simply no alternate route. Yet while this sacred act of preaching is itself powerful beyond all imagination, the one who undertakes it is bound to be a broken vessel just like all the ancients were. Every one of God's honest preachers has a limp. We can't trust the ones who claim total perfection.

Candid or not about this fact in the public arena, a preacher wanders like the rest of us behind that safe, thick, hardened, wooden fortress we call a pulpit. Note: *pulpit* comes from the Latin word *pulpitum*, a "stage." The contemporary church has done a masterful job of treating the pulpit as just that: a stage where we preachers put on our act, donning masks of piety that cover over our real, true selves. But Jesus didn't come that we'd cake over reality with a good performance, did he? Is God's kingdom a kingdom of actors? I don't believe so. Over the years, I've come to appreciate preachers who are up front about their own brokenness, imperfections, and foibles; I've also tried to emulate them as well as possible. I suppose you could say my preaching palate has changed. In times past, I was drawn nearest to those preachers who presented every matter of faith as a series of either/or options—black *or* white, in *or* out, this *or* that. I was enamored with sermons that drew lines in the sand of reality. After years of subsequent reflection, I've come to believe it was the "*or*" I lusted for. Everything just feels safer and more concise when you live under the *or*. The *or* makes things more straightforward and clear-cut, almost surgical. I would have said I liked preachers who offered nothing but black-and-white certainty—particularly, certainty about their own clarities and perfections and opinions on every matter under the religious sun.

Not so much anymore. I've come to believe that truth—at least truth in the Christian sense—is far more complex than a series of either/or options drawn from the perfect life of a pristine preacher. Truth, in Christianity, has wrinkles. I am the first to admit this may arouse uncomfortable reactions within many of us, but it is the very basis of historic Christianity. At the moment Jesus declared that he was "the way and the truth and the life" (John 14:6), he was refusing to offer the same old, tired evaluation on the nature of truth popular in the minds of his contemporaries. Rather, Jesus was offering a fresh, novel way of understanding truth that nobody had considered up to that point. Truth, for Jesus, wasn't something "out there" written in the stars or drawn from the philosophers or revealed from the observation of rolled dice or chicken entrails or clear crystal balls. He—Jesus, the God-man—was *himself* truth. Truth was a person, a person just like you and me. Jesus lived a real human life through and through. Yet before being nailed to the wood of the cross, Jesus's skin would be daily pierced by the tiny slivers common to a carpenter. Jesus, this truth, would have had the wrinkles of a first-century Jewish peasant carpenter who worked rough wood under the sun day in and day out. *He* was truth. Such a way of thinking about truth must not be abandoned for the Christian. For it remains a dangerous temptation to misconceive truth as a series of propositions or statements or ideas trapped in the air-tight coffin of human words. Rather, truth is Jesus Christ—God in human flesh who walked around and had wrinkles. Jesus Christ walked, and talked, and ate, and drank, and burped. He was Emmanuel—God *with* us.

This wrinkly truth, Jesus Christ himself, is the sole content of a preacher. A preacher isn't to be a peddler of opinions, a purveyor of politics, or a door-to-door salesman of religion. A preacher, above all, is tasked with bearing the fact of Christ's *euangelion*, good news, salvation—what we call the gospel, which is the end of opinion, politics, and religion. Indeed, preaching is the crucifixion of *all* opinion and novelty on the cross of Jesus. Nor is a preacher a preacher of theology, something we've more often than not come to abuse as a kind of philosophical zoo to cage the wildness of the Creator. No. The highest calling of a preacher is not primarily to lay forth this doctrinal opinion *or* that doctrinal opinion, this denomination *or* that denomination, this view of the end times *or* that view of the end times. The preacher's task is instead the bold proclamation that each of our lives is being built upon either Christ *or* anything else. There's no middle ground. Rock *or* sand, Jesus said—there are no other foundations upon which to build.

The most effective pulpits aren't sturdy wood; they are broken people. The most effective pulpit is the wobbly, unsturdy, wandering life of a saved sinner who has denied and been welcomed back three times like the apostle Peter. Preaching Jesus is best done from behind the pulpit of our wandering, broken lives. The most succinct definition of preaching I've come across is that preaching is "truth mediated through personality."[2] What this suggests is that preaching Jesus Christ must be done through the *actual* life, story, struggles, wanderings, and personality of the preacher who proclaims him. I agree wholeheartedly. Amen and amen. The preacher will soon find that the best platform from which to preach this gospel is an authentic life of a real person who is struggling to live it out. Anything else just won't do.

Still, more often than not, we don't actually allow preachers the space or freedom to teach from the textbook of their wandering experiences. We demand preachers, sadly, to be perfected celebrities above all else. The pressures we've put on the backs of people who help lead us in our faith have reached ludicrous proportions. We expect preachers to be saviors, not servants; lawyers, not witnesses; CEOs, not shepherds. And it's because we want celebrities, not real broken servants. Celebrities bring in the cash. And so pastors have become celebrities, by and large, trading in their holy role of being "a guide on the side" to serving as "a sage on the stage." We've *idolized* them. Don't misread me, please. Celebrity Christianity is *everybody's* fault, not just that of a few. It's as much our fault for propping someone up as it is theirs for allowing it to happen.

To protect our idolized expectations of the celebrity pastor, we give them only so much space to speak about their wandering experiences. As I recently toured our nation's churches and universities sharing my own story of a struggle with alcohol that I had recounted in my book *A Glorious Dark*, I found time and again people caught off guard that my struggle came to a head just three and a half years ago. They couldn't seem to believe it. People couldn't conceive of it—it happened such a short time ago *while* I was a pastor, *while* I taught at their seminary, *while* I was writing books on Christian faith. This is a sign of the problem at hand—it is like we are permitted to struggle and wander in our faith so long as it happened decades ago. But if it happened just three short years ago, or last year, or last week, well, that's just inappropriate. We've created a church culture where we are permitted to struggle and wander in the far distant past but not in the dangerous present. It's our statute of limitations on wandering; it is acceptable as long as it happened a long time ago.

In short, we ordain only the safe parts of our preachers. The dangerous parts—their struggles, wanderings, doubts, and sin—we kindly ask them to leave in the parking lot. And, in turn, we do this to each other. Why? Because we're addicted to certainty, not faith. It shouldn't be surprising that pastors are burning out, walking away from ministry, or leaving faith altogether. We've systematically replaced Jesus Christ with certainty machines—a class of preachers expected to be perfect. The pressure of the world has been put on them by the church to be perfect and assertive, and by golly, to never ever wander. Those in my trade have become certainty machines, pumping out a steady stream of safe truths meeting the emerging market of consumer Christians who yearn for cliché more than Christ. And pastors are leaving because of it. Most pastors don't leave the ministry because they're rejecting God; they leave the ministry so they can find God again. I no longer believe being a certainty machine is preaching in the primal, or biblical, sense. You can only preach as you are. Preaching is "truth mediated through personality"—the life of Jesus as told through someone's *actual* and *real* efforts at following him. We must relearn to discuss Jesus as we are actually experiencing him, not as we would ideally like to be experiencing him if we were perfect and never wandered.

Again, the world has only seen one Preacher who could boast of perfection. Light shines best through cracks. For that matter, cracks are the only way light can actually get through. Indeed, the truth of Jesus shines brightest through something that's broken. Following Jesus is hard for the simple fact that Jesus is wild, not caged. Jesus, one finds, isn't tame. He isn't docile. God is feral, wild. This wildness of truth can't be trapped in words or phrases or idioms; truth is the very wild God in Jesus. Yes, words can convey and convince and help bring people to the truth in the way a train can get us somewhere. But a train shouldn't be confused with a destination. Or you might think of it this way: if it fits in a spoon, it can't be the ocean. God can't be contained by the boxes of our words, ideas, or theologies. Truth goes beyond all that stuff. God's bigness is always bigger than our spoons.

In the words of Norm from the movie *Jaws*, truth, like a shark, always necessitates "a bigger boat."

A god completely understood isn't God at all. This is why so many people are increasingly dissatisfied with the preaching they find in churches today. We will never be satisfied by safe truths being ladled into our broken hearts through "flawless" preachers. The last thing we need is safe truth through safe people. We need the wild, dangerous truth of Jesus, which is wild and dangerous through the shattered lives of saved sinners. Preaching involves a preacher drowning in the furious grace of God and inviting a bunch of people to watch. Preaching shouldn't always fit in the spoon of the American mind; it must embody the full-bodied idea that truth is always bigger than the sermon itself. I'm a connoisseur of what I call "rough preaching," that is, preaching that tells it as it is. I've learned the most about following Jesus from those with the greatest failures. Perhaps the greatest commentary any of us has for preaching the good news is our own textbook of mistakes, which helps us exegete our own failures that quietly whisper the eternal mysteries of grace. Maybe the best preaching advice I've ever received is this: if we preach to the perfect, nobody will listen; if we preach to the imperfect, we won't be able to keep folks away.

Again, years ago it would have been different. I would have told you that I liked everything to be straight and ironed out during Sunday's sermon. But things have changed, and not because I'm opposed to eloquence, or allergic to explanation, or don't believe in absolute truth. On the contrary—I believe in clarity and explanation and truth with the best of them. I just happen to think that a wrinkle in a sermon is a preacher's most eloquent way to actually hold high the beautiful truth about Jesus Christ. We can preach about one of two things: Jesus or anything else. Our witness should always say, "Hey, Jesus is the way. *Really.* But let me assure you: this preacher of Jesus has got quite a ways to go. Jesus is the way. I'm not."

One might conclude this is precisely why Paul wrote that we preach "not ourselves" (2 Cor. 4:5). It strikes me that preaching self seems to have been a temptation in the early church. To lie to the world from our stage and say we've arrived in our faith is to preach *ourselves* and not Jesus. For any of us to stand up and pontificate—wrinkle- and wandering-free—that we don't continue to wander on our way toward Jesus is to lie. We all wander. We all know we wander. But to stand up and hold ourselves up as having arrived is, in the end, to preach the wrong savior. When our message about Jesus comes off *too* slick or too much about ourselves, it's more about the preacher than anything else. When I am the hero in every story I tell, I am most certainly proclaiming a false gospel. If people see me more than Jesus, I need to get off the stage.

That's why I like preachers who talk about their wandering—they become the palate for the beauty of God's love. They're honest. They don't have to make things up. This is what you get—me and my silly life drowning in the grace and mercy and love of Jesus Christ. And I guess this is as good a time as any to say it: the best preachers wander, stumble, and scratch their way through the life of faith like the rest of us but keep going. They aren't any different. Only the best preachers are willing to talk about it. True preaching isn't reality modification. False preaching sweeps reality under the rug of the "sermon."

Love the preachers who talk about their sin. Be skeptical of everyone else.

—⚹—

St. Paul the preacher was the first to publicly confess in his own writings to other Christians of his sin and struggle in his ongoing journey to follow Jesus. In so doing, Paul sought to illustrate the contours of his own spiritual weakness with such vivid conviction and passion and repetition that one is left wondering if perhaps he is actually inviting us to model the same. For example, we find in 1 Timothy 1:15 Paul giving himself the title "the chief of sinners." In Ephesians 3:8, Paul refers to himself as "less than the least of all the Lord's people." He doesn't end there—the language with which he opts to discuss his own internal strife and struggle regarding his flesh's love for sin in Romans 7 leaves the reader clearly aware that this was a man who experienced internal anguish and toil.

Paul was aware he hadn't yet arrived. His brilliance lies in the fact that he never tries to fake it. "I press on toward the goal," Paul writes to the church in Philippi (Phil. 3:14). Paul's words here—most likely written as he was strapped by the ankles to a burly Roman guard while under arrest for treason against the Roman state—are reflective of a unique attitude toward the Christian life that one might find surprising from its apostle par excellence. Paul wrote of pressing on from within a prison cell where he awaited trial for his subversive crimes against the Roman state. What would lead him to pen such words? It seems almost silly to consider that someone could "press on" toward anything as they sit in a prison cell, doesn't it? But Paul, ironically, was apparently advancing even though he was chained to a burly soldier. There's nowhere to go while in prison, is there? How can someone "press on" when they're so stuck in life?

One can tell Paul never "preached himself." Rather, Paul preached Jesus from the dank prison cell of his own life. Yet, in so doing, he relentlessly talked about hope and joy and grace as though he wasn't disturbed by his plight. I've often wondered if he was simply out of touch with his dire situation. I appreciate Rodney Reeves's words about this hope in his book *Spirituality according to Paul*, in which he discusses Paul's optimism in such toilsome situations. Reeves writes that either Paul had something otherworldly going on in his heart that could allow him to be this free and optimistic and hopeful in a prison cell, or, frankly, Paul was in complete denial.[3] Which is often how hope comes across—it can easily be interpreted as denial. Hope isn't denial; hope is taking in your real-life situation and finding God smack-dab in the midst of it. Hope is not denying reality. Paul wasn't in denial. Paul had hope that in his wandering, he would someday arrive. He could "press on" in a prison cell because a physical wall was no match for his gospel freedom. The prisoner Paul knew that his journey was not really a physical one, such as going from one city to another or from a room downstairs to a room upstairs. Paul "pressed on" not physically but spiritually.

What's similarly striking is Paul's incessant humility. Paul was pressing on to take hold of Jesus Christ within a prison cell he believed couldn't hinder him. Paul seems aptly prepared to admit that he hadn't arrived yet, that he had quite a way to go. "Not that . . . I have already arrived at my goal," writes Paul, "but I press on to take hold of that for which Christ Jesus took hold of me" (Phil. 3:12). As has been discovered by countless of the faithful who have gone before us, Christian maturity isn't ever ironed out this side of heaven. This is not to discount the many brave souls who have striven for arrival, of course, an attempt that should be applauded. But to claim it has happened is nothing short of hubris. Perfection, for the Christian, comes at death and no sooner.

Paul humbly admitted he still had a long way to go. This kind of humility should be part of the Christ follower's comprehensive outlook on life. That Christians derive their outlook on their life not primarily from science, Hollywood, or politics but from an executed carpenter should make for great humility. And, like Paul, Christians understand that their journey isn't merely physical; rather, it is a journey toward the all-encompassing love in Jesus Christ that can take place while being strapped to a Roman soldier. We haven't arrived at our destination yet. In our own journeys, we should seek to embody the same "press on" attitude of Paul in his dank prison cell.

Truth be told, the best growing and maturing one will ever experience will most likely take place in contexts that are very similar to prison cells. A Christian grows most where they are stuck. A family can be our prison cell. Work can be our chains. Having children can be holding us down. Our prison cells are different, but we all have them. And it is the wrong way of thinking about things to assume we can only experience breakthrough or growth when we can escape those things. Quite the opposite: Paul spoke, ironically, of being free in a prison. It turns out that freedom in Christ does not necessarily include freedom spatially, or relationally, or vocationally. More often than not, we will blossom most in those stuck places we'd never want to be or dreamed we'd be in in the first place. This process will require first and foremost that we cease trying to escape our prisonish environments for better lands where we think real growth can happen. Maturity can only happen right here, right now. Christian growth has never been dependent upon ideal environments or perfect conditions. Prison cells have always done the trick. And so, like Paul, we must learn to embrace following Jesus precisely where we are. Nowhere else will do. We will never be able to follow Jesus anywhere else other than here and now.

I guess what I'm saying is that there is no "somewhere else" in God's kingdom. That the kingdom is "at hand" means it is right here, right now.

Christian spirituality is a slow train that must inevitably stop at every little Podunk town in our life—nothing can be skipped over. Our efforts to learn to love and follow Jesus must meander through wherever we are as we wander our way through life. "Not all those who wander are lost," wrote Tolkien in *The Lord of the Rings*. Tolkien, brilliant literary genius that he was, certainly knew that wandering and lostness aren't exactly the same thing. One can wander and be right on track, just as being in the desert doesn't necessarily mean we are deserted. Wandering and discipleship go hand in hand for the Christian. Keep in mind that Paul preached and wrote and ministered as one who claimed to have not yet arrived. That should say something to us. Paul spoke openly of his sin, struggles, and lack of ministerial success—he was a prototype wandering preacher who embraced the wrinkles of his own life as a platform for the truth of the good news. And he was the apostle who brought the gospel message to the gentile people. Not bad, when you think about it. If Paul still pressed on in his wanderings, then we probably need to as well.

We press on down the bumpy path, as it were, along the roughest of terrains. This path is straight but never smooth. This may be sad news for any of us who were duped into following an easy Jesus who bears an easy kingdom. Jesus clearly left the hard stuff about the kingdom of God in place—he asked people to abandon possessions, leave families, and give of themselves with wild abandon. His kingdom wasn't easy.[4] The Japanese theologian Kosuke Koyama once wrote that Americans love the cross; or, rather, they love the cross so long as it's conveniently handed to them in the size of a lunch pail and comes equipped with an easy-grip handle.[5] Christ's kingdom wasn't convenient. I guess those easy-grip, convenient preacher types have the right to make the cross comfy, but the kind that rings true is the kind that comes with all the slivers it would have originally had. One knows truth has been discovered when it hurts but leaves you wanting more. The road of truth is painful but worthwhile. It is always bumpy but always worth it.

Like John the Baptist, I wish to "make straight paths" (Matt. 3:3). But there's a big difference between straight and smooth. The path is straight, indeed, but it is almost never smooth.

Wandering, like the truth, can't be fully explained. It can only be experienced. Wandering is, as I like to say, a sermon without an explanation. I can talk about it from the pulpit all Sunday long until I am blue in the face. But you have to do it to really get it. Don't misread what I am saying. It's not a sermon without a *point*. Rather, it's a sermon without an *explanation*. The best points of truth are often best unexplained, and an explanation can deter from that point. It's kind of like the book of Job. I've read the book countless times. Job, in his suffering, has friends telling him *why* he is suffering. And, as I read it, the point of Job is simple: when encountering someone suffering, silence is golden. In terms of suffering, explanation can't replace experience.

There's a subtle danger in writing about wandering like I'm giving a lecture or something. Because talking about the wandering that comes with faith is a lot like taking a Lamaze class. You can talk about how to deliver a child, but every mother who has given birth would be hesitant to say that a class is adequate preparation for the actual birth process. Lamaze and having a child are not the same thing. And neither are talking about the terrain of faith and walking the terrain of faith the same. Along that path, Christians will wander. No one else can do it for them. There are no surrogates. And there certainly are no anesthesiologists to make it more comfortable. One must walk the painful wandering road themselves. We each must "press on" over the painful terrain of the Christian walk.

As the saying goes, the map is not the territory. Having a map and walking the terrain are very different experiences. All of faith is like that. The same goes for suffering. I can go on and on about the experience of suffering and pain. But *why* God lets it happen so much, I've got no answer. I can't tell you why we wander, but I can tell you it's unshakably important. You can try to walk around it. I've seen people fake it and make it look like they aren't wandering. But they are wandering, and we can't avoid it, and all the while we have no explanation for the *why* of it all. Wandering is a mystery—a beautiful mystery. And while mysteries might not always make sense, you can't live life without them.

Mystery is the fresh air that keeps the faithful alive.

—⁂—

A cursory reading of the Bible reveals wandering on just about every page.

The sacred writings of Scripture are a wanderer's handbook, of sorts—an honest and loving friend for the wandering journey. One biblical scholar, in a conversation with me, referred to the Bible as a "wandering text," a term I've come to believe bears great weight and truth. The Bible is written for wanderers *by* wanderers. I appreciate the words of Jill Bledsoe, who captures the Bible's ability to speak to humans in the storms of wandering. "The storms in my life," Bledsoe writes, "have become workshops where I can practice my faith in God's sovereignty."[6] The people of Scripture weathered great storms. And we must not imagine that the Bible is a book of hollow, ethereal, dry, intellectualized information about a distant god who himself never weathered storms. The Bible does not merely offer musings on life; the Bible points to Life himself. In a time where most have bought into the lie that the key to Christian formation is information, the last thing we need is data. We need models, sponsors, and Sherpas who have walked the high ridge of faith before us. And if the Bible is the inspired Word of God for the Christian community, we can expect to have to go through what the ancients went through.

Given the amount of wandering the ancients did, wandering must not be caricatured as some extracurricular activity that only a few immature Christians do in their seasonal times of sin or disobedience. That would assume that good, churchgoing Christians never wander. Or that wandering would never happen for the person who is squarely in the will of God. But I want to suggest otherwise: wandering will be, at times, the very will of God the Father. Any caricature of this won't do. Christian wandering isn't extra credit; it's often the class itself. The topsy-turvy walk of the Christian faith eventually leads through a series of peaks and valleys and wanderings on the way to the destination.

Wandering is my sweet spot, one might say. As I've done in the past, I could have drawn on a wide array of subjects to talk about the Christian life. Yet my own experience of wandering is the deepest well. In writing on wandering I've consistently found myself surprised at how snug and well fitting the topic feels. And my own familiarity with wandering gave me such a deep well to draw from that writing about it was done with a relative ease I've been unaccustomed to in writing. This is an anomaly for someone like myself, who, lacking a degree in creative writing or literature, has not found the skills pertinent to good writing easy to come by. Whatever formal training I do have—in biblical studies and theology—is not known for producing excellent creative writers. Often, biblical scholars and theologians write with the creative juices akin to a bag of oats. This isn't all that bad, for a good theologian or biblical scholar isn't paid to be innovative. Christian history has a word for creative theologians: heretics.

"Creative theology" books are not the kind I often like to buy. In my humble opinion, far too many Christian writers are attempting to write *creative* theology that seeks to create new truths. But there is no *new* truth out there. Creative theology, I've long held, is an oxymoron. The task of a theologian such as myself is faithfulness to the message that has been received, not provoking ingenuity as though I bear to the world something God hasn't already gone on record about. The Christian faith, wrote Vincent of Lérins, is "what you have received, not what you have thought up; a matter not of ingenuity, but of doctrine; not of private acquisition, but of public tradition; a matter brought to you, not put forth by you, in which you must be not the author but the guardian, not the founder but the sharer, not the leader, but the follower."[7] God is after faithfulness, not ingenuity. Christians are like used-car salesmen—we faithfully pass on that which was not ours in the first place. We are proclaimers of Someone we never owned.

The truth is not from within ourselves; rather, it comes from without. We're not, as many in our time have come to believe they are, orthodox unto ourselves. Truth is beyond us, not from within us. The minute I'm my own basis for truth, no one can teach me a thing. And so my task here is creative writing, not creative *theology*. Even my writing isn't all that creative. As with any writer, whatever words and order of words I opt to use I've picked up from or been taught by others along the way. The turn of the phrase, the timely adjective, the terse connective sentence—none of these are unique to me. And in the same way, my message isn't mine. As a theologian, I pass on that which I have received from others, who received from others, who received from others from the deep well of Christianity. As a Christ follower, the gift of faith was passed on to me from that ancient generation. It is not my own, nor will it ever be.

Authentic Christianity is found precisely by that person who throws all caution to the wind and chooses to borrow the life, death, resurrection, and teachings of Jesus in their entirety as a pattern and model for their own life. In that way, true Christianity is plagiarized. Christian faith isn't yours, nor can you make it your own. Faith is a gift, not a do-it-yourself project. All that one can effectively do is receive it the way a bull rider receives the straps on their beast and goes along for the ride. In receiving faith as a gift, Paul says, we are freed from any temptation to "boast" (Eph. 2:8–9). To boast is mostly to treat as a wage what has been received as a gift. A boastful follower of Jesus has become so self-referential that they believe truth can be made up, or chosen, for oneself.

To be sure, the very notion—quite popular in our time—of one seeking to "find a faith of one's own" fundamentally distinct or separate from one's parents' or the tradition of Christian history is unfounded in both the biblical narrative and Christianity. All such inventive faith is boasting. Boasting is a self-created faith. Such a faith can't be received as a gift because it came from within. Some, again, might even call such faith heresy. I don't know if I'd disagree. "For what I received I passed on to you," wrote the great St. Paul to the church in Corinth (1 Cor. 15:3). Faith is a gift from first to last, not a do-it-yourself project for the morally and spiritually capable. Paul was so keenly *against* the idea of faith as ingenuity or personal creation or fitted to the personal individual that he railed against it at just about any moment he could. Whatever faith you have, he would say, is a faith that has been given to you as a gift from someone else. And a good deal of our wandering is probably owed to the fact that we are trying to re-create something that we can't re-create.

This is so freeing. For when we actually take the time to examine the lives and stories of those faithful who have gone before us, we will quickly find that those great heroes all wandered in their faith. In short, your bumbling about in faith like a drunken, lost sailor in a foreign

15

land is anything but new or ingenious. Our faith struggles aren't all that inventive. Others have wandered too. And, again, this is freeing, for you have a long family tree of wanderers who learned how to do it mightily and faithfully. Just like these heroes, I've wandered a lot. And I feel exceedingly confident that I am qualified to write a book about the disciplines and realities of wandering.

Those closest to me, it turns out, probably would agree. I know at least my publisher did. After proposing to the acquisitions editors a book on the disciplines of wandering, I was taken aback at their warm receptivity. Carefully reading through the confirmation they sent to me, I was particularly drawn to one line from a note the editorial board had written. It was vague but extraordinarily telling. It read, "As an editorial board, we feel this is a topic you will have a lot to say about."

With such editorial praise that I associate, perhaps unfairly, with a publisher that I'm sure just wished I'd get writing rather than talking about writing, I found myself a little wounded at first. Do people see me as a wanderer? Do I have a reputation? At any rate, while initially offended, I chose to sit in that sentence for a few moments only to find it began to feel more and more comfortable by the minute. I am a gifted wanderer! I wander with gusto! I have something to say about this topic! And I'm proud of it. I guess I have become known as a leading scholar on the topic of Christian wandering.

It's not *if* you wander. It's *how* you wander.

Still, few seem to feel as though they have the skills necessary to wander the Christian journey of life for the long haul. Let me be emphatically clear in my point here: we all wander, but few of us do it with gusto. Wandering is a lost Christian art. We are all expected to put on our good face and pretend we know what we are doing. But more often than not, we put our heads on our pillows at night knowing we've tricked the world into thinking something that is not true. Wandering isn't mere happenstance or only a result of a mistake. And the question of our reason for our wandering doesn't always have an easy answer. One might hope that the strongest predictor of why we wander would be because of our sin, but it is not. Wandering is more complex than that. Wandering should be seen as a discipline. We *learn* how to wander with God the way we learn to love and hope and think rightly. Up to this juncture, I've written three books for a more general audience on Christian spirituality. The first, a book titled *Messy*, sought to conceptualize faith and life as an ongoing process that entails a good deal of struggle, challenge, and, as the title suggests, messes. The second, *A Glorious Dark*, included a section I called "Awkward Saturday," which considered Saturday of Holy Week. What follows, I am coming to believe, is shaping up to be a culminating book in the process.

As I began writing this book, I encountered a surprise. Few, if any, books on the topic of wandering are available to the popular market. In fact, it's worse than that. I've discovered that Christians almost feel the obligation to be dismissive of thinking through the theme of wandering out of some fear that all wandering is the result of sin or a lack of faith or a sign that they are off kilter—all assumptions, I've come to believe, that are off kilter themselves. This moratorium on the topic of wandering is unfortunate given the amount of wandering we all do on a daily basis in our attempts to follow Jesus. I find this to be a lamentable neglect in our conversations about Christian spirituality.

What I offer is this: a description of and hopeful vision for the wandering Christian experience. So much of faith wanders. This kind of experience is reflected in the words of the psalmist: "I walk through the valley of the shadow of death" (Ps. 23:4 KJV). The Christian walk often goes off the safe road. I want to invite you, my reader, to embrace this dangerous road of wandering so that you might find the life you most seek—life in Jesus. The church's approach toward spirituality has been riddled for years with trying to get us as far away from the wandering experience as possible. Too much of our church language, advice, and even preaching is about minimizing the amount of wandering we will do. This book doesn't do that. I intentionally sidestep age-old tricks to avoid the life of wandering. We must face it head-on. Wandering will happen whether we like it or not. Wandering is fundamental, even necessary, to the journey.

Christianity has never been nor will it ever be a movement of those who have found an easy path of walking *around* the shadow of death. Real Christianity, in its truest sense, is found in going *through* the valley of the shadow of death. There, in the dark shadows, will we find life—true and eternal life.

Mom's Gazpacho

The spiritual journey is not a career or success story. It is a series of
humiliations of the false self that becomes more and more profound.

Thomas Long, *The Human Condition*

What does the image of *wandering* provoke in your mind's eye?

Wandering is a surprising image to pay attention to in the Bible.
Similar to a good many other biblical images, wandering is an image
that's repeated with relentless consistency throughout the Good Book.
But even such a relentlessly consistent image inspired by the Holy Spirit
does not guarantee that the reader will appropriately interpret the image
in the way it was intended—we've become masters at misunderstand-
ing biblical images. That an image is inspired doesn't necessarily ensure its proper understanding or use by the user. It takes great work to
unpack the meaning of a message. To help us not make some common

mistake about the image of wandering as has often been done, let's settle ourselves on this image for a bit in order to give it some clarity.

Like words, images are easy to misinterpret. Because words have the power to create *and* kill, as the book of Proverbs tells us, one must be careful to use words appropriately and accurately. Images have a similar power. Therefore, they demand the same caution. A good reader of Scripture should learn not only the skill set necessary for reading but also the skills to see, and hear, and smell the Bible. The Bible is multisensory, inviting all of our senses to partake in its beautiful bounty and provocative artistry. It isn't surprising, then, that Jesus's nearly unending torrent of parables about fishermen, coins, and sheep constantly confused, confounded, and frustrated his audience and disciples alike. If words can be confusing, images can be even more confusing. If we are going to speak about the image of wandering, we must be willing to interpret the image with great care.

Despite the ever-present danger of a misinterpreted image, Scripture continuously uses images from everyday life to make its point. In fact, the Bible opts to utilize images more than anything to convey deep spiritual realities—it speaks of invisible realities by discussing visible ones. Broadly, there are many ways the Bible uses images. I'd like to draw your attention to a few. For one, the Bible will often take two entirely conflicting or contradictory images and awkwardly place them side by side to make a point about God or reality. In short, it uses seeming contradiction to reveal a more full-bodied understanding of reality. Consider for a moment the prophet Hosea's approach to images. In one chapter (Hosea 5), God is simultaneously described by the author as a "moth"—that little fluttery, graceful, soft creature that can't be touched without being killed—and a "lion"—that fierce, strong, powerful king of the forest.

Hosea describes God as a "moth lion."

How could God have the attributes or qualities of both a lion *and* a moth? Of course, Hosea was after a big point in making this very odd connection between two very different creatures. What was he after? In harmony with so many other sections of Scripture, the paradoxical nature of God is being highlighted. God is as tender as a moth yet as fierce as a lion. God isn't a mean old curmudgeon in heaven doling out rules. Nor is he a kind "bro" who softly loves and admires everything we do. God is at one moment a fierce lover, a graceful judge, and a demanding friend. Paul would later give great clarity to this idea when he wrote to the church in Rome: "Consider therefore the kindness *and* sternness of God" (Rom. 11:22, emphasis added). The minute we see God merely as a moth, he becomes in our minds a fluttery, sentimental, personal-improvement coach who never says anything hard. And the minute he is solely a lion, he is furiously unapproachable.

That is why God is a moth lion. He is simultaneously graceful and fierce.

Along the same lines, consider that the apostle Peter opted to speak of Christians as "living stones" (1 Pet. 2:5). Such phraseology is akin, I would argue, to speaking of a peaceful tornado or a gentle star implosion. Peter's point was that Christians have both a life and a strength available to them unlike anything else in all of creation. They're alive like a baby but strong like a rock. Again, this is the same exact lesson that's being offered by John the apostle when he speaks of Jesus as "grace and truth" who came into the world (John 1:14). John not only begins his Gospel offering these conflicting images, but he will draw an illustration of this in the following chapter. In chapter 2, John tells us Jesus first goes to a wedding and turns water into wine. Then he enters the temple with whips to drive out the animals and turn the tables over. Now, I suspect many may think that such passages reveal a Jesus with an acute personality disorder. But Jesus didn't suffer this way. John, like any good preacher, was making a point utilizing images to convey that Jesus was both graceful and truthful at the same time. John was illustrating the "grace and truth" of Jesus Christ. Jesus is the one who brings grace (new wine) into the world but also bears truth (a whip) in the world. And John's way of telling us this is that Jesus bears both wine and whips, grace and truth, simultaneously.

These images reveal a spiritual world of conflict, or paradox. Similar to these conflicting images, the Christian life is a life of holy conflict.

21

The Christian life reflects a knowledge and respect of this paradoxical nature. Isn't it telling that in the New Testament, a Christian is called both "God's child" (Gal. 4:7) and "Christ's slave" (1 Cor. 7:22)? We are at once welcomed into the family and invited to a life of radical obedience. In the same way, Christ followers are both followers and finders. They have found eternal life, but they will need to take a lifetime to learn all about it.

To embrace the cross is to embrace a life at odds with itself. A Christian invites personal conflict as a pathway to Christlikeness in the same way the cross consisted of two boards going against one another that eventually became the scene of the salvation of the world. This conflicting-image approach that I've described is one of many ways the Bible plays with images to convey a point.

A second way that the Bible uses images is through offering the same image or picture in two very different ways. For example, the image of sexual intercourse is a mixed bag in the Bible. Sex, as we will see, is used in many ways to get across different points. For one, it is used in the Song of Songs as an elongated, play-by-play love scene depicting two people on their first night together. It is downright provocative, erotic, and sensual.

Of course the Bible isn't using erotica for mere erotica's sake. The point of the Song of Songs is that God loves his people in a way similar to a husband's physical love for his wife. The Song of Songs is an inside look at *how* God loves his people, and his love looks very intimate. But the use of the erotic image is so diverse that we find it used in the book of James to describe sin. James describes sin as a sex act. "But one is tempted by one's own desire, being lured and enticed by it," writes James, "then, when that desire has conceived, it gives birth to sin, and that sin, when it is fully grown, gives birth to death" (James 1:14–15). James would tell us that sin is the process of someone being lured into the act of sex. What is the point? Sex, as an image, is used in the Bible to describe both intimacy with the living God and walking away from God in sinful desire.

Enter the image of wandering. It turns out that the image of wandering is likewise a conflicting image. In short, the image of wandering cannot be seen as either merely good or merely bad, angelic or demonic. Wandering is both a virtue *and* a vice in the Bible—it is good *and* bad. The people of God wander in the Bible as a result of sin and disobedience. However, the people of God wander in the Bible as an act of obedience and being in the will of God. It is neither one nor the other. Now, I am keenly aware that one might critique my use of wandering as a thematic framework for this book by pointing out that the image of wandering is almost exclusively used in negative terms in the Bible. I concede this point. Generally speaking, wandering does have many negative elements in the Bible. However, this is not universally the case. The image of wandering is used both negatively and positively. Wandering is what happens when God's people sin, worship another god, and lose track of who they are and where they are going. But wandering can simultaneously be a by-product of following God.

Consider the words of the author of the book of Hebrews, who wrote of the ancient saints,

> And what more shall I say? I do not have time to tell about Gideon, Barak, Samson and Jephthah, about David and Samuel and the prophets, who through faith conquered kingdoms, administered justice, and gained what was promised; who shut the mouths of lions, quenched the fury of the flames, and escaped the edge of the sword; whose weakness was turned to strength; and who became powerful in battle and routed foreign armies. Women received back their dead, raised to life again. There were others who were tortured, refusing to be released so that they might gain an even better resurrection. Some faced jeers and flogging, and even chains and imprisonment. They were put to death by stoning; they were sawed in two; they were killed by the sword. They went about in sheepskins and goatskins, destitute, persecuted and mistreated—the world was not worthy of them. They *wandered* in deserts and mountains, living in caves and in holes in the ground. (Heb. 11:32–38, emphasis added)

That phrase "not worthy of them" should hit hard on the floor of our spirits. The ancient faithful were of a different league; the world was not worthy of them. And because of it, they were never really at home here. And so they "wandered." Wandering, we can see, is a unique image in the Bible that can be used of those ancient saints who epitomized the life of godliness. Wandering can be good *and* it can be bad. I have reflected on that fact from time to time—the holy ones were all relegated at some point to wandering in deserts and mountains and caves and holes. Wandering, the author of Hebrews tells us, is the way of the faithful—the world was not worthy of them, and because of this, they never really found their home. And the faithful never really do. For this reason, Jesus had no place to lay his head at night (Matt. 8:20). The world was not worthy of him. Christ wandered for thirty-three years to his eventual death on the cross for the world. And so we must enter into the complexity of wandering. Wandering can be good, bad, hurtful, and unhelpful. Wandering, as an inescapable theme of the Christian experience, is just as much an inescapable theme in the grand story of the Holy Bible.

Søren Kierkegaard, the ever-so-wise Danish Christian philosopher, was known to be quite the storyteller. He told the parable of an auditorium filled with people sitting in their seats. In the room were two doors. Above one of these doors was a sign that read, "heaven." The other door, however, read, "lecture *about* heaven." Everyone in the auditorium, said Kierkegaard, eventually made their way through the door labeled "lecture *about* heaven."[1] Kierkegaard's words are as worthy today as they were in his day in that they speak to human nature. For, I suspect, when given the chance, most would rather hear a TED talk about God than actually know God. We are more enamored of good content than we are of reality. That's our time. It's who we've become.

We love knowing *about* God the way we love knowing about biology or about the state capitals or, vaguely, about what goes into Aunt Diane's Thanksgiving Jell-O. Our knowledge is *very* heady. Yet Christianity isn't solely concerned with knowing *about* God the way we know about photosynthesis, Olympia, or Jell-O. A problem arises when we frame the Christian faith primarily in terms of objective, sterile, test-tube knowledge about God that we would get from a lecture. In the early twentieth century, there lived a famed German Protestant theologian by the name of Helmut Thielicke. In a small book called *A Little Exercise for Young Theologians*, Thielicke said there are two kinds of theologians.[2] He began to notice that when seminary students entered into their various studies about God—learning the languages of the Bible, learning doctrine, memorizing Scripture—their newly acquired knowledge would lead them down one of two paths. There are, of course, true theologians—those bold souls who put into practice all they learn. True lovers of God metabolize into their lives all the great truth Christ has spoken. But the danger of another type of theology always lurks—Thielicke called it "diabolical theology." This kind of theology, like the first, is known. The problem is that it is *not lived*. This, Thielicke says, is the theology of the demons.

We know so much more *about* God than we know *of* God himself, a tragedy indeed. I think if we actually got to know God as he is, we'd appreciate him so much more than our objective knowledge about him. He is more incredible than our facts about him. Don't mishear me: the objective knowledge of God is important. But nothing, including perfect facts, can replace him. The words of A. W. Tozer still ring true:

> There's scarcely anything so dull and meaningless as Bible doctrine taught for its own sake. Truth divorced from life is not truth . . . but something else and something less. . . . No person is better for knowing that God, in the beginning, created the heaven and the earth. The devil knows that, and so did Ahab and Judas Iscariot. No one is better for knowing that God so loved the world of people that He gave his only begotten Son to die for their redemption. In hell, there are millions who know that. Theological truth is useless until it is obeyed. The purpose behind all doctrine is to secure moral action.[3]

In short, truth divorced from life isn't truth. Unlived truth hasn't actually become true yet for us when it stays up in our brains. Knowledge, it goes, is nothing but a rumor until it has moved its way into our muscles. In the end, the truth of Christianity is found by those who are gutsy enough to walk it out, not those who are heady enough to merely reflect on it. Nor is it found by those who know the most facts about it, have the most wisdom concerning it, or know a lot of others who have done it. Christ is primarily found along the journey, not in a lecture. And anyone who desires to actually know God for God's sake is in for quite the journey—a journey, mind you, that doesn't just happen for happening's sake. God has an agenda. He always has. And he always will.

We come back to Paul's personal mantra of the Christian faith: "I press on." Paul didn't end there. Paul also said that in his pressing on, he had a goal in mind; he didn't seek without intent to actually find. He had a goal. He pressed on "toward the goal to win the prize" (Phil. 3:14). Paul seemed to love sports metaphors. And he utilized them to get a very important message across. Paul knew that the Christian life is a race with a finish line—a place where it all finds its goal. The Christian walk isn't some amorphous, ambiguous journey that never comes to completion. Quite the contrary. Christianity, for Paul, isn't just about the journey; there's a concrete destination, a goal, an end, a completion. At the onset of his letter to the church in Philippi, Paul puts it succinctly in such a way only Paul could: "He who began a good work in you will carry it *on to completion* until the day of Christ Jesus" (Phil. 1:6, emphasis added).

But what is this goal to which God is working to bring about completion in us?

As we will see, there is an ongoing work of God in every one of our lives. It will be completed at some point, but it is still in motion. If you are reading this, then it isn't done yet. And it must be continuously walked out. In the meantime, we press on. Our pressing on has a hope. Our pressing on has a goal. Our pressing on has a purpose. We don't just do it to do it. Paul was not into head games or knowing *about* God. Paul wanted to know God. He wasn't into intellectualism for intellectualism's sake. He wasn't into academic knowledge about God. Paul wanted to know God. And in Christ, Christ alone, Paul was complete.

—⁓—

I started a garden because I wanted to make mom's Gazpacho. A garden is like a poem—it teems with life. The poet Marianne Moore once defined poetry with eloquence. In her poem called "Poetry," she describes poems as "imaginary gardens with *real* toads in them."[4] Poetry and parable are often fictional. They don't necessarily concern themselves with real stories, but they are unquestionably about real truths. Poems are where made-up stories bear eternal truths. Poetry may be imaginary, but it bears great truth. Likewise, a garden may seem useless. A garden—plants, dirt, tomatoes, hoses, blueberry bushes, compost, chickens, and fences—may seem mundane and uncomely. But a garden bears great truth. I've learned a good deal from the garden. I swear.

It's like there's something in that dirt.

The Bible begins in a garden. In that garden, Eden, Adam and Eve are thrown into their vocation of caring for and tending it. Immediately, I'm aware that some of my more critical, suspicious readers will retort that Adam and Eve weren't real, and neither was Eden, and neither were those vegetables that they grew with God in the cool of the day. To be clear: I would disagree. I find no reason to believe that they weren't real people in a real place with real carrots. But even if you are tempted to envision Adam and Eden and the carrots as some mythical invention, try to suspend your suspicion for a moment and imagine that even perhaps in the "imaginary garden" found in the Bible, as you might suppose, there are some *very* real toads of truth.

Adam and Eve find themselves in a garden. What a jostling experience that must have been. To be sure, Adam and Eve didn't first take a correspondence course on agriculture. There were no lectures *about* gardening. They just *did* it. No one learns to garden in an auditorium. You have to learn to garden in a garden. That's at least how all gardeners begin—they are thrown into it. I certainly was.

When I was a child, my mom didn't teach me the mechanics of gardening, wax eloquent regarding nuances in gardening philosophies, or give me a book on the topic. Mostly, my mom taught me in her *love* for the garden. That love is my good fortune. In that little garden of my distant childhood, she would hand me, unknowingly, a passionate love—a love deep in her own bones—for that little parcel of land in our backyard. My mom was the best teacher in that way. And as with all the best teachers we have in life, we find that we learn more from their *love* of the content than the content itself. I still can't remember a darned thing old Mr. Krumdick taught us in seventh grade American history; what I do remember is far more important. I remember his *love* of history. To this day, his love has infected me with a love for history in the same way my mom's love for the garden has transferred into my bones.

We learn most from people by what and how they love, not what they tell us. Now that I have a child and a home and a desire to grow my own food and have my own chickens, I've come to love and appreciate gardening as I've practiced it. You learn quickly as a novice gardener. Or I should say you must learn quickly. If you don't, you won't have a garden. Every year you learn just a little bit more. While I received a *love* for gardening from my mom, her gardening skills were anything but intellectual or theoretical or abstract. Her knowledge of the seasons and soils were tacit, felt, and instinctive—the way a bird knows where a worm passes underground unaware. Few gardeners have a deep, academic knowledge about the various components or origins of soil. Nor do they need these kinds of intellectual tools. My mom could almost *sense* the soil. She knew what it needed. She could almost talk to the wind. And her magic knowledge of our backyard paid off.

More than anything, I remember Mom's tomatoes with vivid clarity. Her tomatoes were almost famous in our family—big, thick, luscious tomatoes, the kind of tomatoes that look like they're full of life. Year after year, I'd watch from my bedroom window as Mom planted those famous tomatoes—I'd sit on my bed in my upstairs room and peek out the dusty window to see her prepare the ground. Like a nun praying, down on two knees in the sacred soil below, head in the bushes, bucket at her side, she'd till and sweat and get soil under her nails.

Then, like the parable, she'd *sow* the seeds in the good soil. Even the soil took work. Good soil doesn't just happen. Indeed, good soil takes sweat, she'd say. Mostly I'd sit there and dream of the gazpacho that was to come in a few months' time. I bet there's still dry drool on that windowsill.

People who are used to shopping at the supermarket don't often like the cost that comes with caring for their own garden. Gardening isn't convenient. "Sure," they might say, "I'd love my own carrots and tomatoes and asparagus, but the smell of the compost rotting in the corner of the yard, the work it takes to water everything, the sheer time it takes to keep it all going—well, it's just too much." Gardening is a messy venture. The gardener is constantly putting his or her pride to death, knowing that the backyard is eternally a work in progress.

God was in Eden. And I swear, he's been in my garden too. When all is said and done, my experience of gardening has had a deeper transformational impact on my reading of the Bible than just about anything else. Living life actually makes the Bible come to life, in a certain sense. It is only possible to understand certain aspects (not all, of course) of the fatherhood of God if one has been a human father. One can truly appreciate the book of Job only if one has experienced a great loss. Likewise, having a garden has unlocked whole sections of the Bible for me. Alongside years of attentive reading of the Bible, a good deal of what I know about the garden of Eden I've picked up from our garden. It's funny how you learn so much about "tending the garden" and "naming the animals" when you actually have to do them. There's something holy and fixed in our bones about gardening, like we were made to do it or something. I mean, if the Bible is right, gardening was the first thing we did as a human race. I've come to see how Adam might have seen the garden of Eden.

—※—

It's funny to me that the garden *preceded* Adam and Eve in the creation story. That is, the garden was not the result of Adam's work and toil and knowledge of gardening. God gave the gift of the garden before

Adam would have known what to do with it. Adam's work was the result of receiving the gift that came beforehand. Sometime—roughly, I'm told—between seven thousand and 13.8 billion years ago, everything that can be seen, tasted, touched, and felt in this vast, expansive, blow-your-mind universe showed up inexplicably as if from nowhere. Whether its origin was that of a big bang or a heavenly word (or both), few can agree, but one thing is sure: it appeared out of nowhere at some point in history. To imagine the chaotic moment of creation is difficult. What a brilliantly picturesque sight the whole ordeal must've been.

The stark reality, however, is that the epic creation narrative of the Bible relays to us a simple, almost humiliating, fact: in his infinite sovereignty, God elected to insert the human cast members into the ancient script of creation *last*. Humans were the final physical creations of the Creator. In fact, one is quick to discover, human beings weren't even created and placed in all their majesty into the garden of Eden until the sixth day. And that is *after* five other entire days of God creating all other kinds of things, from light to artichokes to topsoil.

One wonders why. What divine rationale led God to choose such a late act to insert the humans? It's very likely that some will say that God did this because God saves his best for last, like the way Jesus gave the best wine at the *end* of a wedding in Cana. Jesus Christ is the same yesterday, today, and forever—right? Indeed he is. But such a notion of human exaltation is rooted above all in human arrogance. We humans are not the only part of creation that God takes a liking to; God loves everything he makes. And any idea smacking of the notion that we are the pinnacle of God's handiwork is both rooted in pride and bound to fall to oblivion in the age to come. Narcissism is never holy.

There is a lurking temptation for all of us to think that we are far more important than we really are. I was reading the story of Corrie ten Boom. She was a wealthy Dutch woman who rescued countless Jews during World War II by hiding them in a room in her house. She was a hero. She was also a follower of Jesus. Ten Boom wrote a book called *The Secret Room* about her experience. At the end of her life, she is thinking back on her heroism and what she got to do with her life's energy. She poignantly reflects on the donkey that brought Jesus into Jerusalem, and wonders what that donkey thought about itself.

Jesus rode into Jerusalem on Palm Sunday on the back of a donkey, and everyone was waving palm branches and throwing garments on the road and singing praises, do you think that for one moment it even entered the head of that donkey that any of it was for him? . . . If I can be the donkey on which Jesus Christ rides in His glory, I give Him all the praise and all the honor.[5]

Humans tend to be prideful donkeys, really. To see everything as being about merely us is to be the donkey that brought Jesus into Jerusalem and think people are clapping for us. The story of creation, of course, has a story that is greater than just us. Yes, we are important, but we are not the sole character in the story. I think the creation narrative does not permit such arrogance to think the whole story is about us. What other rationale might there be for God creating humanity so late in the game? The reason, one might consider, is humility. That's it: humility. I would maintain that God created humans so late in the creational game so that we would eternally know how little we know. Being made so late is kind of a built-in humility for humanity. Think about it: slugs and dung beetles and bacteria came before us in the biblical creation story. A day-six creation would leave in the back of our minds the eternal notion that there were five good days of work in there before we had the gift of showing up on the scene. Humanity wasn't in the front row for creation. It certainly gives God great pleasure when we realize—no matter how much we think we may know about everything—that even the dung beetle had a better front-row view than Adam and Eve. Listen: My grandfather's birthday was on the fourth of July. He grew up thinking the fireworks were about him. I think that we too often think all the fireworks of creation are just for us. They aren't.

Perhaps that's precisely why nobody can agree about how or when creation came about. None of us was there. Some would say it came about in seven literal days; others that it took billions of years. Regardless of where we stand on that question, we're stuck with one unquestionable thing: only God was there on day zero. We weren't. Or if one of us was actually there, it's about time that person spoke up. Tell us what happened, won't you? Write a piece. Do an interview. Podcast. Begin a blog. Start a denomination. At the least start a Twitter account.

No matter how energetically certain one might be about what exactly one thinks happened at creation, we must at the least reserve a humble space for the simple reality that we just weren't there. In a rare fit of humility, a scientist and a Christian agree: neither was there at the beginning. "In the beginning God . . ." implies, well, in the beginning *weren't* people. The Bible doesn't say, "In the beginning Adam . . ." God was there. No one else. When you're this late to the game, humility is a must. But we like to act as if we were made on day one.

That is not to say that we weren't in the mind of God, which I believe we were. In a way we were created in the mind of God first. Humanity wasn't an impromptu add-on to the creation story. God created everything knowing us before we were in our mother's womb (Jer. 1:5). Certainly God knew about Adam and Eve and you and me before the creation of the world. And so we've been around quite some time in idea more than in flesh. I've heard rumors of an African tradition that states a person's birthday is not the day they were physically born but the day their mother first thought of them. How beautiful is that? God knew us way before we actually came along. Our true birthday isn't the day we were born; rather, it was the day we were imagined.

The garden was a gift. Regardless of when humanity came along, one thing is for sure: humans weren't there at the very beginning. The garden was prepared for us. By definition, a gift is something that's originated from outside one's own self. In that sense, the garden *preceded* Adam and Eve. The garden was a gift. The garden was not the result of their efforts or sweat or tilling. Adam did literally nothing to earn it—they could only work it. They inhabited and kept the garden with the love they had seen in the Creator for it. They loved it because

God loved it. No other reason. It is interesting for me to consider the fact that the word "to keep" (Gen. 2:15 KJV) used in reference to Adam's task is the same word in the Hebrew language as "worship." Working the garden was Adam's way of worshiping. Worship, in short, could be described as what we do with the very gift that originated from outside our own selves.

Adam's world was a gift from God. The land. The animals. The sun. The stars. The water. His wife was received as a gift. The first words off Adam's tongue after Eve is created are words of poetic ecstasy—literally. He says, "This is now bone of my bones, and flesh of my flesh" (Gen. 2:23). Of course, to say he "said" this is quite the understatement. The first words Adam says are actually a song as he beholds the naked woman. The minute Adam saw Eve for the first time, all he could do was be filled with the Holy Spirit and speak in poetry. That is what a gift does to you. It causes you to be overwhelmed with the knowledge that someone loves you more than they should.

Mom didn't just garden to garden. There were other purposes in her mind indeed. Namely, in our case, a cold vegetable soup known as gazpacho. I can't really describe gazpacho, for it would be like trying to describe looking at the earth from space. Gazpacho transcends description. Gazpacho was pretty much what our garden existed for. After the harvest—taking the tomatoes, carrots, cucumber, and spices—Mom would magically mix it all together in her white blender and out came the best cold, summer gazpacho you could imagine (if you can even imagine it). I've searched the world to discover something similar, but assuredly, my mom's gazpacho is the best gazpacho. And every year, as she would set out planting, sowing, watering, tilling, gardening, and reaping, she would have that gazpacho in mind.

For my mom, gardening had a purpose, a destination, and an end-game. It was gazpacho. For others, it's simply the sustenance of food for the winter. But a real gardener has an end in sight, a direction, and a reason behind the whole thing. Yes, there are certain psychological and physical benefits to being out in the garden, but gardening, in the real sense, is about something that is yet to be complete.

The parallels between the Christian life and gardening are endless. For one, gardening reminds us of the *ongoing* work of God in our little lives as we try to follow Jesus. God works in our lives the same way a gardener works the soil. Salvation is as much a process as anything. In recent years, Christians have increasingly been comfortable discussing the life of faith as "a journey." In one sense, the metaphor of faith as a journey is good and helpful and should be appropriated. For truly, Christ followers are, at their core, pilgrims on the way. Yet this image of the Christian "journey" isn't by any stretch of the imagination a novel one. Teresa of Avila's iconic *Interior Castle* narrates one walking through a mansion as a metaphor of the life of Christian faith. And in recent years, this metaphor has become all the rage. In his very helpful little book *The Journey*, Alister McGrath wisely looks at the Christian experience as akin to a road trip or a hike. Clearly, the themes of journeying and wandering harmonize quite well in that they both assume we still have a long way to go.

Yet as with any trend in Christian theology, the image of spiritual "journey" is one I hold some major reservations about. For to describe the Christian life merely in terms of "journey" is to describe gardening merely in terms of "tilling." But it ain't just about the tilling. A journey, as such, can only be an authentic journey if it seeks to go somewhere—if there's the proverbial gazpacho at the end of the line. In the end, the inherent danger of constantly talking about the "journey" is that we can easily become duped into thinking we never have to *arrive* somewhere. In fact, I might show my own cards and suggest that this is one of my own critiques of using the image of wandering as a way to look at the Christian life. The danger is we see spirituality as one big walk with no destination. But we are called to arrive. Paul "pressed on toward the goal." A journey without an arrival is a race without a finish line. And Paul would have none of it.

I contend that our "journey" language needs to be nuanced. If the Christian life is a journey as we say it is, it's a journey unlike any other.

When we imagine a journey, we often think of an ongoing, smooth, uphill hike. But the language of conversion in Scripture isn't really described this way at all. New Testament language regarding conversion is much more dualistic—in *or* out, black *or* white—than we're likely comfortable with. Colossians contends, "He has rescued us from the dominion of darkness and brought us into the kingdom of the Son he loves" (1:13). Jesus similarly spoke of being "born again" (John 3:3). Such in/out, black/white language is far removed from that progressive, uphill, smooth-over-time journey we imagine. Rather, we transfer from one kingdom to another in the blink of an eye—one moment we are in the womb, the next we are in someone's arms. The moment of birth isn't a process—it's a moment. Yet therein lies the contrast between conversion and salvation. Certainly, while conversion remains momentary, the ongoing process of salvation is a progression, a journey.

In a sense, we have arrived; in another sense, we continue to walk. Funny paradox, isn't it? For this exact reason theologians are prone to speak of salvation as a "punctiliar process." By that, we mean it is an experience marked simultaneously by a period and a comma. We are converted in a moment, but salvation is a work in process. Rethinking this helps us rethink the metaphor of journey in a more thoughtful way. While in a sense we have arrived (at conversion), we have, in another sense, a long journey ahead ("to work out [our] salvation with fear and trembling," as Paul writes in Phil. 2:12). The journey is a lot like a marriage. Often, we see the wedding ceremony as the endgame, the finale, but of course it is anything but. A wedding ceremony is a conversion to the married life, but that is merely the beginning. There is then the whole marriage thing. Conversion and salvation are just that: a ceremony and a marriage. In a sense we have arrived, but boy, there is a long way to go. That is why Jesus could tell his disciples who had left everything to follow him to ask, seek, and knock. Being a disciple does not preclude our need to continue striving. As one brilliant theologian has put it, conversion takes a moment, and salvation takes a lifetime.[6]

We see this exact same theme through the lens of Israel as they wander in the desert after leaving Egypt. Israel has been redeemed from Egypt's controlling oppression, but there is a long way to go to the promised land. In a moment's notice (like a birth) Israel leaves Egypt. But it would take years to enter the promised land. Salvation is always entered *and* worked out. We don't just leave Egypt and go about our business. We leave Egypt and continue to enter salvation. Conversion is the first word; salvation is the whole book.

God's plan is a finished and ongoing process with a goal, an arrival. To journey for the sake of journeying is to garden for the sake of gardening. When Jesus spoke of asking, seeking, and knocking, we have to assume he meant that there was something that could be found and that he wasn't sending us on some kind of eternal goose chase. Seeking merely for the sake of seeking isn't true seeking. *Seeking after something is what makes it true seeking.* The Christian journey always has a goal in mind. My mom would tell me, when you sow, remember the gazpacho. That's *why* we garden in the first place. Don't forget that there is an end to all of this toil. Sometimes, when we talk about faith as a journey, I wonder if it gives us permission not to have to land anywhere. But faith without a goal is shallow sentiment.

Sometimes I think we're scared to actually *arrive* anywhere.

—⁂—

Like grace, a garden must be cared for. One can have grace, but unless they learn to work with it, grow stuff in it, get it under their nails, it is just a plot of dirt. Gardens take time—lots of time. And they are way messier than you'd ever hope. Gardens and grace both share this: they are gifts that must be kept.

It's easy to forget that there is a vast chasm between receiving and keeping a gift. A gift must be kept, not just received. It's become our family's liturgy two days after Christmas to go all over town to return all the gifts we received but didn't necessarily want. Even the week before Christmas, we are doing everything we can to regift the things from last year we want to give away. Again, it is one thing to receive a gift; it's quite another to keep it, care for it, and hold on to it. One can be given the gift of a garden but choose not to keep or tend it. If people procrastinate in their gardens for too long, they put themselves in the position of one long year of buying foods at the local supermarket—or, worse yet, going hungry. In times past, there was a word for procrastinating gardeners. They were called *dead* gardeners. Procrastination, of all things, isn't the gardener's privilege.

Again, there are striking similarities between a garden and the Christian life. One can believe but never fully inhabit, keep, or live out the gospel to one's fullest capability. Again: one can receive the gospel only to give it away because it didn't fit one's desires. That's precisely why, in the timeless words of St. Paul, we're invited to "*work out* [our] salvation with fear and trembling" (Phil. 2:12, emphasis added). Paul never suggests that we work to get our salvation—Paul would never endorse such a putrid theology in his writings. Rather, we "work out" the salvation we've already received. We receive it only to find that we are simultaneously provoked to till it and care for it and steward it the way my mother would her garden. You are given a garden; *then* you work the garden. You don't work and earn a garden. Nonsense.

A garden is the gift; garden*ing* is what one does to keep and live out the gift.

Mom didn't garden just to garden. Nor does God start a garden just to garden. God is after something. There is an end point. A goal. An arrival.

I guess what I am saying is that our lives are kind of like God's gazpacho.

BANISHED

Return, O wanderer, to thy home,
Thy Father calls for thee;
No longer now an exile roam
In guilt and misery;
Return, return.

Return, O wanderer, to thy home,
'Tis Jesus calls for thee:
The Spirit and the bride say, Come;
Oh now for refuge flee;
Return, return.

Return, O wanderer, to thy home,
'Tis madness to delay:
There are no pardons in the tomb
And brief is mercy's day.
Return, return.

> Thomas Hastings,
> "Return, O Wanderer"

"In the beginning God . . . " (Gen. 1:1).

As we've been discussing, that's the beginning of creation—four words that capture the essence of everything from the sunset to raccoons to the very book in your hands. Before *everything*, was God. Sure, God eventually gets around to creating a garden where he will place Adam and Eve. And soon God will move in and give directions. God tells Adam and Eve to make kids and eat. Look at the first two commandments to Adam and Eve in the Bible (Gen. 1:28–30): "multiply" and "eat." I suspect most Americans will appreciate that. The Bible begins with food and sex. Who isn't going to like that? And then, almost immediately (and I mean almost immediately), the rules established by God begin to break down. Adam and Eve step over the boundaries, transgressing the way of things. They not only forget the rules, but they ignore and break the rules.

It all began so wonderfully—*Sound of Music* wonderfully. Running-through-hills, spinning-in-daisies wonderfully. And then it all went downhill from there.

It is often called the fall. It changed everything.

What happened in Eden didn't stay in Eden.

Eden, literally translated as "paradise," was most certainly a paradise. But it was also a unique kind of paradise with boundaries established by God. We mustn't imagine Eden as some free-for-all, all-inclusive resort where anything could be freely done, consequence-free. By venturing in to take a closer look at the garden scene in the early pages of Genesis, we discover that the garden of Eden was not, as one might say, a "cage-free" existence for its original inhabitants. Eden had very clear, established boundaries pertaining mostly to food. It is interesting that *the* boundary God establishes—"eat from every tree except the tree of knowledge"—was about food. And it is all the more interesting to see that the first sin took place in regard to food as well. Most of my sins are like that, about food. The first thing I stole was a cookie.

Garden life, paradise, was not "free" in the way we think of free. Nor are our own existences free of the confines of boundaries and limitations and lines of demarcation. A cage-free, boundless, infinite, limitless, "do whatever you please" sort of life is a myth unsupported by both experience and the witness of Scripture. Real life had, and still has, boundaries. Real life knows that it won't last forever and can't attain everything it wants.

In the creation story, there were two levels of boundaries—physical boundaries and moral boundaries. As it pertains to the physical boundaries of creation, there were many to be noted. For example, God established boundaries between the sea and the land, between the sky and the earth, between the fishes of the water and the animals of the land. There were boundaries of time—days marked by darkness and dawn. Creation had boundaries of seasons. And, of course, there were boundaries between animal and plant species. Eden teemed with all kinds of living beings that reproduced within their given boundaries of its species community. The place had a purposeful and thoughtful infrastructure. In fact, the structure of the physical space in creation has reminded some of a very-well-thought-through set of architectural plans. To that end, a number of Old Testament scholars have sought to examine the story of creation in architectural terms; like an architect, God separates light from dark, land from sea, all acts of delineation that an architect would be doing.[1]

Alongside these various physical boundaries, there were boundaries pertaining to how humans were to exist in relationship to God and one another. These were also *moral* boundaries. What this means is that there were clear, concise, divine boundaries, directives, and rules for humanity that God opted to establish before inserting Adam and Eve into the world's plot that basically existed to sustain them. For example, note that God·extended Adam and Eve the freedom to eat from *any* tree in the garden of Eden—every tree, that is, except the one in the middle of the garden known as the tree of the knowledge of good and evil (Gen. 2:16–17). All of this came before they would eventually eat the fruit from the off-limits tree in the center of the garden. Moral boundaries existed before Adam and Eve ate the fruit and sin entered the world. Boundaries, as it were, were not a result of the fall. Boundaries, as such, mustn't be falsely understood as a result of humanity's disobedience, sin, or the fall. Boundaries predated the fall; a good creation had rules before the serpent came slithering about. Boundaries are good, not bad, and helped create a world that would flourish and be good.

This notion of moral boundaries unquestionably rubs up against almost all of our cultural sensibilities, doesn't it? For example, an American will feel entitled (almost from birth) to a set of "inalienable rights" to freedom and happiness and do whatever the heck we want to do. Then, along comes the Bible, telling us we *can't* do everything we want to do. No wonder the Bible has grown wildly unpopular in our time as an ancient, unnecessary document—it refuses to offer us a vision of unimpeded freedom. Take sexuality as an example. Time and again, the Bible offers a kind of sexual ethic that says sexual intimacy is ideally only to be enjoyed by two people in mutual, covenant relationship with one another. Anything else leads to destruction. Now, because of this, the Bible gets hammered for being closed-minded and archaic. But imagine for a moment a world in which this kind of sexual ethic is actually embodied. Imagine a world in which human sexuality only takes place in the context of mutual, loving covenant— completely removed from our world would be all rape, sexual abuse, child pornography, all pornography, and sex trafficking. Far more kids would have two parents as divorce rates would plummet. Now, one might critique the Bible's sexual ethic as being outdated. But it's difficult to deny that such a world is a lot more like heaven than whatever it is we're doing now. In general, boundaries are only hated by those who refuse to respect them. Boundaries are loved and respected when their Creator is loved and respected.

No wonder we see the Bible as archaic: an upright God will never be praised by the crooked.

Telling, isn't it, that with all these physical and moral boundaries, the garden environment had no barbed wires or walls or watchtowers?

Eden wasn't a gated community. It wasn't a prison. There was a remarkable sense of freedom to disobey what God had established. Adam and Eve could have left if they pleased. Likewise, as we've observed, they were entirely free to eat from the one tree they weren't permitted to—in short, God is the Creator of choice. And so there is an essential lesson to be learned from the epic Eden story: with great freedom comes the great possibility that disobedience may ensue. The cost of freedom is potential disobedience. Likewise, true freedom is only true if there are boundaries. Imagine a free world with no stop signs, speed limits, or lines on the road. That isn't freedom; it is chaos. While there were, as there *are*, boundaries and rules, there was such creative freedom in the garden that was pregnant with great possibility. Adam was invited to name the animals. Eve was free to walk around in the garden. Adam and Eve were free to enjoy a sexual relationship.

Eden had freedom *and* boundary. I like to call this *bounded creativity*—an existence marked by brilliant creativity that simultaneously respects the divine boundaries. Within the context of creation's bounded creativity, humans are invited to color, so to speak, within the lines drawn before the foundations of the earth. God desires us to be creative and bounded at the same time. The splendidly intentional way God creates the world with bounded creativity suggests a nuanced brilliance behind the whole thing.

The problem is, we think in terms of either creativity *or* boundaries—it can only be one or the other. Generally, we're good at one but not the other. A problem surfaces when we ignore one side of that tension, when we are merely "bounded" or merely "creative." In so doing, we greatly neglect our God-given vocation of being creative within the lines of creation.

Many forms of Christian religion misread the creation narrative and forget a whole side of the garden's creative dimension that invites us to cocreate, name, make, and keep the garden. Religion does rules really well. It says do this, do that, don't do this, don't do that. Religion emphasizes the boundaries. A neat and tidy religion based on such rules naively comprehends life as nothing more than an environment of black-and-white boundaries that exist primarily to keep us from having any fun whatsoever.

While religions are good at the rules, progressive culture like Portland, where I live, is good at the creative side of life, often ignoring life's boundaries and choosing only to see the side of human life that respects one's ability to do as they please. Life becomes, in this light, whatever we want to make of it. We become who we want to become. Any boundaries are bad, progressives would say, so just be free to be yourself. Eat what you want to eat, drink what you want to drink, sleep with whom you want to sleep with; do whatever you want whenever you want to do it. But we are deceived when we ignore both tensions of creation. To be only creative or only bounded severely undermines the way God created us to live, and it will lead to an impoverished existence.

The gospel of Jesus reinvites us into this kind of *bounded creativity*, an invitation that demands great creativity and boldness and also great obedience and faithfulness. The Christian life is to be both right-brained and left-brained. On one side, in creative freedom, we are called to push ourselves to make and create and work the way God created us to. On the other, we do so while faithfully living within the limitations of our lives. More on this later, but suffice it to say that we will wander from that creative tension the minute we ignore the other side. We will stall if we are only creative or only bounded.

I think this awkward tension is why so few Christians willingly choose to enter the creative world of the arts—we're afraid. For many Christians, there's almost a fear of creativity, of making, of doing. It's like we see creativity as the opposite of faith when faith should be what awakens creativity. Similarly, I think that this is why many people wouldn't be caught dead going to church; church and the religious life are caricatured as a kind of death to all true creativity and ingenuity. But, ironically, Christian doctrine has long argued that any sense of creativity is a part of God's image, the *imago Dei*, in each and every person. The artist—Christian or not—is evidence of a Creator. For true creativity is what happens when the *imago Dei* in any person comes out and takes a walk. All artistry is a sign of this divine brilliance. But this false dichotomy between Christianity and creativity is stunning. Christ followers are called to be the most valiant of creatives. Yes, their creativity has boundaries, but creativity without boundary could bring down the whole world.

When the boundaries aren't respected, we can almost assuredly expect that destruction will come as a result. I was reading the story of a megachurch pastor who started a church that exploded into massive proportions. He wrote tons of books that influenced the masses. He became famous. He traveled the world and taught. Then, after a personal crisis, he stopped pastoring. After he left the church, he started changing his views and theology and began to reject the story of Jesus. He did an interview in which he said that once he'd left the boundaries of the church, he finally felt free to "be himself." Some might applaud that. I don't. Christians are not to "be themselves." They are "hidden with Christ" (Col. 3:3). Some of us want to leave the church because once we leave those boundaries, we can be and do whatever we please. But that can be very harmful to our souls. The church is the rope that tethers us to the good news.

So we are invited to be creative *within* the boundaries of faith, church, and Scripture—not outside of it. True creativity is possible only in the context of boundaries. Some of the most incredible literary works are done by people who have found their freedom in prison cells. Is this a mistake? Nope. It is without question, for me, why the best writings come from prison. When you're in prison, you're stuck to be free. You are stuck by space but free to be you. It was in prison that Martin Luther King Jr. wrote "Letter from a Birmingham Jail," some of the crispest and clearest testimonies to freedom ever considered. It was in prison that Dietrich Bonhoeffer could write with majestic clarity his *Letters and Papers from Prison*. It was from prison that St. Paul could write letters that would become Scripture. Creativity is often best exercised in a prison. It is best exercised when there are some boundaries. I resonate so deeply with these words of Bonhoeffer, written from prison: "I think that even in this place we ought to live as if we had no wishes and no future, and *just be our true selves.*"[2] Perhaps that is why Paul could write as much about freedom as he did from prison. Jesus said the truth would set us free (John 8:23). He never said that "being free" always led to truth.

We don't arrive at our true selves by throwing off boundaries of truth; rather, we arrive at reality and truth by accepting these boundaries that God has graciously given to us. A river without banks is called a flood. A flood destroys. A river brings life; a flood annihilates. But we also don't find life by merely living the rules. We live a life of creativity within the boundaries. We find freedom in coming to respect the boundaries of God. It's true: accepting that we will die sets us free.[3] In the end, I'm eternally perplexed by God's brutal willingness to allow his own creation to wander into sin. The cost of bounded creativity is that one can always go too far. While deploring sin for all it is, God seems wildly comfortable to put his people in places where they have great possibility for sin. The God of the Bible, one finds, is no helicopter parent. Despite what any other parent may or may not let their child do, God *allows* his people to freely wander into the trap of sin and disobedience.

But in its prickly arrogance, human pride has done everything in its power to erase (or at least erode) divine boundaries in order to refashion human existence as boundless and "free." And any sense of freedom without boundaries is not freedom. Freedom can only be freedom if there are boundaries. Sin might best be described as ignoring boundaries and seeking a cage-free existence without boundaries. By saying "cage-free," I am not suggesting that we live behind barbed wire. Rather, I am using an image of bounded living. And cage-free, as far as I can tell, is not just something we want for our chickens. *We* want to be cage-free.

Modern life is increasingly identified as a world of individuals who are doing everything in their power and control to do away with all boundaries and limitations—boundaries around sexuality, our bodies, our relationships, and what is right and wrong. In short, we are becoming a world without boundaries. The contemporary obsession with "cage-free" is perhaps the best metaphor for the way not only Portlanders but also most Americans seek to embody an existence of supposed freedom, health, and well-being free of any moral or ethical restrictions or boundaries that hold us down. We want to be cage-free people in a bounded creation. And anything that gets in the way is seen as a real threat to our "freedom."

This very well may account for why the church is resisted so vehemently in our time. God doesn't play well in the twenty-first century to many people. People opt for relationships where one doesn't have to hear about the boundaries and limitations that have been established, which is most likely why people are more interested in having a dog than they are in God. This is why, I suspect, Portlanders love their pets, particularly their dogs, as much as they do. Everyone in Portland owns a dog. They walk their dogs—big, small, loud, slow, blind, old—through my neighborhood. Why do we love our pets as much as we do? It seems we spend more money and time on pets than at any other time in history. Why? I would suggest that in our efforts at creating a cage-free life, we would go through whatever is necessary to be free of the cages of responsibility and judgment. A neighbor once told me he loves his dogs as much as he does—perhaps even more than his children—because a dog won't look at you and say, "Hey, you're wrong." A dog just gives affection. A dog never judges. Around a dog, one can be *whatever* one wants to be. Children, on the other hand, will judge. Greatly. Maybe this is why our dogs often get more attention than our children.

We want to live the way we want our chickens—cage-free and happy. Again, perhaps that's precisely why religion (particularly Christianity) often gets a bad rap in places like Portland. Religion gets caricatured as a kind of barbed-wire cage that holds us back from being and doing just as we please. Certainly, there is little doubt that humans will, by instinct, gravitate toward the relationships where we get affirmation from the other. And God doesn't always affirm us. Sometimes God judges. If we merely desire affirmation and affection, a dog is a better option than God.

Despite our secret desires that it didn't, creation had and still has boundaries. Humans were not made to live limitless lives. Likewise, the life of faith that Jesus invites us into today is one that beckons us to once again respect those boundaries and limitations. We are invited to eat, but we are invited to eat with limitations. We are invited to enjoy sexuality, but in the way established by the Creator. Like Adam, we are told which tree we *can't* eat from and what animals we *can* name. Still, within this bounded creativity, God's human creatures are created as *free* beings in a bounded world who can (if they so choose) eat from whatever tree they darn well please. Adam could have named the animals the last names God would have ever chosen. It was a world where humans were free to rebel. And because God didn't create one machine or automaton in the creation, we are designed to be free, to do as we want. He created real, free people who could, if they so wanted, eat from the forbidden tree.

The boundaries can be ignored.

But doing so will always lead to death.

Wandering—the theme we're working our way through—is like the moon: it has a light and a dark side to it. There is *good* wandering and *bad* wandering. The Bible doesn't portray it in just one light. Sometimes it is praised, sometimes it is not. While one essential aspect of the Christian life deals with learning how to wander with God faithfully through the desert of this life, another part that we are dealing with here is the wandering that we do as we wander away from God. Again, wandering can be a necessary part of the journey of holiness that one will eventually tread one's way through in order to arrive at new places of promise and refreshment. But on the other hand, sometimes—*sometimes*—wandering is not good wandering. In short, wandering can be the result of sin and disobedience, like the wandering of Adam and Eve.

Sin is a prickly topic indeed. We are wrong to think that sin has always been around. Of course it hasn't. Sin was not originally created but came along after the creation of the world. Sin is, in a way, a kind of undoing of God's good creation. Sin is taking the vat in which sloshes the wine that Jesus made and doing everything one can to turn it back into water. Sin is the wanton deconstruction of God's good. Similarly, evil wasn't created. Satan was an angel named Lucifer originally created by God as a good agent in his creation. It was only later that Satan turned against God. In that way, there is no such thing as "original" sin, for originally God only created good. Originally, there was no evil or sin.

Sin, I've heard it said, is the only part of Christian doctrine that is, beyond question, empirically verifiable by everyone. Every person recognizes there is darkness in the world. And Christians aren't the only ones to recognize a blip in the human personhood. Like many of his contemporaries, Sigmund Freud had a long-standing tradition of writing letters of response to his readers who took interest in his work. One such letter has been published in recent years. In a series of brutally transparent correspondences with a Lutheran minister by the name of Otto Pfister, Freud sought to respond to one of his Christian readers' criticisms. Freud writes, "Well, praise can always be brief, but criticism has to be more long-winded. One thing I dislike is your objection to my 'sexual theory and my ethics.' The latter I grant you; ethics are remote from me, and you are a minister of religion. I do not break my head very much about good and evil, but I have found little that is 'good' about human beings on the whole. In my experience most of them are *trash*."[4]

Trash. That is language used by one of the founders of modern psychology. Freud, of course, stands out as one of the most brilliant and creative psychoanalysts known to his field. Freud's work would shape a whole generation of thought about the human person in the modern world. Of course, Freud wasn't a Christian. It's shocking, isn't it, to see Freud, the leading psychologist of his time, make such a bold proclamation?

The great missionary and theologian John Wesley defined people as "human sharks."[5] I suppose what's odd is that Sigmund Freud, a renowned psychologist, and John Wesley, one of the church's greatest theologians, seem to largely agree on this point. The religious—and nonreligious, for that matter—recognize something off about the human person. To be certain, humanity isn't so much trash as *loved* trash. Christianity—probably because it can overemphasize the fact— gets quite a bit of grief for its point that all humans are "sinners." Many psychologists today assert that this claim creates within a person a great deal of unnecessary grief and can even cause someone to be depressed. But at the risk of being brash, you can't know anybody and not recognize that Freud and the Bible are right. The Bible, however, takes it one step further. While humanity is "trash," it is the kind of trash that God takes a liking to.

—⁘⁘⁘—

The first story after the fall is the story of Cain and Abel. And in this story we can see firsthand the brutal results of this sinfulness we have been talking about. Cain, Genesis 4 recounts, is a farmer. He works a piece of land, as farmers do. In a jealous fit of rage one day, Cain kills his brother, Abel. After cursing Cain for his sin, God sends him to a place called the land of Nod. When he banishes Cain from his parcel of farmland, God tells him, "When you work the ground, it will no longer yield its crops for you. You will be a restless *wanderer* on the earth" (Gen. 4:12, emphasis added). Cain knows he will be hated among men for his actions (see Gen. 4:14). As a direct result of Cain's sin, we find, he becomes a wanderer. In an interesting play on words, Genesis reports that God sent Cain to Nod, a riff on the Hebrew word *nad*, meaning "wanderer"—a person who would never find rest for his soul. Interestingly, neither Nod nor Cain is ever mentioned again in the Bible.[6] It's as though Cain is still wandering, displaced, as it were, somewhere in the land.

John Calvin, interestingly, wrote that Cain's sin caused him such internal "homelessness" in his heart that it was similar to a robber who can't sleep at night because of the guilt of what he's done.[7] Cain's sin caused him to be a wanderer both physically and spiritually. Cain wandered through the earth because he didn't respect the boundaries of God's creation. It is no mistake, in light of the story of Cain, that Paul captures the idea of sin as "wandering" away from the faith (1 Tim. 6:10). Sin, reflects the author of Hebrews, "so easily *entangles*" us (12:1, emphasis added). The apostle Peter—one who was well acquainted with the nature of wandering away—similarly uses *entangling* language to describe the power and nature of sin in our lives (2 Pet. 2:20). This wording would have evoked such clear implications for first-century readers. The word used by the author of Hebrews, *euperistatos*, is only found once in the Bible. It is a kind of military language suggesting being encircled, ensnared, or obstructed. Sin can cause us to wander—wander from God, from the church, from each other, even from ourselves.

Sin traps us. It trips us up. It pulls us down. Above all, it isolates us.

—⁓—

You sin a lot. So do I. But what does that mean?

Martin Luther spoke of humans as *simul justus et peccator*—saints and sinners at the same time. Having pastored a community of saints and sinners for quite some time, I've had the opportunity to watch time and again the process people go through when they are caught up in some sin habit or pattern. Their response is surprising. More often than not, the first thing we do when we get caught up in sin is not to start cussing, gossiping, or sleeping around more. The response to sin isn't first *more* sin. On most occasions, the first thing that happens is that we stop going to church or stop living in relationships. It is odd. The community God has placed us in is often the first victim of our sin—we stop being with others who are seeking to follow Jesus. It's like we are repeating the story of Cain. Like Cain, we begin to wander from the parcel of land God has given us to settle in. Most often our sin isolates us from others.

In that sense, there is an undeniable relational component to sin. Unfortunately, we often minimize the nature of sin by seeing it as merely a bad deed. But that is just *one* component of sin, and it really isn't the heart of what sin is all about. Sin is not primarily about doing bad deeds. Sin is much more dynamic than that. The Bible's description of sin strongly differentiates between the problem with the human heart and the actions that come as a result of it. Theologians, for this reason, are often quick to distinguish between "Sin" (with a capital *S*) and "sin" (with a lowercase *s*). Capital-*S* Sin is the root problem, the disease; our hearts are the real issue. Small-*s* sins, however, are the symptoms, the small problems, the presenting issues of our hearts gone awry.

What is the difference between big-*S* Sin and small-*s* sin? An illustration may help. A few years ago, a good friend of mine started noticing something out of the ordinary with his nine-year-old child. His boy was starting to develop rather pronounced BO, or body odor. Now, of course, this is a normal occurrence for someone who is perhaps fourteen or fifteen. But for a nine-year-old, BO is rather uncommon. This was combined with the fact that he was starting to grow facial hair. Again, very odd for a nine-year-old. They knew something was wrong. After visiting the doctor, they were told that he needed further testing. After undergoing the testing, they found a massive tumor on the little boy's pituitary gland that caused him to go through puberty at a very young age.

Saying that someone's problem is that they sleep around or drink too much or gossip too much is like saying that the boy's problem was his body odor. That wasn't his *real* problem. The real problem was the cancer in his little body. That is the difference between big-*S* Sin and small-*s* sin. The former is a disease, the latter a symptom. This explains why so much of Jesus's message had to do with the heart rather than behavior modification. So little of the gospel message deals directly with the small-*s* sin because the Bible knows, and God knows, that isn't our real problem. In short, God doesn't focus merely on the BO. God gets at the heart of the problem by dealing with our disease. And our disease is this incredible proclivity as people to want to run away.

This may change many people's view of small-*s* sins in that we come to see them not primarily in terms of the breakdown of rules but rather as our disobedience to God's boundaries as a result of something deeper inside us. Again, I suspect that the idea of sin has become depersonalized in our imaginations. We think drinking too much is wrong because the Bible says we should not drink too much. Or we think lying is wrong because one of the Ten Commandments says so. We help our neighbor because, well, it is just the right thing to do. We frame so much of our discussion on whether we are following the rules, when in reality rule keeping and rule breaking are not the heart of the issue.

In fact, it is possible to sin without any rules or boundaries being laid down in the first place. Remember when Cain kills Abel in Genesis 4? Isn't it interesting that God judges him for the murder of his brother before God had gone on record as saying murder was wrong? How can that be? The Ten Commandments wouldn't come for some time. Cain's sin wasn't necessarily a breakdown in rules; it was a breakdown in relationship with God and with Abel. It is assumed that Cain would have known that murder was not God's desire for the world. Ultimately, real Sin is the breakdown in relationship that leads to corrupt living. And that eventually causes us to be "enemies in [our own] mind," writes Paul (Col. 1:21). Because of his relationship to God and his brother, Cain *knew* in his heart that murder was wrong. And even had God not said that murder was wrong, Cain would have still known. The law says what our hearts know to be true. It puts into words what we intuitively know.

Let me put it this way: it's possible to cheat on someone and never have slept around. We can never physically touch another person but still be unfaithful in our hearts. You can *technically* not be breaking the rules but be walking away from God at the same time.

Sin is not primarily about breaking some divine law in heaven or stepping over a book of rules. Sin is, above all, a breakdown in relationship. All sin is against some*one*, not some*thing*. Imagine how silly it is to think that a father would fight to end drunk driving for the rest of his living days because someone once broke Oregon State Statute 3.46. No. People don't fight against evil because they are angry a law has been broken. They do that when their child has been killed in a car accident. If that were me, I wouldn't seek justice because I was offended that my state's laws had been broken. I would seek justice because my son was dead.

—꿔—

Sin is inherently personal. I think that is why sin is depicted in such sexual terms in the Bible. I pointed out in chapter 2 that the theme of human sinfulness is set in parallel to the act of sexual intercourse in James's epistle. James, in risking such graphic parallels, suggests that it is our dark desires, our sinful natures, that lead us down the path toward conceiving the child of sin that will eventually grow up to become death. There is an exceptional kind of rhythm, a kind of progression to any sinful act that begins much deeper than the act itself. Sin begins with desire, hangs around the bar, starts a conversation, makes its way to a hotel room, and eventually has a child. Sin, as such, never *just* happens. Sin isn't just born; sin grows up, gets a job, and becomes death.

In essence, sin snowballs.

The progression of sin is, of course, a reality every day of our lives. Never once in my experience of walking with friends who have been unfaithful to their spouse have they said the affair "just happened." They tell me the emotional affair started long before the physical affair did: when they started hanging out too long, going to the gym too much, answering texts they shouldn't, fantasizing. Similarly, no pedophile is born overnight. Pedophiles are created when, after time, they give themselves over and over again to ways of thinking that are harmful.

This kind of progression is seen, again, in the story of Hosea, the minor Hebrew prophet. Hosea is told by God to marry a woman of "ill repute." He does. The image, of course, is of God's love for his people. Such provocative images would have made their point in the ancient world. Hosea and Gomer soon parent three children. The Bible does something unique at the end of the first chapter of Hosea: it gives us the names of their children. The three names are Jezreel, Lo-Ruhamah, and Lo-Ammi. What do their names mean? Look at this.

Their names, respectively, are "God sows," "Unfavored," and "Not mine." Who names their children such odd names? More particularly, in an ancient culture where the father named the children, why did Hosea choose such awkward titles for his children? One is left to the commentaries on this one because the mystery of the names of Gomer and Hosea's children is odd. And what the commentaries suggest is astounding. The first name is a positive name. It is like naming a child "God provides." It is a beautiful name. But something happens after the first name because the second name is clearly a negative name— "Unfavored." The last name is simply atrocious. Hosea essentially names his last child "Not my kid."

We get a clue from the progression of the story of Hosea. The progression is clear: Hosea 1 is about the marriage of a prophet and a prostitute, Hosea 2 is about Gomer starting to sleep around, and Hosea 3 is about Gomer giving herself entirely over to prostitution. The names reflect this.

The first child was Hosea's. But the next two—and we see this from the names—*are clearly not his.*

Imagine yourself as Hosea. You have married a woman whom tons of your friends have probably warned you about. But you do so anyway. The honeymoon, as it should be, is incredible. You have a blast. You and your new lover experience all that comes with a beautiful new marriage. You come home and settle into your new life together. After a few months, Gomer gets pregnant. You are going to be a dad! What a blessing and a gift from God. Nine months later, you hold the child in your arms with complete ecstasy.

Soon after having your first child, though, you begin to notice that Gomer is acting strange. She is pulling away. Emotionally, you can sense a kind of distance that you have never sensed before. And you notice other things. She starts coming home later for bed. She showers when she comes home. She often smells of foreign perfumes you've never smelled before. And her cell phone is locked—you can't see what she's texting or who she's calling. You also notice an odd book on her bedside stand called *Fifty Shades of Grey*. She then asks if you'd consider an "open relationship."

But all of your suspicions are swept away when you find she is pregnant again. Putting aside your concerns, you wait, and then you hold your new child in your arms. But something in you tells you things are off. The child doesn't look like it's yours.

Then, after a while, you have a third. And this time around, you *know* the child isn't yours. You don't have genetic testing or anything like that, but you know your kid when you know it's your kid. And you know this *ain't* your kid.

There is a textual brilliance afoot here—the commentaries call what Hosea is attempting to do here a "poetic progression." The names communicate something about the internal life of Hosea. It is as if Hosea is naming his children "Mine," "Pretty sure it isn't mine," and "There is no way in the world this child is mine." It is good, then bad, then worse, until all hope is thrown out the window. In the economy of sin, it seems, one thing always leads to another.

Sin is a progression. Most marriages end exactly the way this marriage broke down—slowly and over time. For in the "creeping separateness," in the words of Sheldon Vanauken, there is a breakdown of love, of hope, and of relationship.[8] Idolatry, according to the Bible, is not always quitting God cold turkey. Idolatry is often more subtle. Idolatry is often our attempt at a polyamorous, no-strings-attached, when-you're-on-that-business-trip-do-what-you-want kind of relationship with God. Idolatry is what we do in Vegas before coming home to our wife and three children and BBQ in the backyard. When God's around, we're intimate with him. But we think he is cool if we take up other lovers at the same time. What is crazy, of course, is not that we try to live in such a relational paradigm. It is that we think God is willing to be loved like that.

When we sin, we wander further and further and further from the truth.

What starts with the simple eating of some fruit becomes the outright murder of a brother.

God has some hard words for Gomer as she goes down this path. As Gomer is about to move toward full-blown prostitution, God says this: "I will make her like a desert" (Hosea 2:3). This opens up a new way to understand wrath in the Bible. Wrath, of course, is not God's lightning bolts from heaven against the evil infidels below whom he can't stand. Wrath is God's way of doing hospitality. It is God's way of letting a wanderer who wants to wander continue to wander in their sin. Real life is the result of someone surrendering to God, "Thy will be done." Wrath, I've heard it said, is the result of someone to whom God says, "*Thy* will be done."

The biggest problem with sin is that we want it. Bad. We all *love* sin.

—⟋⟍—

Judgment is God's way of responding to our incessant desires to choose anything else over him. God will tell us about it. He will judge us. But God's judgment is so much more graceful than we might think. They say that judgment can be clouded by love. And that rings true for the Christian. God's judgment is always clouded by Christ's love for us.

I wrote a book a couple of years back about Christians and the environment. I wanted one of my heroes, Wendell Berry—a Kentucky farmer, poet, and Christian—to write the foreword to the book. A friend, Matthew, knew Berry. And so he decided to ask Berry if he would write a foreword to my book.

In the end, Berry said no. He rejected us. But that was okay for me. His rejection was a sign of grace. For rejection simultaneously conveys the idea of acknowledgment. Berry acknowledged me by rejecting me. It was, in my mind's eye, his way of saying, "Kid, I'm not doing this for you—but I acknowledge your request and your efforts." True rejection would have been hearing nothing at all.

Had we gotten a formal rejection letter, I would have considered making it the foreword for the book. That is how much I love Berry. Even his rejection is an endorsement of my existence.

Judgment is a form of grace. In judgment, you may feel rejected, but you are simultaneously being acknowledged as a human being who is loved. By taking time to confront you, God is equally taking time to love you where you are. The Lord disciplines those he loves

(Heb. 12:6). We have forgotten in our culture that there is a huge difference between judgment and condemnation. If we are in his love, we can be judged, but we will never be condemned. In fact, that is why Jesus can say that he did come to "judge" but not to "condemn" (see John 3:17; 9:39).

—∿—

Hosea's redemption is beautiful. God says he will take Gomer out into the wilderness and woo her back into his love (Hosea 2:14). That is the grace of God. We have a God who seeks to reconcile and find us around every corner and at every moment. We are constantly being sought out.

But if we don't want to be found, we can keep on hiding and running and wandering. There is good reason that the writers of the New Testament speak with grave concern of those Christians who "wander away" from the truth and the faith (1 Tim. 6:10; James 5:19). James is speaking of those who have tasted the love of God and have opted to leave it all. Thus it remains well within the realm of possibility for someone who has seen the beauties of a sunset to come to believe there is no sun whatsoever. The fact that we can "wander away" from truth and the faith means that we can, at one time, touch them with great passion and fidelity and at some point completely abandon them. For whatever reason, faith and truth don't always stick. As scary as it may sound, being a Christian is not a "tenured position." One can literally wander away from the truth that has so touched one's life. And most troubling is the fact that God is so hospitable, so kind, so willing to extend freedom that he will let us do as we please. If we want a cage-free life, he'll give it to us.

—∿—

I've often wondered: Why go through all the trouble?

Why—knowing that all this sin was a possibility—did God even start the garden in the first place?

Why would he let sin happen?

Keeping our garden is so much hard work. Then there are our chickens. Our chickens taught me a great deal about Adam's naming the animals in Eden. Having chickens is a lifestyle commitment. I don't know how to describe it, but there's almost a kind of unspoken peer pressure to own chickens if you live in Portland. It is difficult to escape. People don't hiss at you at the grocery store if you buy eggs or anything, but you become some sort of royalty if you live in city limits, keep your own chickens, brew your own beer, and make your own kombucha. I don't know why these came to be the culturally cool things to do in Portland. But it's safe to say that in the coming apocalypse, inner Portland won't be short of omelets or fermented teas.

Once we had Elliot, we couldn't resist any longer. Even before moving to Portland, we'd always wanted to raise our children around God's good creation. This was hard to do when we lived in an apartment. Now we have the space, big backyard and all. No roosters are allowed in the city. And the city allows only three chickens per household, which, while feeling a little conservative for such a progressive town, turns out to be a handful. We bought three very feisty little chicks from Portland Homestead Supply—a Leghorn, a Rhode Island Red, and a Sex Link. The lady who sold them to us could easily tell we didn't have the slightest notion about the difference between the breeds. She assured us, despite our ignorance, that all three would give us what we wanted—real eggs.

Like having a child, there's quite a bit to do to prepare your home for chickens. Chickens need warmth, love, water, food, and above all a coop to protect them. This was only in the realm of possibility because my friend Josh came over and helped me build the cutest little chicken tractor that we could move around in our backyard every other day or so. Today, we have three emotionally unstable chickens—Anastasia, Mimi-Popo-Jojo, and Freddy. Naming the chickens became an important thing for our family. Each of us had authority to name one of them. I have always been taught that when Adam named the livestock, he was naming them by species, kind of the way a scientist would. "This is *Chickenus adamanus*, and it lays eggs for omelets," he would say.

When I told Elliot that Adam named the animals, he asked me if it was like us naming ours Anastasia, Mimi-Popo-Jojo, and Freddy. I think it was more like that. I wonder if Adam was actually giving them names the way we name people. Something changes when you name your animals. You have a direct relationship, a connection with them. You don't treat animals you've named as utilities—they are your family.

But there it is: I suspect that the greatest gift a parent can pass to their child is a simple knowledge of cause and effect. One thing always leads to another. Without grasping cause and effect, life becomes nearly unlivable. I cherish knowing that Elliot in his simple, childlike wisdom gets to observe firsthand our little beasts eating bugs and scraps and dirt, and that out of all of that—*kazam!*—comes the miracle of eggs. Eggs are a gift, like every other good and perfect gift from above. I want Elliot to know that if he asks God for grace or the Spirit or hope, God will, like a good parent, give it. I also want him to know that if you want eggs, you've gotta feed the chickens. Eggs aren't created *ex nihilo,* out of nothing. All things arise from somewhere. Nothing, save God's creation, just appears. The rest is cause and effect. I want him to know that this leads to that, that chickens come from somewhere—cause and effect. If he can learn that, he can pay his bills, handle a marriage, and get his oil changed in a timely manner.

Then again, I mostly love knowing that Elliot intimately knows the names of our chickens. This first-name basis is the foundation of compassion and grace. Without a name, we are tempted to abuse. A name makes things personal. All of life changes when it gets personal. You think about your eggs differently when they come from chickens that you know. When you name a chicken, you start looking at it differently. I want Elliot to know the names of every creature God has made that he comes into contact with. Our detachment from our food has created all sorts of problems, not least of which is that we don't appreciate the animals themselves before we devour them. When you name an animal, when you know it, when you are friends with it, it is much more challenging to abuse it. If slaughterhouses were made out of glass, we'd all most likely become vegetarians.

Still, I know the chickens have changed Elliot. Every night, we pray together for the world and for each other and for his toys. He had always been reluctant to pray. I think there's a part of us that resists the urge to make prayer a performance. But the first time Elliot did pray, it was very specific. It wasn't for the world, for global peace, for a healing, or for his toys. His first prayer, quite simply, was for the "chickens to be happy." God listens to my boy. They are very happy chickens.

Garden moments like these have been everything for Elliot. Our tomato plants go crazy in the summer. Oregon tomatoes are insane. They come like crazy for about two months. So, for two months, everyone is just trying to get rid of all their tomatoes. I eat more tomatoes during that time than the laws should allow. Once Elliot and I were in the backyard in the tomato plants, and we were on the ground weeding together (weeds were thriving in our garden). I don't know why, but he loves to get down in the dirt and work with his shirt off. There is something about being down in the dirt with papa with the sun beating down on him. Not sure what it is. Out of nowhere, he looked up at me and said, "Papa. In my heart . . . *I love you.*"

Out of nowhere. Now, any parent will know that there is something very special about a child who says they love you out of their own free will. It changes things when you have to tell your child to say "I love you." Forced love doesn't go over well in a parent's heart.

A parent loves to be loved freely.

I guess that is why I am squeamish about certain theological systems that remove this aspect of freedom from the life of faith—a freedom that was established by God in the garden. Universalism, for one, says all are saved and will be in heaven in eternity. That seems like a bummer for people who don't want to be there. Universalism is presumptuous in that way. Likewise, Calvinism speaks of the "frowning providence" of God—a phrase akin to saying that God will save you, but boy, he really doesn't like you. Calvinism says that only those whom God desires to save will be saved, and the rest are toast. That is similarly offensive. Calvinism and Universalism are both challenging for me, ironically, because of the same issue—neither fully takes into account the freedom and responsibility that God established in creation. If God is to be loved, he is to be loved freely. We can't be forced to hug.

I am whisked back to the moment God was working with Adam in the garden. Why in his right mind would God save me and put me smack-dab in the middle of a world overgrown with so much sin, distraction, and evil? Why not end it all? I wonder if this world—God's tomato garden—is that much different from my backyard. I wonder if it is just that God really likes to be loved freely. God isn't coercive. God doesn't force. God welcomes.

Like any good parent, God despises *forced* love.

And that is why God created the garden. He created it because he is a loving God. God loves to love. And God loves to be loved, but not in an insecure way. And the cost of loving and being loved is the potential of being rejected.

That's why God is willing to start a garden like he did. A garden inevitably gets weeds. But just because there are weeds, it doesn't mean you abandon the garden.

God will keep putting up with the weeds because he loves gardening with us.

4

DESERTS

It seems clear that the Bible provides nothing like a map that charts the precise path for us to follow into the future. What it does give us is a *travel itinerary* of God's people, that is, the story of their pilgrimage as strangers and foreigners through this world toward the kingdom of God.

Barry Harvey, *Can These Bones Live?*

I get Moses.

Like Moses, I was raised in Egypt-like conditions. In a way, Egypt was my backyard; my mom was my pharaoh. Not that my mom was an oppressive queen. If she was a pharaoh, she was by far the nicest pharaoh of them all. Don't misread me—I've got a marvelous mom. Yet despite her greatness, a mom's got to do the menial tasks necessary to keep a household going.

Mom gave me one of my first paying jobs. When I was fifteen, we bought a new house that didn't have a garden. It was my job to prepare the soil for her garden. Mom kicked off her dream project of beginning a garden in our backyard—she'd long held hopes of a bountiful garden of tomatoes, raspberries, blueberries, and carrots, among other things—by assigning me the task of searching out every big rock (at the rate of something like five cents per rock) hiding underneath the surface in the parcel of dusty land that was, at the time, a vast strip of fruitless dirt. Hours, days, and months passed as I picked out those rocks and tossed them into a giant wheelbarrow to be wheeled down and thrown in the lake that was near our home.

The work was hard. I'm pretty sure child labor laws were broken. Like the Hebrew children, I "cried out" from under the heat, sweat, and exhaustion of it all. I wanted my freedom. I wanted to be out. I yearned to be anywhere else. And like Moses, I'm pretty sure it was not outside the realm of possibility for me to easily start talking to a bush under the hot Oregon sun. But listen, the food was good. Yes, the work was torture. But when Pharaoh knows how to make meatloaf that's *that* good, you willingly endure the oppression with cash in hand and a smile on your face. Those rocks hiding under the dusty surface were nearly impossible to find. It was like they were invisible. We are still finding rocks to this day, rocks that silently lay like they are playing hide-and-seek.

Christianity deals with the realm of the invisible on a consistent basis. Certainly, much of life consists in the realm of visibility—old cars, dirty napkins, crisp dollar bills, diapers, spandex shorts that should have been tossed years ago. So much of life is about the visible. But not *all* of life is visible. In fact, it is most certain that a good deal of human life is lived in a minefield of invisible things that escape the human eye—invisible attitudes, invisible powers, invisible beliefs, and invisible agendas. Sometimes, like those rocks from my childhood, visible things lay invisible, dormant, quietly hiding under the surface of our lives. Or, for another example, consider my son's LEGO addiction. All the signs of a real problem are there. Of course his parents have played no small part in his problem. We got him hooked. We're his enablers. His closet houses a giant green plastic tub of such massive proportions it is almost impossible to get it out. When we finally do, he'll play for hours constructing the most exotic of worlds. Sometimes, after a long day at preschool, he'll come home, close his door, and spend hours in his closet with those LEGOs.

Before dinner, we clean up. And after cleaning up, all *appears* to be well.

But, alas, all is not well. I've learned the hard way. Over the years, I've been trained by experience to gravitate toward a kind of suspicion of that seemingly "clean" carpet. It will happen at some point in the next couple of days. Walking along, minding my own business, I'll step unprepared on one of his invisible LEGOs. The pain always catches me off guard. Those invisible LEGOs-turned-landmines—they're the death of me. And people wonder why I always wear shoes in my house. There. That's why I wear shoes in my house.

Sometimes visible things are invisible. But every once in a while, invisible things can become visible, for example, when the invisible things of our heart manifest themselves in the visible things of our life. John Calvin once likened the Bible to a pair of glasses that help us see the invisible things of life.[1] The Bible refuses to deal only with the surface level of things. It presses in, pushes deeper, and looks at what nobody else is looking at. And it is through these holy spectacles, Calvin believed, that we are invited to see the invisible dimensions of the world. Perhaps more than anything else, that is why the life of faith as described in the Bible is important for us here and now. In life, we will all step on unseen things that open our eyes to a reality that someone has been around our house playing LEGOs. The Bible invites us to entertain the idea that some things—like hidden rocks in the backyard—are not currently visible to the naked eye.

And more than anything, the Bible unveils the hidden things of our hearts. The author of Hebrews writes, "For the word of God is alive and active. Sharper than any double-edged sword, it penetrates even to dividing soul and spirit, joints and marrow; it judges the thoughts and attitudes of the heart. Nothing in all creation is hidden from God's sight" (4:12–13). Like a pair of glasses that can see beneath the visible layers of our lives to what is invisible, the Bible sees right through us into the deepest recesses of our innermost beings. It calls us out. It finds the rocks and puts them away so the ground might be prepared.

—ɯɯ—

Any conversation about wandering in the present day should immediately sweep us into that great story of God and his people as found in the Bible. The notion of wandering has an inescapable connection to the story of Scripture for all of God's people, but it is keenly central to the story of God wandering through the desert. Part of our task, therefore, is to go on an exploration of some of these desert narratives that we might draw out from them the brilliant gold that they house. The word *wandering* is a familiar word for readers of the Bible, as we've discussed. Particularly for those ancients in Scripture who walked with God before anything had been written down in formalized texts like the ones we have now, the word *wandering* would have been very close to their hearts. In the story of God and God's people, wandering was commonplace. They wandered all the time. God's people knew a lot, did a lot, heard a lot, and talked a lot about their wandering experiences when they finally would put their stories to paper.

An astute reader will note that I talk a lot about history. I admit it: by doing so, I've already stepped on some toes. In contemporary culture, there is a pronounced, visceral prejudice against living in and giving authority to the past. This gets Christianity in hot water because it essentially is a religion that keeps on living in the past. Progressive culture has sold the idea that we would do best to escape the past so that we might move boldly into the future. For instance, we're told that morality has progressed and evolved and become something of a different story in the twenty-first century. And if we are to do well, we should update all of our notions according to the times. Antiquated ideas of truth and morality and ethics are removed and replaced with newer, shinier truths.

"I mean, come on—it's the twenty-first century for heaven's sake." These words seem to be on everybody's lips these days. They've almost become commonplace. I consistently hear this appeal for all kinds of things—a new view of ethics, of morality, of how the human community should exist. Saying it's the twenty-first century suggests we have gotten to a point of human maturity where we can move beyond certain boundaries and certain ways of living that we have recognized for countless years. I have two problems with this. First, those who say that the twenty-first century somehow gives us moral authority to move beyond what has been written aren't actually paying attention to the twenty-first century. We still have racism, murder, rape, abortion, slavery, ecological degradation, and genocide. Nothing has changed. We are just better at hiding our sin. And second, the statement seems to suggest that we have permission to move the natural lines of boundary that God himself made. And it suggests that truth is best served fresh.

With this historical arrogance, we've almost come to believe that the distant past should stay in the distant past. But in order to know where we are going, isn't it important to know where we came from? Can we talk about our purpose without talking about our beginning? In his brilliant commentary on the biblical text of 1 Chronicles, Old Testament scholar Andrew Hill hits the nail on the proverbial head as to why we don't spend that much time reading history, particularly biblical history. "We find ourselves living in a society that craves a future without a past. Increasingly, North American culture is characterized by a 'centripetal individualism' that scorns any communal record framed in the 'preterite tense' because of its preoccupation with self-gratification in the 'present tense.'"[2] This "centripetal individualism" that Hill lucidly speaks of is, simply put, an allergic reaction to the written and lived past—the things that shaped us and informed us and molded us to become who we are. I suspect that is why so many of our more recent Christian forbears recommended that we read not only the newspaper but the Bible as well. We need both. We must enter into the fresh pages of today knowing what has been written before.

It isn't really possible to be a Christian and hate history because Christianity is historical. For our faith and our stories and our ideas are, by and large, quite old. "There is nothing new under the sun," the author of Ecclesiastes wrote (1:9). This means that there are no new stories. No new God. No new truths. All we have are new methods of telling old stories, new words to talk about the same God, new perspectives on the same old truths. To learn to have a conversation about contemporary wandering, it is imperative we have a conversation about biblical wandering in the past.

Which is exactly why paying attention to the past—and reading the Bible faithfully—is increasingly important. The ghosts of the forgotten past will always come back to haunt us when we forget them. Forgetfulness gives our demons their power. Memory dethrones those ghosts. It is often not the past itself that haunts us but our unwillingness to move past it.

History is the hammock on which our future rests.

The whole history of Christianity is a history of people who wandered. Why should we think anything would be different today? A plethora of biblical wandering stories is available for us to remember, recapture, and learn from. We read of Adam and Eve wandering their way from the garden of Eden to the east. A few chapters later, Abraham ventures into the land of Canaan in order to establish what God has for him and his future progeny. Years later, Abraham would reflect, calling his journey a kind of wandering—"God had me wander from my father's household" (Gen. 20:13). Even his grandson Jacob would be known as a "wandering Aramean" (Deut. 26:5). In the years following Israel's redemption from the oppressive land of Egypt, they would spend some forty years "wandering" through the desert on their way to the promised land. Even the wandering Psalms—or the Psalms of Ascent (Pss. 120–134) that would be read as people made their way to Jerusalem for worship—give testimony to this wandering theme. Pilgrim worshipers, year after year, wandered their way by foot to Jerusalem in order to worship the Lord their God. In the biblical version of the "trail of tears," Israel wandered to and from Babylon before and after the total annihilation of their homeland. Later Jonah, a prophet, wandered, stumbled, and tripped his way into the mission field toward the evil city of Nineveh. As I have pointed out, we are even told that

67

the earliest Christians identified themselves as the people of "the Way" (Acts 9:2). As time went on, many medieval Christian writers went so far as to call the Christian a *viator*—a wayfarer, a journeyer, a wanderer through this life on his or her way to the heavenly world.

Christians were a people who were going somewhere—on their way. Still to this day, there remains a tradition suggesting the word *Hebrew* comes from *habiru*, meaning "dusty travelers" or "dusty ones"—an image of a people who continuously find their identity in a desert.[3]

The sheer fact of how many times God's people wander in the Bible is telling. Wandering stories such as these, for me, lend to the Bible credibility and truthfulness. In the words of one scholar, wandering stories, as difficult as they are, bring the Bible a kind of "flavor of authenticity."[4] They would have no purpose in the service of making God's people seem flawless or perfect. If the Bible is seeking to create a celebrity culture around the patriarchs and the biblical cast, it is simply doing a horrible job. The Bible isn't a story of celebrities. It is intended for creating a people of God. And if these stories are true, then the Bible must be an accurate account of faithful spirituality.

With wandering came deserts. One observation repeatedly arises from an attentive reading of both the Old and New Testaments: there is an endless number of desert stories. The Bible largely takes place in a desert world. Of particular note, two desert stories immediately stand out: those of Abraham and Moses. In the early chapters of Genesis, God calls to Abram (who later has a name change to "Abraham") and invites him and his family to pack up their belongings so that they might go to a land "I will show you" (Gen. 12:1). Note the complete lack of geographical directions in the calling narrative—Abraham would have to completely trust the Lord moving forward. In response, Abraham packs his bags, gathers his family, and wanders through the desert by the sovereign hand of God to the promised land. The next few generations would be called the "patriarchs," a list including Abraham, Isaac, Jacob, and Joseph. Following Joseph's death, the people of God are left in Egypt and begin to put down roots in a foreign land. At first, this is a good situation for Israel—they have food, protection, and even some power. But as the years go on, the setup deteriorates drastically. Soon Israel becomes a vassal people, oppressed, overtaxed, and ruled over. Beginning in the book of Exodus, the Bible narrates their experience of being slaves in the land of their oppressor.

Later in Exodus, we are told that God's people begin to "cry out" (Exod. 2:23) to God for his redemption. As they cry, God listens with compassion and is moved to action to free them. Hearing the painful cries of his people, God enters in to rescue the people of Israel that they might worship God and God alone. As a nation, Israel is freed from Egypt through a series of God's interventions (through Moses and Aaron), including plagues, miracles, and signs. Now Israel will walk out of their time of captivity into the desert of freedom. Having crossed the Red Sea, they are no longer oppressed by Pharaoh. Emancipated, they are their own people now. In the desert, they will soon come to a place known as Mount Sinai. For a number of reasons, which we will soon explore, the people of God, freshly redeemed from their Egyptian oppression, will wander in the wilderness for forty years. If I were to show you a map of that time, it would look a lot like someone who has no idea where they are going—lots of circles, backtracking, and seeming confusion.

There in the desert, God would repeatedly enter into a unique expression of his relationship with his people. God was very near in the desert. In Exodus 25, God instructs his people to build what he calls a *miqdash*, or a "tabernacle." In these years before the permanent temple in Jerusalem was constructed, the tabernacle would represent a kind of travel-trailer version of the temple among them. There in the tabernacle, God would be with people as they were in the desert and "*dwell* among them" (Exod. 25:8, emphasis added). God was traveling with them in the desert; God was present with his people. God *dwelled*. God was there. God was present. In those desert years, the cloud of God would cover that tabernacle as a sign of his presence, and the terrible power of God's glory would fill it (Exod. 40:34). Israel was in the desert, the dry place, but God was so close.

Pay close attention to the stories of Abraham and Moses, for their stories share one thing in common. Notice that in both stories God does not deliver his people to the promised land *directly*. Rather, they must first go through a desert experience as they make their way to the final destination. Or you could say that God saves his people, of all places, into the *desert*. Through a series of eye-opening stories (narratives found by anyone bold enough to read Exodus, Leviticus, Numbers, or Deuteronomy), the people of God, Israel, will gingerly wander in circles in an unknown, wild desert landscape just north of Egypt—a land, it might be suggested, they undoubtedly never thought before their emancipation that they'd have to traverse to enter true freedom. Along the way, that scary, terrible land that would come to be overflowing with foreigners, fears, and foibles would soon become clear for what it was. The desert, ironically, came to represent not only a place in their minds but also the space where God's people would experience salvation.

And this fact that God saves his people directly into the desert and not the promised land on the way to their final destination reveals an important truth for us: as far as I can tell, there is no streamlined path toward arriving at holiness. Every path I can find seems to endure the same kind of bumpy circles that Israel endured. The real road to maturity is miserably slow. A to B in God's kingdom sometimes includes lots of circles on the journey, a journey that is rarely linear. It would be nice if we were crows and flew the way they do. But God's people never travel the way the crows do.

One has to appreciate the language of Exodus. It speaks so pointedly to the life of the follower of Jesus in the here and now. For "when Pharaoh let the people go, God did not lead them on the road through the Philistine country, *though that way was shorter*" (Exod. 13:17, emphasis added). God didn't lead them the quick way. He rarely does, does he?

God does not often take his people along the short route.

Such an extreme notion runs counter to the prevailing story Christians repeat to themselves about what Jesus's salvation is all about. We imagine salvation as being freed into lush, green pastures of idyllic perfection. But such a story is not provided in Scripture. Salvation mustn't be interpreted as an improved *old* life, just as Israel's salvation into the desert was anything but an improved Egypt experience. The food, water, safety, and environment were far worse in the desert. Salvation isn't God tinkering with our old life; rather, it is God giving us a completely new one—one we never thought imaginable during our years in the old. And such a new life invites us into new spaces and places. Nor does God save his people *directly* or *immediately* into the promised land. God takes them along the twisting path. The path to true freedom almost never goes as the crow flies. The path to freedom never goes through predictable territory. Rather, the path of Israel's salvation went through a very dry, windy place. This is something that should make sense to a Christian. The saved are rarely welcomed into fruitful, lush spaces. Rather, they are sent to a dry place. Salvation takes place in the wilderness, in the desert, in the dry places.

Of course, I am obliged to remind Christians that when they describe their walk or relationship with Jesus as "dry" (as in, I'm going through a "dry" season), they are unwittingly describing the primary desert experience of Israel's salvation. Dryness isn't always demonic in Scripture. Often a desert is the sign that one has begun the process of salvation. Israel's salvation experience was unbearably dusty. And this theme of salvation into the desert is anything but isolated. For instance, while Galatians does not tell us exactly why, Paul, after his own conversion to Jesus Christ, goes immediately into the desert of Arabia for three years (Gal. 1:17–20). To do what, we simply don't know. Paul doesn't elaborate. Ever. But Paul's conversion is followed up by a desert experience, just like Abraham and Moses. Jesus, likewise, following his baptism in water and the Holy Spirit, is immediately "sent" (Mark 1:12) into the desert, where he will be tempted by the dark one. Dryness, as it were, is not always something to be defeated in the Bible. Rather, sometimes it is a sign of God's inbreaking freedom.

God saves us into the desert. It almost seems, in the Bible, that if it is dry, it looks like salvation. Could it be possible that we are "sent" into desert places?

—⁓⁓—

The desert provides the landing pad of salvation, the starting line of all moves toward promise. Like Abraham, Moses, the people of Israel, Paul, and Jesus, we are invited by God into the dry desert to be with him, for it is there that we begin our walk toward the land of promise. But there is a fundamental problem with the desert for God's people. For it is in the desert where we are tempted to abandon the one who has brought us there. In the desert we get lonely, and the food isn't as good, and we secretly start missing the comforts of our old oppressions. The desert is hard. In the desert, the invisible loves of our hearts that are not centered on Jesus begin to come out. Something about the desert pulls us away from Jesus.

The turn away from worship of the one true God happens quite quickly in the story of Moses. In just two short chapters, the people move from worship to what we call idolatry. Israel, in the desert, begins to complain and daydream incessantly about the quality of their food in the desert—it apparently wasn't nearly as good as their Egyptian food. Israel grumbles. Furthermore, as Moses returns from the top of Mount Sinai bearing the Ten Commandments, he comes down only to find that the people are worshiping a golden calf. What did the golden calf have that God didn't? Did a golden calf rescue them out of Egypt? Does a golden calf provide? Does a golden calf love and care and serve? What made these wandering emancipated slaves so quick to worship something other than the God who saved them?

God's people, in nearly comical fashion, almost immediately replace their external enemies of Pharaoh and Egypt and slavish oppression with a whole litany of internalized enemies: distrust, envy, nostalgia toward the Egypt years, and outright idolatry and worship of false gods. Physical salvation did not immediately translate into emotional or spiritual salvation. While having been freed from their oppressive external enemies, Israel so quickly oppresses themselves internally with numerous invisible drives and forces. As I've often heard it said, it isn't hard for God to get Israel out of Egypt, but it's really hard for God to get Egypt out of Israel. The enemy is no longer external and visible. It's now internal and invisible—slavery soon becomes idolatry.

The visible Pharaoh has been replaced with an invisible, internal Pharaoh.

There has been a good deal of scholarly talk about that golden cow that Israel would have worshiped. What's fascinating is why they chose to worship a golden cow, of all things. Why a cow? What about a golden cow was so worthy of worship? A good many biblical scholars have argued over the years that Israel worshiped a golden cow because a cow was the predominately worshiped god in Egypt.[5] The people of God, therefore, in being freed by an invisible God, were reverting to the worship of the god of their former oppressors. Rather than entering into worship of God the way God desired to be worshiped in the desert, they began to worship the way their old oppressors did. And this is further illuminated by the fact that the gold with which they forged the cow was gold that was given to them by the Egyptians as they left Egypt. Only God's people could be saved by God and turn around to worship the provision of God forged into the image of an Egyptian deity.

There is an old saying: you are what you eat. Moses's descent from the mountain after receiving the law has provided endless fodder for conversation among biblical scholars and theologians as to why God responded the way he did. God's response was odd at best: he made Israel grind up their golden calf and eat it. Why?

I was talking to my wife, Quinn, about that story. She has a theory that I believe has merit. She suspects that God did that as a way to teach a lesson to somebody who loves a false god like a golden calf. You know one of them was so in love with that gold that they would do anything, *anything*, to get it back. And I'm sure someone was so in love with that false god that they would have gone through their own manure to find it. It's as if God is saying, "If you really want to worship another god, fine! Just know, you are going to have to go through a lot of crap to do so."

Idolatry will never give us what we truly want.

And so God's people opted to worship the visible over the invisible. Back to John Calvin. He wrote a good deal on this human proclivity to worship golden cows and such. He writes that the human heart is like a "factory of idols. . . . Man's mind, full as it is of pride and boldness, dares to imagine a god according to its own capacity; as it sluggishly plods, indeed is overwhelmed with the crassest ignorance, it conceives an unreality and an empty appearance as God."[6]

Most of our imaginations will quickly try to let us off the hook, because few, if any, of us woke up this morning in front of an effigy of a golden cow. But theologian Richard Keyes has rightly written that idolatry is a much broader category than we might imagine as some kind of overt, golden-cow worship.

> A careful reading of the Old and New Testaments shows that idolatry is nothing like the crude, simplistic picture that springs to mind of an idol sculpture in some distant country. As the main category to describe unbelief, the idea is highly sophisticated, drawing together the complexities of motivation in individual psychology, the social environment, and also the unseen world. Idols are not just on pagan altars, but in well-educated human hearts and minds (Ezek. 14). The apostle Paul associates the dynamics of human greed, lust, craving, and coveting with idolatry (Eph. 5:5; Col. 3:5). The Bible does not allow us to marginalize idolatry to the fringes of life . . . it is found on center stage.[7]

In other words, idolatry is a fluid category. It molds itself into many forms. Idols reincarnate in each person's life in a unique way. In short, I've never met one person who struggles with worshiping golden cows, but we all have proverbial cows—money, relationships, sex. Idolatry is never us entirely betraying God so that we can have one other lover. Idolatry is never that clean.

Why are God's people always inclined toward worshiping visible things rather than invisible things? An idol is a visible god that arises from an invisible love. It is something that can be seen and touched and held. In the Old Testament, the people of God clearly struggled with the fact that their God, unlike others, was invisible. They often asked God to show up in tangible ways, like the gods of the nations around them. They wanted powerful, visible signs to prove his existence. They struggled with God's invisibility.

I began this chapter by talking about invisible things. In the desert, there is a problem. For in the desert, we often begin to desire to worship the visible things. Life isn't just about visible things. There are invisible realities. And Israel, in the desert, begins an invisible love affair with a visible god that isn't a god after all.

5

INVISIBLE LOVES

Why did you bring us up out of Egypt to this terrible place? It has no
. . . pomegranates.

Numbers 20:5

"I love being a writer," a famous writer once said. "What I can't stand
is the paperwork."

God isn't into busywork or paperwork. He despises the purposeless
work of bureaucratic red tape and procedure. The process of Christian
maturity requires a lot of work, certainly, some of which is appealing.
A lot of it may feel like paperwork or busywork. But we can stand
assured that any work of God in our life is anything but work for the
sake of work. He is seeking to make us into a people who look, smell,
and act like Jesus. He never wastes his own time.

We will find, as we make the journey, that it takes us along paths we
never thought we'd wander down, or want to. As Israel wanders through

the wilderness in the book of Numbers, the people of God begin to complain with great regularity. It seems reasonable that, as they wander from hill to hill, they start seeing everything as a bunch of meaningless adventures. But every little wandering is another wrinkle of maturity on their face. Losing patience, they have to blame somebody. Coming to Moses with their problems, they complain about a whole litany of issues: the lack (or quality) of the desert water, the difficulty and lack of ease the desert life brings, and the mundane flavor of the food God is providing for them. Most memorable is their complaint about "no pomegranates" (Num. 20:5), which apparently were plentiful in their years in Egypt. In cycle after cycle of complaint, Moses responds as any leader of God should respond—by approaching God for direction. But a key observation must be made: these complaints happen over and over and over again as Israel experiences its first years of freedom from Egypt. Israel responds to their newfound freedom by complaining. One of these complaint cycles, as they're often called, aptly illustrates the people's hearts as they walk through the desert: "The rabble with them began to crave other food, and again the Israelites started wailing and said, 'If only we had meat to eat! We remember the fish we ate in Egypt at no cost—also the cucumbers, melons, leeks, onions and garlic. But now we have lost our appetite; we never see anything but this manna!'" (Num. 11:4–6).

In responding to their liberation by complaining, Israel commits the sin of nostalgia—living in the past and failing to recognize the holiness of the present. Nostalgia is seeing God as the Alpha of our beginning, the Omega of our end, but not as the God of every letter in between.

Nostalgia refuses to see God in the now.

Israel's nostalgia didn't come out of nowhere. In the end, that nostalgia was deeply interconnected to what was going on in Israel's heart. Consider what has just happened for Israel: they have just been emancipated from years of slavery in Egypt. These complaints about food and water and pomegranates are coming from a people who have just been set free from four hundred years in Egyptian slavery. Striking, isn't it? It almost seems impossible that God's people could start complaining about the melons, leeks, and free fish given the freedom they are now walking in. What could make a freed people spend all their time thinking about the food of their slavery? The same thing that could bring someone who has been saved from the power of hell to spend all their time complaining about the volume of the music on Sunday mornings or whether a sermon "feeds" them or not. The critical word is "crave" (Num. 11:4). God's people had a secret, quiet *love* for the food from Egypt. They hold an invisible love. And so in experiencing their new freedom, all they can bring themselves to do is complain about the quality of their food.

We tend to be like Israel in so many ways. The scary thing about these complaint cycles remains that it is possible to be freed by Jesus Christ from our sin and depravity yet still function with the desires and cravings of our Egypt years. We must remember that there is a price to be paid for freedom in Jesus—the price of our freedom in Christ is that the food isn't always as tasty and good as it used to be. The food is a bit more bland, predictable, manna-ish. Life isn't as spicy. But at least the food is the kind that can feed our souls. The cost of emancipation in Christ is that we will be asked to leave the comfort and predictability of Egypt to enter the chaotic wilderness of freedom. The food may not be as tasty, but we're free.

This brings up a fascinating interplay between food and deserts in Scripture. As we've observed, desert experiences appear in the stories of the Old and New Testaments. Israel and Jesus both wandered into the desert. In both cases, one thing remains the same: Israel and Jesus were tempted to worship a false god and give into their cravings. Israel was tempted to worship a golden calf. Jesus was tempted to worship his own power, his own authority, and Satan. Israel gave in to their cravings; Jesus did not.

—⚬⚬—

Why is the desert a space where we are often tempted to abandon our love for God and take up love for another? What is it about the desert that makes temptation much more heightened? The desert is a dry place. It is a lonely place. It is an isolating place. The desert is a place where you begin to wonder if you are serving a real God or not. And in the desert you realize that you are there, in the dry place, precisely because of your love of God. Your desire for worship got you there. The desert is a place where we all will be tempted. In the desert, it can feel as though God is gone, distant, disinterested, far away, doing something else. And so in the desert we're going to face the temptation to abandon God. In the desert, God is often invisible. It's easy to think God is with you when the food is good and tasty. It's easy to abandon that belief when there is nothing to eat.

Israel was tempted to worship the false god of their cravings. Jesus was tempted to worship the false promises of the devil. Both were *tempted* in their own desert story. "Idolatry" is the general term to describe what happens when God's people turn their worship, their ultimate love, toward something other than God. Idols are anything we worship other than God.

Be cautious, though: most of our idolatry isn't rooted in outright rejection of God per se. By that I mean we don't run around participating in idolatrous pagan worship ceremonies (at least few that I know do). Our idolatry, our worship of false gods, is rarely overt like that—it is almost always quiet and invisible and hidden in our hearts. But it can spring up out of nowhere. What is remarkable to me is how quickly idolatry happens for Israel following their emancipation from Egypt. It is almost immediate. They are literally just starting to celebrate their freedom—they are freed from their oppression to the Egyptian forces, and in a new relationship with God. And here they are worshiping false gods. It reminds me of an athlete who, after scoring the winning point, jumps up and down in glee only to break his or her ankle. God's people have just tasted victory, and here they are throwing themselves into the arms of a false god. This isn't exactly biting the hand that feeds them as much as cutting off the hand of the one who feeds them and throwing it into the ocean.

In becoming new people, we will always be tempted to revert to the old ways we used to live. And this reversion is almost always incremental in nature, slowly taking over more and more of our hearts.

The temptation to idolatry is always the temptation to live an open, polyamorous relationship with God—to remain in a relationship with God but have a little fun on the side with the other gods. Years ago, I traveled to Tunisia. On one of our first days in the country, our group was touring the ruins of modern-day Tunis, which was the famed city of Carthage in antiquity. Nearing the end of the tour, we came to a house from the first century that is known to archaeologists as "The House of Idols." The house, it turns out, belonged to first-century Christians who had converted to Christianity from paganism. The front room was decorated with Christian pictures revealing a family that had converted to Christianity. A few years ago, however, some archaeologists had accidently bumped the back of the structure, causing the back wall to fall down. What they found behind the wall was a secret room of idols. What they determined was this: it was a family of new Christians who, in their new faith, struggled to give up their old idols.

Those earliest Christians kept their idols in a secret back room and held dearly to their old ways of life. It was as if they loved their freedom but wanted to keep a quiet, secret love for other gods in another room.

—⁂—

No one worships *nothing*.

I have a friend who became an atheist a few years ago. Mostly, he stopped believing in God because he thought faith was a cop-out to not have to think. My friend and I have talked from time to time about his decision to reject belief in God. Certainly, it would be easy to think that in ceasing to believe in God, he has stopped believing altogether. Quite the opposite: he is still a believer in science, reason, and philosophy even if he no longer believes in God.

We are worshipers. Everyone is. We can't help but worship the way we can't help but breathe. I think it is fair to say that if we cease worshiping God, we quickly aim our worship at something else. When we remove God, we in turn put *anything* in God's place—sex, power, identity, comfort. Anything. Without worshiping the Creator, the creation can basically turn to worship anything it wants to. In fact, Paul spoke of this when he wrote that people cease worshiping the Creator and begin to worship creation itself (Rom. 1:25). We were created to worship. The very act of worshipful adoration—a primal, symbolic act that sociologists, archaeologists, and religious historians continue to discover among both contemporary and ancient peoples—has proven to be a faithful mark of *homo religiosus*—humans who are inherently born to be religious.

People are inherently worshipers. We are bowing, worshipful creatures who have the rational, emotional, and religious capabilities and capacities to exalt something beyond ourselves; we are, in the apt words of James K. A. Smith, "liturgical animals."[1] As liturgical animals, we are creatures created to need a Creator.[2] Even when people deny such theistic claims, or remain at least ambivalent toward them, it should be argued that they *still* worship. All—be it faithful, ambivalent, or opposed to the idea of God—are created to worship. In the iconic words of G. K. Chesterton, "The first effect of *not* believing in God is to believe in *anything*."[3] Or, put simply, one cannot *not* worship something; we can alter our altars, but we cannot alter our nature.

When we turn from God to anything else, it is called idolatry. The Bible teaches us that idolatry is a fluid category. By that I mean that people will always be inclined to worship different gods other than God himself. But rarely are two people's idols exactly the same.

It has been said that without God, everything is possible. This oft-quoted and oft-debated phrase that has been attributed to Dostoyevsky may appear, at first, as a bit of an oddity to the general reader. It implies that without God, one can do whatever one pleases. The idea goes that if there is no God, then we are ultimately freed to act and live and be however or whatever we want to act, live, and be. Without God to ground all of our actions in what is right or wrong, we become the basis for all right or wrong. Without going into the debate as to whether one can be moral without God, what does remain true is that removing God from our understanding of the world frees us from having to worry a lick about what he thinks about stuff.

I suspect that when one chooses to remove God (or at least the idea of God) from one's understanding of reality—when one dictates that there can be nothing beyond ourselves, that God is at least an improbability and at most an impossibility—one is left to one's own moral devices to do as one darn well pleases. In short, the person who removes God can do, be, and become everything and anything his or her little heart desires. But if there *is* a God, it's suggested, we will come up against moral limits and boundaries. We will be restricted. Life with God is a life of restraint. We *won't* be able to do anything we please because there is a God who wrote life's owner's manual. But without God we are, in the words of Sartre, "condemned to freedom" to be and will as we desire.[4]

Like I've said, idolatry changes from person to person. For instance, one might be inclined to have an invisible love for comfort. For this person, God is caricatured as a cage, a box, an oppressive limit to our human freedom in today's culture. For so many today, it is as though moving beyond God is the ultimate act of freedom. On the other hand, faith in God can be a way to make ourselves feel better about our cruddy lives. I admit that faith has destroyed me time and time again. Faith has pushed me off the ledge of a comfortable life into an abyss of pain, dissatisfaction, and frustration. For me, faith has annihilated most of my comfort. To push it even further, I guess I feel jealous of those who have rid themselves of the need to believe in God. I grow a little jealous of the atheist and the agnostic. *They have it far easier.* It's almost a gift to not be tormented by belief and faith. I imagine it being so freeing. I wish I could just move on. Life would certainly be easier.

But I can't just move on. God torments me. God won't let me go. My comfort keeps getting crucified. I think that more often than not, each of us struggles with the same pull toward our idols throughout our life. If we struggled with worshiping comfort early on, we probably will struggle with that later on. Salvation that Jesus brings creates a kind of pull in one's life away from the old ways that he seeks to free us from. But those old ways don't just dissipate and go away. They pull and push at us to revert, go back, and return to the false things we used to cling to. I think of the magician in Acts 8 named Simon, who blew everyone away with his magic tricks. He became a Christian. Then, after his conversion, he tried to use Christianity as his new magic trick—something he was wrong for doing. We are all like Simon. Our idols often move along with us through life.

Jesus, then, who seeks to help us remove those idols from our hearts, gives us the Holy Spirit to resist loving them. There is little denying that entering into a relationship with God has the capability of creating a whole new, shiny set of problems in one's life. I'll admit it never ceases to confuse me when I hear someone say that a Christian has bought into faith to serve as some kind of crutch, as if to suggest that they talk themselves into buying a lie in order to make their lives *feel* better. Does this work in the long term? Lies, at least the ones I have believed in the past, never brought me any semblance of long-term comfort. Lies have always ended up costing me way more than the initial deposit. The lies I've bought into have, in the end, been wildly unaffordable. And, furthermore, I guess the idea that faith is a crutch confuses me because faith has rarely proven to be therapeutic in my own life. By that I mean Christian faith is anything but comfortable. In the words of Flannery O'Connor, "What people don't realize is how much religion costs. They think faith is a big electric blanket, when of course it is the cross."[5] If comfort is our god, we will be sorely disappointed with the Christian experience.

Again, in removing God, we can easily turn to worship anything else. Take, for example, our worship of altruism, of doing good. Doing good is not the only goal of being a Christian. Yes, it is important to do good, but one can do good and still be inherently a child of the devil. Historians of World War II continue to be surprised by how so much evil was perpetuated, practiced, and preached by everyday people, not just those in control. The evil was planned from the top and executed by others. German Nazi doctors actually saw their role as procuring a bright future for the state by eliminating the sick, handicapped, and non-able-bodied people. In fact, they viewed their work of either killing or sterilizing them as a "healing work."[6] Hitler called these *Gnadentod*, or mercy killings—putting people out of their misery. The policy of "ethnic cleansing" of Jews, Jehovah's Witnesses, gypsies, and homosexuals was executed largely by simple, everyday people. They just got caught up in it all. This atrocious sweep is described in Christopher Browning's book *Ordinary Men*. The Nazis sent Reserve German Police Battalion 101 into Poland in an effort to massacre the Jews. Over time, these men became mindless and ruthless killers; very few resisted. The killings became routine.[7] Normal, everyday people got caught up in all the evil. We are like what John Wesley described as "human sharks"[8]—normal people caught up in the sin of the world.

People were caught up in the evil. But that was not the whole picture. I was reading a book years ago by Simon Schama called *Landscape and Memory*. He talks at length about what appears to be the most environment-friendly organization in history, an organization that started recycling programs, taught children about the outdoors, and initiated conservation movements—the Nazis. Schama writes, "It is of course painful to acknowledge how ecologically conscientious the most barbaric regime in modern history actually was. Exterminating millions of lives was not at all incompatible with passionate protection of millions of trees."[9] Even evil can be altruistic. Even evil can do good. Even evil can recycle. Doing good is not the final goal of Christianity. Worship and love of God are the ultimate goals. This brings me back to my point: in *not* worshiping God, we can worship *anything*. And that anything isn't always evil. Sometimes we turn to worshiping the good rather than worshiping God.

Worshiping the good is not the same as worshiping God—one can do endless deeds of good but be worshiping good over God. Portlanders generally see themselves as good people. And I would not disagree that Portlanders go out of their way to do all the good they can. Yesterday I was driving down a street and saw one of those Oregon Adopt-a-Highway signs. They're everywhere here; the state budget issues have forced the state to let lots of their highways get adopted. At the bottom, the Adopt-a-Highway signs mention some church or youth group or Cub Scout group that takes the time to clean up a given stretch of beautiful Oregon highway a couple hours once a month. That's the *one* place in Oregon the state advertises religion. But sometimes it's not just religious folks.

The sign I saw yesterday said that stretch of highway was cleaned up by Multnomah County Atheists—it was the cleanest stretch of highway I've ever seen. Maybe it's because there are lots of atheists in Multnomah County, or maybe it's that atheists are really tidy. I'm not sure. And I guess, in hindsight, I'm not all that sure why that little sign caught me off guard like it did. Maybe there's this really ignorant part of my heart that still seems to think that Christians, of all the peoples in the world, are the only ones doing any good. But that sign proves to me that it isn't true—you can do good and not believe in God. An atheist can care about a dirty highway just like a youth group can.

One of the challenges of being a Christian in Portland is that if we are honest, many non-Christians do more good than Christians often do. Christians in Portland have to answer a really tough question: Why are so many non-Christians doing so much good? The church in Portland has had to learn that Christians are not the only ones in the world doing good. The old-school argument that there are no atheists feeding the poor is just simply not true. One does not do good only because of belief in God. People of all kinds of belief do good. And the church has had to recognize this. The church does not have a monopoly on doing good. But the truth of the matter is that doing good is not the thing that defines the church—the worship of the living God is what defines the church. C. S. Lewis was once asked why so many atheists are such good people who do so much good. Lewis responded as only Lewis could: "Well, they have to be good, don't they? If you don't believe in a God who forgives, you are damned to unrelenting goodness."[10] When you *don't* believe in God, Lewis is saying, you are not bound to doing wrong. You are often bound to doing "unrelenting goodness." You are bound to doing good because there is nothing else. Good becomes your god. But good isn't a god. Only God is God.

In fact, we must remember that belief in God—even *perfect* belief— isn't something that will assure that one is either doing good or actually worshiping God. It may seem odd to my readers, but Satan has a better orthodoxy than Christians do. Satan believes in the Trinity. Satan believes Jesus is Lord. Satan acknowledges the power of the Bible—we know that because he kept quoting it to Jesus. Satan has right belief. But he didn't worship God as God.

Right belief does not ensure that one is worshiping God, and right action, doing good, does not ensure one is worshiping either. That is why, in the end, Christianity isn't merely about altruism. In fact, it is entirely possible to desire to do good and be entirely outside the will of God. When the woman sought to pour the most expensive nard on the head of Jesus, the disciples complained that it was a waste, for the money could have been given "to the poor" (Matt. 26:9). Their good intentions were wrong. Sometimes doing something that is good in our eyes is not the will of God.

I am reminded that Jesus, in the desert, was not necessarily tempted by doing bad. Rather, he was tempted to do that which, in his time, would have *looked good*. Satan tempted Jesus with good, admirable things. That is the nature of temptation. We can be tempted by good, or we can be tempted by evil. We can be tempted by anything. Our hearts are messed up. We long to find love in all the wrong places.

We have done a great job of replacing God with doing good. In Portland, people volunteer, run nonprofits, and fight for justice—our city has more nonprofit organizations per capita than any other city in the world. But we need to recognize that we can turn even something good like altruism or justice into an idol that replaces God. We aren't called to worship doing good or seeking justice—rather, we are called to worship God above all. One can even worship justice over the God of justice. One can worship doing good over the God who is good. That is incredibly interesting to think about, isn't it?

I have come to find that the idol of perceived goodness is one of the most challenging ones to overcome in sharing the good news of Jesus. Like the rich young ruler who comes to Jesus thinking he has done everything right and perfect, confessing he believes he "lacks" nothing. It is in thinking we "lack" nothing that we lack everything.

But people's perception of their own inherent "goodness" is going to be a problem if they are interested in Christianity, because Christianity doesn't dance around the concept of "sin." In fact, I would even suggest that our own ideas about how "healthy" we may be become the very "sickness" that we are blind to: Jesus said he came for the sick, not the healthy (Luke 5:31). That doesn't mean that Jesus believed there were sick people and healthy people—rather, it means there are the sick and the terminally sick who buy into the lie that they're actually healthy.

If this is true—that we all worship something—then everyone is a believer . . . in something. In reality, atheists are some of the most religious people in the world. Madeleine L'Engle, the literary genius, hits the nail on the head: "It has often struck me with awe that some of the most religious people I know have been, on the surface, atheists. Atheism is a particular state of mind; you cannot deny the existence of that which does not exist. I cannot say, 'That chair is not there,' if there is no chair there to say it about."[11] L'Engle's point was that atheism is faith based, not reason based. I think there is something to be said about that. Everyone believes in something or someone—the whole world is a faith community, not just the people who go to church.

If this is true, it completely undermines the assumption that idolatry is something that only evil, malicious, horrible people do. One can do good and miss God. The road to hell is indeed paved with good actions.

Our hearts are driven by a whole set of invisible loves.

These cravings cause us to go after all sorts of things we aren't created to go after. We crave Egyptian food. But the food of freedom is the only food that sustains us, even if it is more bland. My whole week is centered around communion. Every week, it is that moment where I orient myself once again to a visible loaf of bread and a visible cup of juice and return to the sustaining bread of life. When you think about it, communion is the one thing in our week that *visibly* represents the grace of God for us. Without communion, I would wander. I would wander toward the meaningless. I would wander toward the unnecessary. I would wander toward that which brings death. I would wander toward busyness. I would wander toward wanting Egyptian food. Once a week, at the same time and in the same place, I turn, walk forward, kneel, put out my hand, receive a piece of bread, dip it in juice, and drown again in the graces of our God. "Jesus is the image," writes the apostle Paul, "of the *invisible* God" (Col. 1:15, emphasis added).

God knows what we need. And we need visible things to orient us toward an invisible God; that seems to be human nature. Humans are created visible. And, as we've seen, humans are drawn to worship visible things, both good and bad. God, however, is invisible. While God would dwell with his people in the tabernacle, he did so invisibly. In fact, on multiple occasions when people tried to see God for themselves, they were killed. God even said that if anyone saw his face, they would die. Of course, he let some people see parts of him. But nobody could see his *face*. And there is a reason. We *literally* can't handle the truth. If truth were visible in its truest form, we would wither and die.

It is almost as though God knew how humans are used to worshiping visible things. So God came to be visible: Jesus is the image, the picture, the representation, the manifestation of the invisible God. If Jesus is God, then the incarnation represents an incredible change in the world's experience of God. For now, in Jesus, one can look into the face of God and live. We can see all of him. We even saw him naked on the cross and lived. Long ago, if someone living looked at God's face, they would die. Now, if someone who is dead looks at God's face and believes, they will live. Christianity deals in the visible and the invisible, particularly the invisible things of the heart. What's powerful about Christianity is that God opts not to remain invisible. God came, God was seen. We saw, we heard, we touched him, John says (1 John 1:1).

The imagery of this is powerfully seen in the beginning of John's Gospel. John says that Jesus came and "made his dwelling among us" (John 1:14). His word usage is telling; John opts for the word *eskēnēsen*, the word rendered "tabernacle."[12] John is saying God "dwells" with us *as* God dwelled with them in the desert. He uses the same word used in the desert narratives when God "dwelled" with his people in the desert. Eugene Peterson's translation of the text remains timeless—God "pitched his tent" with his people (MSG).

And today we center our worship on the visible. When Jesus called himself the "bread of life" (John 6:35), he knew what he was saying. We celebrate the Lord's grace with bread and wine. When the psalm says, "Taste and see that the LORD is good" (Ps. 34:8), I wonder if it has in mind the people of God in the desert. For certainly, the food of freedom is an *acquired* taste. Some just don't like the taste of Jesus Christ. Eucharist is not something the church does. It is imperative we learn to see it another way: the church is something the Eucharist does. Christ's church is broken by the bread. The church doesn't create the Eucharist; the Eucharist creates the church. We gather around, in love and worship, something that existed before we did.

We become the food we eat. It is true. And we become not only what we eat but *how* we eat. That is why there are no stipulations surrounding what kind of bread or wine are to be used in communion. But there are lots of commandments around *how* one is to eat. The visible pulls us back into a love for the invisible.

6

WALKING

All that is gold does not glitter,
Not all those who wander are lost.

J. R. R. Tolkien,
The Lord of the Rings

If you pay close attention just following a national tragedy, or a major
social decision by the Supreme Court, or some history-making event
with widespread moral implications in America, some Christians will
offer a surprising kind of narrative in response: *Jesus must be coming
back.* There are two things at play here: one a misconception, and
the other, a truly understandable, and important, belief. Of course,
the fact that someone would suggest Jesus's return due to what is
going on exclusively in America is a truly American concept. Jesus
will return, I am sure, but I am not as sure it will be directly related
to how America is doing. That aside, the fact that the church would

yearn for the return of Jesus in times of societal pain and struggle is understandable. It would seem natural, of course, to desire a kind of escape in really difficult societal times. I would even suggest that feeling is biblically attested: even Paul himself seems at moments in his Letter to the Philippians to want to escape and just go to heaven. In the face of major personal upheaval, it is natural to want it all to end.

I think we shouldn't see Jesus's return as an excuse to escape a hurting world. Rather, it should be the very reason we *stay* and help out. Jesus's return shouldn't be escapism. I hold unflinchingly to the inspiring words said to be from Martin Luther: "If I knew Jesus was coming back *tomorrow*, I'd plant an apple tree *today*."

The key, of course, was that Paul *didn't* escape. He chose to stay and help. He remained for the sake of those around him. The lesson of the life of Paul is that we are created to strive, press on, and not escape. The desire to escape will probably never go away, but despite it, we are created to "press on."

Humans are made to strive, to press on. The only time in my life that I have been depressed was after I finished my PhD. After working for years and years and pouring my heart and soul into the project, I finished. It was with great elation that I finally reached the goal. But shortly thereafter, I began to grow sad and weary and depressed. They never tell you this, but finishing a degree, writing a book, having a child—these are not the finish lines of the projects. These are the starting lines of whatever comes next. And when these wonderful things happen, you can trick yourself into thinking you are "all done." I started getting depressed because I believed I had "arrived." And the minute I thought I had "arrived" was the minute I started losing my purpose in life. That's when I got depressed.

Humans are created to strive, to be heading somewhere. In the words of Thomas Schmidt in his phenomenal little book on Christian maturity called *Trying to Be Good*, we are created by God to constantly be "striving" while not "arriving."[1] That is, we are created to push forward, to press on, to be on our way somewhere. This is the kind of thing Paul spoke of from prison when he said, "I press on toward the goal to win

the prize for which God has called me heavenward in Christ Jesus"
(Phil. 3:14). Paul *presses on* toward the goal. We were created for that
kind of ongoing striving.

I've learned a great lesson about myself: I thrive when I strive, when
I am pressing on toward something. And the minute I start arriving is
the minute I start dying.

All steps forward in maturity in Christian spirituality are starting
points, not goals.

—⁓⁓—

In his book *Reflecting the Glory*, N. T. Wright suggests that one of
the frightening things about the wilderness experience is how many
voices one hears in it.[2] It's hard to discern between those voices—which
ones are truthful and worthy of our attention and which are dangerous
and should be ignored. What is the devil and what is an angel? The
desert is the place Jesus debates the devil and is comforted by the
angels—imagine the chaos had he confused the two. The wilderness
is the place where we wonder, "Will I make it, or is this the end of the
line?" Everything depends on which voice you listen to in the desert.
Certainly, the desert is a scary place, but it can be a God place. Just
because it is dry doesn't make it evil. The wilderness is scary, but
sometimes, very holy.

As were all the patriarchs, Abraham was a man well acquainted
with deserts. If he had written an autobiography, Genesis 12 would
have been a cornerstone experience in his story. There, Abraham and
Sarah are called by God to go to a land called Canaan. It is there, we
see later in the story, that God will establish a place for his people
known as the promised land. When God calls Abraham, the calling
remains rather vague—God invites him to come to "the land I will show
you" (Gen. 12:1). God does not give Abraham a map. God does not
tell him which way to go. God does not give specifics. God just invites
him to the land God would show him. And so Abraham and Sarah
would wander through the land together on their way to this place of
promise in Canaan. But this mapless adventure would have been so

foreign to Abraham. In the story in Genesis 11 preceding Abraham's call, Abraham and his family had set out from a city called Ur (where Abraham grew up) and settled in a city called Harran.

That path was an interesting one. The path from Ur in to Harran runs alongside the gigantic Euphrates River. The whole way between Ur and Harran was along a big, visible river that one could easily follow. Now, when we contrast these two journeys of Abraham—between Ur and Harran and Harran and Canaan—it reveals something very interesting. The first leg of Abraham's journey was a safe, watered, predictable path. A river is a safe place when you live in the desert. A river is a safe place because you aren't concerned about being attacked from one side. A river is a good place because you can fish. But mostly, a river is a natural path, a road, and a predictable journey. You just *follow* the river. But along the second leg of the journey from Genesis 12 on—the journey from Harran to Canaan—Abraham and his family had no such safety. That path went straight through the desert. That path had no river. It had no protection. It had no fishing. And mostly, it had no predictability. Abraham must have learned quite the lesson from these two journeys, a lesson we must learn as well.

Sometimes the path runs along the safety and predictability of the river. But sometimes the path goes away from the river through the danger and dryness of the desert. There are rivers and deserts.

The difference between the two is similar to the difference between preaching from a script and preaching off the cuff. This is not to say that one is right and the other is wrong. There are times for both. I once learned that some of the earliest Pentecostal Christians believed preaching from a manuscript was a sin because it did not demand that a person rely on the Holy Spirit. Of course, this assumes that the Spirit *couldn't* be involved in the writing process of a sermon. Certainly, the Spirit can be, and is, involved in both. I also once heard of a preacher who stood up every week and preached by reading a manuscript. We need both, don't we? There are times we stick to the script. Then there are times we have to wing it. God can be in both. God is along the river, and God is in the desert.

There are river times and desert times. There are times the path is clear and times the path is unclear. Regardless of the time, we must still continue to walk. These two ways of following God—along the path and through the mapless territory—are seen elsewhere in the Bible. The same kind of idea is at play in the life of the magi, those distant kings who left their homeland to find and worship Jesus, bearing gifts. Standing and worshiping before the baby Jesus, these travelers reveal to us so much about the way in which God operates in the world. For the manger had quite an open-door policy. *All* were invited to worship. But it is the magi's journey to the manger that stands out to me. They followed a star, we are told. It would have been easy to travel by night, for it is only at night that the star is brightest. But during the day, they had to use an entirely different set of senses to go in the direction they were to go. Walking the walk of worship will always demand that we know that discerning the way at night may very well be different from discerning the way in the day.

I find that I walk out the footsteps of Jesus *before* I am aware they were the right ones. Clark Pinnock is a theologian whose work and career have given so much shape to my own. He described in a similar way how he learned about the kingdom of God: "I approach theology in a spirit of adventure, being always curious about what I may find. For me, theology is like a rich feast with many dishes to enjoy and delicacies to taste. It is like a centuries-old conversation that I am privileged to take part in, a conversation replete with innumerable voices to listen to. More like a pilgrim than a settler, I tread the path of discovery and do my theology en route."[3] In harmony with Pinnock, I can agree that so much of my own understanding of God happens "en route," as it were, after or even during trying to do what he has said to do. Some would say that you can best "love your neighbors" by doing a complete study beforehand to know exactly the best way to appropriately love others. I think learning about loving happens en route, as we are trying to do it.

My big point is this: discerning the path of our journey with Christ doesn't always happen the same way. At one moment we find ourselves walking along the river; at another we trust in God's invisible hand of guidance because the path is unclear. Sometimes we use one means to discern the voice of God. At other times we rely on other sources. Like Abraham, at different times we must use different ways to discern the way forward. In the beginning of the journey, often it feels like Abraham's first leg. There are times—perhaps earlier in our faith—when the journey is predictable and safe and watered. At other times, however, we no longer walk alongside the safe path of the river. Once we leave the path of the river, we begin to walk into the scary lands of unpredictability. One might say Abraham entered into the new paths of trust. While I am not sure he would have used the same language as we would, I do think that this second stage of his journey involved his learning to "walk in the Spirit." Of course, in the Christian story, we believe that God literally dwells within us as we walk around. Everywhere we go, the abiding presence of Jesus Christ in the Holy Spirit goes with us.

"The Spirit indwells," writes the German theologian Jürgen Moltmann. "The Spirit suffers with the suffering. The Spirit is grieved and quenched . . . indwelling in wandering and suffering created beings."[4]

The Spirit indwells wanderers wherever they walk.

Often, somewhere in early adulthood, we stop having much patience for the path that doesn't run along the river. As we get older, we want things to be predictable and safe. We dream of idyllic certainty. But the story of Abraham is one that begins along the safe Euphrates but emerges into the scary and unknown desert. I remember those early years before I lusted for such a predictable, safe life. When I was a child, my parents gave to me—along with a treasure trove of other toys that have been lost to time, or one of many local Goodwill donations—a giant, metal spinning globe of the world painted in many colors. Other than school, that spinning globe was my initial introduction to the geopolitical world outside my little hometown. Most of all, I recall some of the colors of the countries on the spinning globe. Madagascar was brown, *bright* brown against the backdrop of the bright blue Indian Ocean. China, unsurprisingly I later came to find out, was bright red. (Communist countries were always either red, purple, or black.) And finally, we, the great U.S. of A., were as tan as a field of Iowa wheat. (I suppose I always thought Canada was made up of women because Canada was bright pink.)

Looking back, that globe had a subtle effect on my emotional psyche. Having that globe made me feel powerful, like the way you feel powerful when you see an anthill. You feel almost godlike. The spinning globe made me feel almost sovereign over the world. Alongside my prized baseball card collection that I'd been perfecting for years, I treasured my multicolored spinning globe of the world. I embrace vivid memories of sitting there cross-legged in my room, right there before the globe, closing my eyes, spinning the world violently with all my upper-body strength, only to stop it with my pointer finger. *I'm going to live there,* I thought. Except for the few hiccups when my finger committed me to living the rest of my life smack-dab in the middle of the Pacific Ocean or the Mojave Desert, my luck put me in exciting places.

As most of us do somewhere down the road, I stopped spinning the globe. We all stop spinning the globe at some point and want to "settle down." I guess you stop spinning the globe when you have kids or get a mortgage or something like that. My globe was lost over the years alongside many of the other relics of my childhood. And, as life would have it, I never moved to Canada or the middle of the Pacific Ocean or some exotic island. Life has turned out rather mundane compared to the excitement my childhood held for the future. Not that I'm sad about it. It is just way less exotic than I'd imagined it would have turned out. Now I have a wife, a child, a house payment, a church to pastor, three chickens to feed, a mother and a father to call, and a neighbor's yard to mow. However, before all of life's commitments and responsibilities took root, I felt so free. I truly believed I could have moved anywhere and been anything. The whole wide world was literally at my fingertips.

If today I somehow found that lost globe, sat down in my room, spun it, and decided to go where my finger landed and leave everything behind, there would be a lot of devastated people. If I went where my finger led, a delightful wife would have a very different life, a sweet little boy would no longer have a father around, a wonderful church would lose their pastor, and my neighbor's grass would grow too long. It's probably good I lost the globe. But that doesn't mean I don't dream. I do. We all do. We all think about running away, escaping, getting out of Dodge. For all of us, there's a kind of seductive attraction—almost a lust—to get our globe out, spin it, and start pointing the finger. I constantly feel this tension inside me, this craving for liberation.

—⁂—

Last year at Easter time, I did my best to explain to my three-year-old boy the story of Christ's resurrection. I told him about how on Friday, Jesus was placed in the cave, dead. Saturday, Jesus lay in that grave alone in his death. But on Sunday, when everyone woke up, Jesus was no longer in the cave. "Where did Jesus go?" he asked me. I told him he came back out, that death couldn't hold him inside for longer than one day. Elliot then asked me a provocative and thoughtful question: Did Jesus walk out the *other side* of the tomb?

I've been asked a great many questions about resurrection, but that one takes the cake. Of course Jesus didn't go out the other side of the cave. It wasn't a tunnel, it was a cave—there was one way in and one way out. But Elliot's question begged a deeper insight that I'd never fully considered. In not going out the other side of his grave, the resurrected Jesus chose to come out the same exact path that took him in. True resurrection isn't the result of an escape door out the back of our death. True resurrection requires real death, and the ones who are resurrected go back across the same terrain of pain that brought them there. Jesus came out the same path on which he'd been carried in.

Walking is a very important theme throughout the Bible, a theme I want to take a brief look at. For example, the Bible begins with walking. After creating the world, Adam and Eve walked with God throughout the garden of Eden. God himself walked—"The man and his wife heard the sound of the LORD God as he was walking in the garden" (Gen. 3:8).

God walked with humanity. Why did God create the garden of Eden? Was God in need of more vegetables? I think not. God created Adam and Eve because God wanted some friends—someone to walk with and talk with and explain how he invented cucumbers.

Then came sin, as we've discussed. Immediately after the fall of humanity, nobody walks with God for two whole chapters. Then something happens in Genesis 5 when we are introduced to a man named Enoch, who, the text conveys, "walked with God." "When Enoch had lived 65 years, he became the father of Methuselah. After he became the father of Methuselah, Enoch *walked faithfully* with God 300 years and had other sons and daughters. Altogether, Enoch lived a total of 365 years. Enoch walked faithfully with God; then he was no more, because God took him away" (Gen. 5:21–24, emphasis added).

Enoch walked with God, the Bible says, the same way Adam and Eve walked with God. To make the point stronger, Scripture uses the same word in both instances of Enoch walking with God as it uses for Adam and Eve walking with God. Once again, people begin walking with God as they had before. When you think about it, there's nothing particularly spectacular about that fact. Enoch didn't die on a cross. He didn't build a boat to save the world. He didn't rescue a people from annihilation. What he did, his special mark, was that he "walked with God." That was special enough for the Bible to take note of. There's actually an old Jewish commentary on the story that suggests Enoch was a cobbler who made his own shoes and was known for being a good walker.[5] And he would need them, because Enoch walked with God.

The God who walked with Adam and Eve was walking with Enoch. God, throughout the Bible, is a walker. So when God comes to the world in the form of a human being in the person of Jesus, what does he do? Well, Jesus walked. Jesus walked a lot. Jesus walked by the sea of Galilee (Matt. 4:18); he walked by Matthew at his tax collector booth (Matt. 9:9); and Jesus walked on water (Matt. 14:25). And all of this in just one Gospel! When Jesus speaks to the seven churches, he "walks among" them (Rev. 2:1). Jesus is most often walking, and so are his disciples with him. When one looks at the terrain of Jesus's teaching and ministry, it is fascinating to consider *where* it was that Jesus was teaching his disciples. Next time you read the Gospel of Matthew, Mark, Luke, or John, look at how many of Jesus's teachings took place as he and his disciples were on their way somewhere. Given the fact that almost none of the recorded teachings of Jesus took place in a synagogue or a religious setting (although there are a few), we can come to appreciate how important walking was to Jesus. Jesus taught as he walked. I once read a New Testament scholar who suggested that some 75 percent of the teaching of Jesus in the New Testament took place as he and his disciples were walking between places. Jesus taught on the walk.

The word for "walk" in the New Testament is *peripateō*. This is why we call Jesus a "peripatetic" teacher—his walk was his talk. Or, more precisely, he walked and talked, and the two were one.

It may be helpful to point out that throughout the New Testament, *walking* is an operative term used for the Christian life. Faith is like walking. Of course, we've updated our metaphors for the Christian life in recent years, updates I'm not entirely a big fan of. Now, God is our "copilot," borrowing the image of flying somewhere. But anyone who has ever tried the Christian life knows that the Christian life never happens "as the crow flies." The terrain is real and difficult. In an age of automobiles, we talk of God "taking the wheel," emphasizing getting places with God faster rather than at a slow pace. We have largely rejected the slow walk as an operative way to understand faith. As for the walking metaphor, Paul continuously spoke of the need to *peripateō*, or "walk" out, the Christian life (Rom. 6:4; 8:4; 14:15). Paul exhorts his readers to "walk by the Spirit" (Gal. 5:16). In his Letter to the Ephesians, Paul writes that we should "walk in the way of love" (Eph. 5:2) and "walk as children of light" (Eph. 5:8 ESV). And this new walk is different from previous walks; in Christ, they weren't to walk as they did before (see Eph. 2:2–3 ESV; 4:17 ESV; Col. 3:5–7).

This use of the walking image continues in the early church. For instance, St. Augustine is quoted as saying that the Christian must always keep walking, never growing satisfied. "If you would attain to what you're not yet," wrote Augustine, "you must always be displeased by what you are. For where you are pleased with yourself, there you have remained. Keep adding, keep walking, keep advancing."

Faith is to be walked out.

When God invites a follower of Christ into a desert, the Spirit goes with that person. And that is so important for the times when we don't have a river to walk along, when the path isn't perfectly carved out, when the geography gets a little murky. As we wander, God's Spirit gives us fire by night and a cloud by day, going with us, walking with us, being present with us.

If we walk in the Spirit, then technically *nothing* is wandering.

Yes, there are periods in the journey of faith during which walking seems clear, as one would walk beside the river. But sometimes the journey isn't clear. Sometimes we walk through the desert to "the land God will show you." There will be seasons of time when we have absolutely no idea whatsoever what we are supposed to do with our lives, with our future, with our hands. And in those times when the river isn't beside us, we have hope because we "walk in the Spirit." And when you walk in the Spirit not knowing *where* you are going, you let go of the destination and merely take the hand of God, who is with you. When you walk in the Spirit, every step is the "point B." For the one who walks in the Spirit, everything—going to the post office, a root canal, or a workout—is a mission trip. Why? Because God's Spirit is with us.

Walking in and with the Spirit doesn't look all that pretty to outsiders.

Had we watched Israel walking through the desert on their way to the promised land and taken note of how many loops, circles, and mistakes they made, we would have thought that they looked like complete fools who aimlessly followed no God. In fact, Pharaoh looked at Israel in the desert and thought to himself, with hardness of heart, that they were "wandering around" (Exod. 14:3) out there in the desert. Pharaoh probably saw their wanderings and thought to himself, "Man, they're just a group of lost, bumbling, confused people." But of course, God was with them. God went with them in the cloud and the fire.

More often than not, it's possible to appear as though you are lost when in reality you are on the right track. Whether we are on the right path or not is not for Pharaoh to decide; it is God's business. One may be tempted to look at a person of faith and say, like Pharaoh, "They're lost." But that would be to misunderstand the nature of faith. In God's economy, often those who look the most lost are the ones on the right path. And that is because those on the path everyone is on will look down on those who are on the path few are on. And the pharaohs of the world can only look down skeptically on those whose journeys look way more chaotic than theirs.

Israel left the predictable life of Egypt only to embrace the chaotic wilderness of their freedom. Walking in freedom is hard. It is lonely. Few others are interested in walking it. But, like Israel, we do not walk alone. "Walking in the Spirit" is a funny but critical way of describing the life of faith. As an illustration, I liken it to the making of a movie that came out a number of years ago called *The Blair Witch Project*. The story of the film is of three hikers who are caught in the hills of the wilderness at night while being chased by some ghoulish sounds. The makers of the movie wanted it to be as realistic as possible, so the acting was not scripted. The actors were given a camera, and the directors would place a box with directions in their camp every morning. During the filming, the reactions of the actors were real and unscripted.

Walking in the Spirit is a bit like the filming of *The Blair Witch Project*. It is an unscripted walk. The reactions are to be real. We wake up every morning and are open to doing whatever God has put in the box the night before. The Christian walk is also a lot like a scavenger hunt; we seek out the next task God has for us. It is that holy process of waking up every morning and honestly asking God, "What does today hold? What are you doing today? What would you like me to do?"

—ᨆ—

On my first historical tour through the city of Istanbul, Turkey, our tour guide took our little team to an old Eastern Orthodox church in the heart of the urban matrix. From the literature, we quickly discovered that the church had been there some seventeen hundred years, welcoming some of the first Christians in the Eastern world. The space was holy. The simple knowledge that the little halls have held the worship of those lifting their hearts, hands, and lives before the Lord their God was profound. When we visited it, we were overwhelmed by the history as we walked the vestibule, the sanctuary, and the quaint gift shop.

Just before leaving, I was taking pictures of the artistry on the ceiling in the corner of the sanctuary. And there, I saw something odd. There was a picture of Mary and Joseph with their arms outstretched like they were waiting for someone to grab their hands. And there he was, Jesus, a child of about two, walking toward them gingerly. He was halfway walking, halfway crawling. And it dawned on me what it was. I was looking at a picture of Mary and Joseph as they watched Jesus Christ, Son of God, Creator of heaven and earth, through whom all things were made, taking his first steps.

Even God, in Jesus, learned how to walk.

And he didn't learn to walk just one time, but two times. Jesus walked as a child, and he had to learn to walk again after his resurrection. He took his first baby steps, and he learned to take resurrection steps.

What did Jesus do after his resurrection? Two things. First, he ate a ton of food. This is a distinguishing mark of his resurrection body. On multiple occasions, Jesus keeps eating food. I think resurrection is not the end of our human appetites but rather the renewal of them. For instance, when Jesus raises a little girl from her death, the first thing he instructs the people to do is get her something to eat (Mark 5:21–43). Resurrection, it turns out, doesn't end hunger. Rather, it makes one hungrier. Jesus eats after his resurrection. Yes, there will be food in the new heaven and the new earth.

But second, Jesus walked around a lot. He walked through the city. He walked the road to the tomb. He walked among his disciples. He walked around the city where he had been crucified. And he had some powerful capabilities in his resurrection body. Jesus could walk through walls. On one occasion, the disciples are huddled together, and all of a sudden he is standing in their midst (John 20:19). Karl Barth pointed out in his *Church Dogmatics* that Jesus both can walk through walls and "stands at the door and knocks." Barth was caught by this paradox: Jesus asks us to invite him in, but he also has the power to walk through walls uninvited. Barth writes, "It is quite true that a [person] must open the door to Jesus. . . . Another thing also remains unreservedly true, that the risen Christ passes through closed doors (John 20:19)."[6]

Jesus can walk into a room even if the door is closed. In his resurrection state, Jesus can walk through any wall and get where he pleases. What is significant about the fact that Jesus walked around Jerusalem in his resurrection body? He walked during his earthly life, and he walked during his resurrection life. And, so, my boy's Easter-time question still knocks on my own heart: "Did Jesus walk out the other side?" No. Jesus walked the very path that led to his grave. Jesus went to his disciples who had abandoned him at his death. Jesus went to his disciple who forsook him three times. Jesus went to a disciple who doubted him. Who revisits such painful places? Why would Jesus use his resurrection walk to revisit such harsh memories?

It is telling that the psalmist in Psalm 23 never confesses that he "walked *around* the valley of the shadow of death." The psalmist walked *through* the valley of the shadow of death. Nor did Jesus walk around the grave. He really went there. And he really came out the same way. Christianity is not a death- and pain-denying religion. Christianity does not invite us to walk around death or the way therein. Christianity does not invite us, as one author put it, to have a "hidden but cherished illusion of immortality."[7] Why? Because if you are in denial about death, then you can't experience resurrection. We don't walk *around* death; we enter it with Jesus. We walk *through* it with him. Jesus goes back to the places that hurt him dearly. He revisits painful stuff.

Unlike us, Jesus had hard skin but a really soft heart. We reverse it. Often we have soft skin and a really hard heart. We neglect to recognize that as we are resurrected with him, the same Spirit who lives in us will actually lead us to places that hurt, to places of pain, to places we don't want to go. Paul's Letter to the Romans says, quite simply, that "the Spirit of him who raised Jesus from the dead is living in you" (Rom. 8:11). For followers of Jesus, that is important. The same Spirit who caused Jesus to rise out of the grave and in whom he walked through such painful places is in us. And if in the renewing life of the Holy Spirit Jesus revisited all of his painful places to see healing take place, then shouldn't we?

When Paul says to "walk in the Spirit," we are being invited to walk the same path that Jesus did. We revisit the hard stuff. We reconcile with people who crucified us. We walk the same city that rejected us. That is why people who are living the life of the Holy Spirit can engage pain and don't see it as an enemy of faith. We don't skirt around it. Like Jesus, we walk bravely in the life of resurrection, a kind of walking that demands great strength and courage. For the first time, the words of Parker Palmer are starting to come alive for me: "For years I shared the common Christian notion that Jesus' greatest courage was in his willingness to go to his death on the cross. But now I am not so sure. His life was a continual struggle, and the thought of death may have been restful. Perhaps his greater courage was to accept resurrection—after all, sitting at the right hand of God for all eternity is hardly a job without burdens."[8] Resurrection walking isn't easy walking. And the ultimate enemy to it is the kind of fear that is the direct result of hatred, rejection, and ultimately crucifixion. I don't think people who don't have some kind of limp in their Christian walk can be trusted. I think one should be wary of Christians who don't have any problems. They aren't real. And they aren't walking in the resurrection life.

There is something powerful and necessary about revisiting painful places. I remember watching a documentary a few years ago about one of the concentration camps from World War II where countless Jews were murdered. The documentary focused on one of the German towns near one of these camps. After liberating the camp, the soldiers led the townspeople through the camp so they would know what they had been complacent about for years. Some Germans who saw what they'd turned a blind eye to committed suicide. Some simply refused to believe. Others sat there and wept. Jürgen Moltmann, one of the most important theologians of the last century and a German soldier during World War II, says that the only way to wake up from our complacency is to come face-to-face with those who are paying the price for our unjust ways of living. In *Spirit of Life* he writes,

It is only the victims who make the perpetrators aware for the first time of what they are doing. That is why it is a vital part of collective self-experience for Germans to see themselves and their own world through the eyes of the Auschwitz victims. That is why it is essential for northern industrial society to see itself through the eyes of the hungry children in the Third World. And that is why one should see one's own car and one's own refuse with the eyes of the groaning earth and dying nature. We then experience our world as others experience it, and *wake up out of our self-complacent illusions* to the realizations of our own reality.[9]

Moltmann, a former German soldier who converted to Christianity in a POW camp after being captured by the British, could only wake from his stupor of complacency after he was willing to learn of Auschwitz and what had happened there. Seeing reality is a part of resurrection. Revisiting the pain we've inflicted is a part of resurrection. Reloving those who rejected us is part of resurrection. Resurrection isn't the sand we put our heads in; resurrection wakes us up to the pain of the world.

The Holy Spirit does not lead us away from the truth of the pain we have caused others or has been caused to us. The Holy Spirit leads us to that and *through* that. In walking in the Holy Spirit, we are called to reconcile, to the best of our ability, with those we have hurt. It is often along the terrain of pain that we find the closeness of God infinitely apparent. Forgiveness, therefore, is the art not merely of "letting pain go" but of bringing pain into the glorious future in hopes of resurrection.

We are able to walk this terrain of pain because we know God is with us; he walks with us. An overview of the life of Moses reveals that his entire life included a series of mountainous experiences. Moses walked four mountains. The first was as he worked in the hills, caring for his father-in-law Jethro's sheep. There Moses met the burning bush and received his calling from God. The next was Mount Sinai, where he received the law from God. The third mountaintop experience was when his brother, Aaron, died tragically before the people were to enter the promised land. And the final was Moses's own mountaintop death. Moses must have loved hiking. And some of his mountain experiences were really painful. How could Moses be so patient, so gracious, so fervent in finishing his journey? Simple: he spoke to a bush. That calling experience made patience along the journey possible.

Without a bush experience—without knowing *who* we are in Christ—a painful mountaintop experience is useless. But when you know who you are, you know why you are walking.

The fact that God can show up and speak to someone through a bush should remind us that God has the capability to show up anywhere and speak to anyone. If a bush can be God's pulpit, then any place can be sacred. The calling of God often comes in the desert. "In the life of Christ," writes Miroslav Volf, "the call comes in the wilderness; the mission takes place in the villages and cities."[10] God calls us in the dry place to go and do a task somewhere. This point reshapes our understanding of our role in the world. Christianity does not become our avenue away from the world but our avenue back into the world to bring healing to it. Christianity is not a world-denying movement. For instance, there is a worship song in which we sing, "the cross before me, the world behind me." The problem with the theology of this song is it seems to indicate a need to abandon the world—a posture, I would argue, that completely undermines a life of Christian responsibility. What does this song say to the person who has left a trail of broken relationships, violence, or abuse? It says: head toward Jesus and don't amend anything you've done. I can't buy that. We need to reverse that worship song. We don't use the cross as a way to escape the world. We encounter the cross that we might enter into the world and embody Christ's "ministry of reconciliation" (2 Cor. 5:18). Perhaps the song should go: "The world before me, the *cross behind me*."

Our ability to serve the world is contingent upon the grace of Jesus at the cross for each of us. The Maori of New Zealand have a phrase, *I nga ra o mua*, which means "to walk forward, looking back." Wherever you go into the future, remember your roots and stay faithful to them. We walk forward because of where we come from.

Resurrection walking is walking out a life of redemptive responsibility. It involves facing the world that hurts you with great pain. It involves facing the world you have hurt. Resurrection walking bears the reconciliation of the God of reconciliation.

—⟋⟋⟍—

"Blind faith," as it's called, isn't really faith at all.

Nobody actually believes anything *blindly*. At the least, most commitments of faith are a set of responses to some kind of movement of the senses, perhaps even microscopic or minuscule—a tug on the heart, a licked, wet finger held up in the wind. People give their faith to something for one reason and don't give their faith to something for a whole array of other reasons. Behind the story of many nonbelievers is a story of pain and hurt toward a church that wronged them at some critical point in their journey. Blind faith, as such, is as nonsensical as blind Republicanism or blind geometry or blind atheism. Faith is a response to something. And this does not ignore the fact that the idea of blind faith is actually quite offensive. Quite simply, one has to imagine that the notion of blind faith is most repugnant and offensive to the blind themselves, who, incidentally, would be the quickest to point out the many other God-installed senses they utilize to get from point A to point B. The blind, the *actual* blind, would tell us that no act of walking is accomplished *blindly*. For even after eyesight has long departed, there remains a whole set of resources to be used—feeling, smell, taste, intellect, touch, even friendship—in getting from here to there.

Christ invites us to explore the idea that perhaps some of us are too quick to rely on eyesight as the lord of all senses. Or perhaps logic or experience is our lord. But Jesus is the Lord above all of these. And by virtue of that, Jesus can optimize a number of our senses to lead us in the direction we should go. When one unthinkingly judges faith as "blind," one ultimately fails to recognize that we've walked to where we are in faith by a whole constellation of senses. "We walk by faith," the Holy Scripture says, "not by sight" (2 Cor. 5:7 ESV). Visual impairment and blindness are not the same thing. One merely has to learn to walk another way.

Spiritual direction is a kind of holy triangulation—we simultaneously lean on Scripture, prayer, God's Spirit, friends, the church, a book here and there, a corrective professor, an epiphany in a movie. We may say we lean on the Bible alone, but we are simultaneously leaning on a whole series of people who are helping shape our vision of what the Bible says. Again, this is triangulation. All of the God-given senses work together to help us discern our way forward with the Bible as our key source. We all (particularly Christ followers) listen to all kinds of things to help discern the voice of God. My choice of the word *discern* is not arbitrary—Paul specifically chose the word in describing why he prays. Paul says that in prayer he learned to *discern* between good and evil (Phil. 1:10). His use of the word *dokimazō* would have awakened the ears of the readers of the Letter to the Philippians; it was originally a word used by metalworkers in figuring out if a metal was pure or not.[11] A good deal of life consists of this process of "discernment," of seeking to discover what is "of God" and what is "of myself." And the sources of discernment are often odd.

God spoke. And in God's speaking, the world came to be. In our understanding of learning how to follow Jesus, the emphasis must be placed on the fact that God is simply a darned good communicator. When God desires to make himself clear, he gets the job done. As a preacher, it always catches me a little off guard when a listener in the gathering passionately relays to me something that transformed them in the sermon. Often what they heard was nothing I said in the sermon.

The Spirit speaks. And the Spirit speaks well even through such a muddled source as a half-baked sermon. My friend Kurissa told me that she felt called by God to go and serve the people of New Zealand as a missionary. The journey changed her entire life. She tells me she did not receive this call while in prayer, reading her Bible, listening to a sermon, or having some ecstatic experience while she was all alone on a mountain—she heard Jesus tell her to go to New Zealand as she watched one of the *Lord of the Rings* movies, which were filmed in New Zealand. I admit it: I've never had a moment quite like that. But I don't doubt Kurissa. Even *she* couldn't say her faith was blind. Even that act of faith had some direction. And I guess the lesson is that God can use even a Peter Jackson movie to help make his will known.

There is a tension here. Certainly, I don't advocate basing our entire faith journey on contemporary films about orcs and hobbits. Nor do I think that bad sermons should become the norm of revelatory moments. But I do advocate being open to the full array of God-given senses that God has installed in us to discern what he is up to. Again, eyesight is only *one* way of seeing.

Someone like Judas can see a miracle with his own eyes and still abandon Jesus Christ in the end. Seeing with the physical eyes is not enough. And I'm not alone in thinking this. Luckily, the Christian tradition has employed all kinds of ways for a person to "discern" the voice of God. Faith and reason are like two feet. At times, we walk through life using our brains. At other times, we walk through life utilizing our intuition or emotions, or we walk in relationship with those who we know are less neurotic than ourselves. We lean on different things at different times to get where we know we are to go. The key is that we never cease walking forward.

7

Our Need for Needs

We taste Thee, O Thou Living Bread,
And long to feast upon Thee still;
We drink of Thee, the Fountainhead
And thirst our souls from Thee to fill.

St. Bernard

What I wouldn't give to be invisible.

Still, I can't imagine it being a good thing. Invisibility would be disastrous for everyone involved. If we could be invisible, we could only fear the worst. Imagine being invisible. Imagine your husband being invisible. Imagine your fourteen-year-old son being invisible. I'm pretty certain that if I *were* afforded the opportunity to be invisible for even one day, I'd be given over to doing some rather, shall we say, un-Christian activities. I think all of us would be in the same boat. And that's why we aren't invisible; someone *knew* we couldn't handle invisibility. A society couldn't function if sinners were able to be invisible. Even our penal system would fall apart. Humans would simply be horrible invisible creatures.

Being invisible would not encourage sinners toward altruism. Sure, it'd be real fun and we'd get to do some things we've always wanted to try out. But few of us have ever dreamed about being invisible and thought about doing really kind, benevolent, helpful things. I doubt anyone, if given the chance to be invisible for a day, would ever consider using their invisibility to secretly wash their neighbor's car or feed the poor. Only a nonhuman—someone like a hobbit—would use his or her invisibility to save the world. Humans? Nope. So, if you haven't made up your mind about whether you're a sinner, just think about what *you* would do if you had one day of invisibility.

Trust me, you're a sinner.

Humans are best *seen*. Visibility is a kind of brilliant, created, built-in accountability system for human beings, keeping us in check and preventing us from doing anything we want to do on a whim. This is an important feature of a world created by a God who actually knew what he was doing. Had *we* invented a world, we would be able to fly, be invisible, and have laser beams coming out of our eyes. But, alas, we would make horrible creators. Creation is the result of brilliant design work by a Creator who knew what was necessary in a creation—a Creator, mind you, who has intended life to be lived in a certain way. I remember a line in St. Augustine's *On Free Choice of the Will* that always comes back to me when I think about the incredible nature of creation. "For you," Augustine addresses his reader, "cannot conceive anything better in creation that has slipped the mind of the Creator."[1] Augustine's point is simple—someday down the road, sometime in the future of human history, we will come to understand exactly why it is we have an appendix. We may not know now. But we will someday. *Nothing* has escaped the mind of the Creator. Creation has been made the way it should be, perfectly crafted in the eyes of its Creator. And so our visibility isn't a mistake. Our appendixes aren't a mistake. Our human limitations aren't a mistake. Our hopes aren't a mistake. *We* aren't a mistake.

Our needs are not a mistake.

And our needs keep us from wandering too far from God.

—⁓—

Needs ground us in God because needs ground us in dependency. In our needs, we cling to him. Look at all the deserts we've seen: in Scripture we discover God repeatedly calling his people away from their normal water sources into dry wastelands. As we saw, God takes Abraham away from the predictable path of the Euphrates to walk the scary uncertainty of the desert. Elsewhere, God delivers Aaron, Moses, and the people of Israel into the desert, where there are few, if any, water sources to depend on. At one place in Numbers 20, Israel quarrels and complains that they don't have any water at all. Moses and Aaron approach God at wits' end and plead for his miraculous assistance. He instructs them to speak to a rock, telling them water will gush out of it. They go to the rock, hit it, and water comes out.[2] The Spirit sends Jesus into the desert, where there will be little water. I've often contemplated why God frequently takes his people to places where they lose their water source. Water is everything. Without it, we wither. Without it, we die.

When we lose our water source, we gain dependency.

Let's be clear: at some point God will intentionally remove us from the fertile, wet, lush expanse we've grown used to and place us in drier places. But just because there appears to be no water doesn't mean there isn't any. Go to him. Ask for water. Be dependent. Refuse to be self-sufficient. The people in the Bible were almost always thirsty. But maybe it is because in thirst we are most trusting and dependent.

Ironic, isn't it, that in the desert are the most tears? We cry out for water, for comfort, and for solace. In the place where we are most thirsty, our eyes produce the most water. In the place where there is not enough water, our eyes well up.

Be hopeful, thirsty wanderer. One of the pictures the Bible gives of heaven is one in which a river runs right through the new Jerusalem (Rev.

22). In that future city, there is plenty of water. But, Revelation continues, while there is a river with plenty of water for everyone, there will also be no tears. Heaven is the desert reversed. In that new Jerusalem, we are invited to drink the water of life forever. No more loss of water source. The present desert has many tears. But the future river has none. Be hopeful, wanderer. Need him. Cling to him. Cry out to him.

A missionary who had traveled the world told me once that there is an almost universal law of belief in God. She told me that when you go to places where everyone has their needs and wants met, the percentage of people who believe in or worship God goes down. But, she pointed out, in the places where people do not have their basic needs or wants met, they are *more* likely to believe in and worship God.

I think God only makes true sense to people who need him. God will be worshiped by those who *need* him. It's like our needs to be touched, held, loved, spoken to, and fed are created by God to drive us to him. If we don't have needs, then God becomes irrelevant to us.

—ᴍᴍ—

A distinct mark of a totalitarian regime is that its leader must rule every conceivable dimension of the people's day-to-day lives. Also, the leader must be a phenomenal golfer.

Case in point: North Korea. In modern-day North Korea, it's required that a picture of the "supreme leader" be placed in every house. In the North Korean totalitarian world, the supreme leader must be *everywhere*—literally. Furthermore, the sacred public image of the supreme leader—or at least the perception that everyday people have about him—is of upmost importance; it must be constantly trimmed and groomed and managed. Popular legend holds that their current leader, Kim Jong-un, has never and will never have to go to the bathroom.[3] Another popular national lore is that Kim Jong-un can talk to dolphins. The groundwork for such a radical public persona was laid by his father, Kim Jong-il, who—according to the seventeen security guards who were present—shot thirty-eight under par for eighteen holes of golf during the opening of the Pyongyang Golf Complex in the capital city. That included eleven holes in one in a single round of golf.[4] Local legend suggests it was Kim Jong-il's first round of golf ever. In a less-than-serious tribute to the passing of this golfing great, ESPN writer DJ Gallo eulogizes the loss.

> What we do know is that no matter how many more majors Tiger Woods does or doesn't win, the debate of Tiger vs. Jack is really an argument about who is the *second*-best golfer in history.

> More than his undisputed greatness on the course, it's probably Kim's simple approach to the game that will be his enduring legacy. While other great golfers have written books full of tips, tricks and swing thoughts, Kim had the best approach to conquering the sport of golf: Have your national propaganda department lie for you.[5]

The image of a totalitarian leader is always a groomed image. It is with great consequence that we come to the Gospels and see a radically different, nontotalitarian human: God. Jesus is anything but subhuman, or suprahuman, in the Bible. He is *fully* human. Jesus even went to the bathroom in his full humanity, and he probably would not have shot a hole in one his first time on the golf course.

John's Gospel goes out of the way to deconstruct any notion that Jesus was interested in forming such a managed, primped persona. For instance, in John 4 we find Jesus speaking to a Samaritan woman by the Sycharian well. Jesus is described as being tired, hungry, and thirsty. Such human depictions make one do a double take—particularly for someone like myself, who holds unswervingly to the divinity of Jesus Christ.

So we mustn't forget the theological position of the New Testament about Jesus being God. Jesus was "the exact representation of his being" (Heb. 1:3). Jesus said, "I and the Father are one" (John 10:30). Jesus was God. But Jesus was human. Pulled together, we have a unique picture of a God who gets hungry, lonely, tired, and thirsty. Sadly, we often cut out one side or the other. He is either Jesus *or* he is Christ. He is a human being *or* a divine being. This creates a bit of a problem. Either God is really not that powerful at all, has needs, and sits in heaven with cravings and appetites like us, or God models a life of need even if he didn't exactly have to.

If Jesus is God, then God got thirsty, hungry, lonely, and tired. And the Bible doesn't shy away from this fact. The greatest leader the world has ever seen had real, legitimate, pressing needs that others helped him with. To have needs is human. It is also divine—that is, if Jesus is God in his humanity. And he is. There is no sin in our need for relationship, food, friendship, or a job. Needs are simply not a result of the fall. We were made to need.

How could it be that Jesus would be thirsty, hungry, or tired? How is it that God could have needs?

Now, admittedly, Jesus had a unique relationship to his needs. Unlike more feeble people, he did not bow at the feet of his needs. He had needs while never worshiping them. For instance, consider Jesus's sleeping record in the Gospels: Jesus slept when he wasn't supposed to and didn't sleep when he should have. The same God who slept in the back of a boat in a storm did not sleep late at night in order to have a lengthy conversation with Nicodemus. John said that this is the mark of one upon whom the Spirit would fall: "The wind blows wherever it pleases. You hear its sound, but you cannot tell where it comes from or where it is going. So it is with everyone born of the Spirit" (John 3:8).

But such a way of life is distant, foreign to contemporary readers who not only have everything they need but have come to worship having their needs met. In so doing, we cease our worship of the living God and turn in homage to what Paul calls the god of our stomach (Phil. 3:19). Jesus had needs. Jesus didn't sin. Therefore, needs aren't sinful. Yet Jesus did not worship his needs or do whatever it took to fulfill his needs. The main goal of his life, what he called his "food," was doing the will of his Father (John 6:38).

Oddly enough, Kim Jong-il is depicted as more of a deity as humans would imagine deity than the Gospels' portrayal of Jesus. And people follow him. But totalitarianism always needs an adjusted image—a lie—to get people to follow. The Bible refuses such a lie. The Bible offers a brutally honest picture of who Jesus was—needs and all. Jesus wasn't, it turns out, merely human or merely God. In the greatest mystery of all, Jesus was both at the same exact moment. While David, his distant ancestor, was "a man after [God's] own heart" (1 Sam. 13:14), Jesus, the King of David's descendants, would be a God after man's own heart. He was both human and divine.

Only a perverted form of Christianity would say that all one needs is God and nothing else. Nobody actually believes that. Nor is it even close to being true. I could have God but no food, and I would die. Such a theology departs entirely from the life of Jesus, God in the flesh. Jesus himself modeled a life of needing. As Christians in this time and place, we have been provided a kind of script. This script—whether we're aware of it or not—is one of complete self-completion and needlessness. Again, we may or may not be conscious of it. But we all read from this script.

This conception of faith—of being people without needs—raises a bunch of perfectly legitimate questions. Is faith really about self-fulfillment? Is Christianity about making people who don't need others? If so, isn't this different from the way Jesus lived his own life?

The implications of this are quite powerful. To need a job isn't ungodly. To need a friend doesn't make one carnal. To need food and drink does not make one fleshly. To need sexual intimacy isn't a result of the fall.

The young college guys who come to me and say that they can't wait till they can have sex are, candidly, on the right track. They were *created* for that need to be fulfilled. To desire to have sex does not make someone wrong in the same way being hungry doesn't make someone a glutton. A need isn't bad.

It's what we do with our needs that becomes critically important. Needs were created by God so that we would be dependent on God and one another. God did not give Adam and Eve the garden of Eden— full of lush food and rich resources—*after* the fall of humanity, as though the need for food was a result of the fall. Adam didn't desire a wife *after* sin had entered the world. Sleep wasn't something that took place *after* the deception of the serpent. These are things God created human beings to need.

God isn't offended at this. When God saw that Adam needed food, rest, friendship, or water, at no point do we see God saying, "Hey, Adam, aren't you fulfilled in *me*? Why don't you just need *me*?"

Still, unmet needs are not good. The story of creation has an interesting pattern in which God says "It is good" after every succeeding part of his creation. When God makes Adam, it is *very* good." But then God looks at Adam in his loneliness and says, "It is not good." Keep in mind the fall has yet to happen. It is noteworthy that something was "not good" before sin entered the world. There is a reason that when people become Christians, they still need to eat, breathe, sleep, and drink until the day they die: God isn't the only need in our lives. Yes, our need for God is a big need, one that must be filled for us to be truly human. But hear me clearly: it is just one need, not the only one.

In fact, the brilliance of Christianity is that it reveals to us what our true human needs are. Christianity tells us what we truly need. When we say that a Christian needs to be generous, that is literal. Giving, being generous, and being openhanded are actual human needs in the same way that breathing, eating, or sleeping are. When we aren't generous people, we begin to die. We can gain everything and lose our souls.

Our greatest hang-up, of course, is that we rarely understand the difference between a need and a want. Our wants, oftentimes, are a result of sin. We want what cannot help us, nor should it. For this reason precisely, Jesus said to his disciples: Don't worry about your needs, your clothes, your food. Your father in heaven knows and he will help. Seek first the kingdom of God (Matt. 6:25, 32–33). Listen to what Jesus *never* says to them. Jesus never says, "Don't worry about your wants—phone, television, or new gadget."

Why?

A disciple must learn the lesson that God isn't primarily in the *wants* business. Hopefully, reexamining the life of Jesus—a life marked by real needs—will help the age-old belief that *all we need is God* retreat into the obscurity it so deserves.

—⚬⚬—

117

Finished with teaching my class at the seminary, I was finally driving home after a particularly long day. Mondays were long days; it was the one night of the week when my teaching schedule required me to arrive home after the family went to bed. Just a few minutes earlier, I had gotten into my car and driven onto the freeway as my routine dictated. I did this every week. It was just past ten o'clock.

As was normal, few other souls were on the road that wet and cold November night. Traffic consisted mostly of me and a few passing cars coming from the other direction. The drive usually took me about fifteen minutes from the school back home, so I expected I'd see my wife before she fell asleep.

When you have a routine, you easily notice things that are not normal. As I drove in the dark Oregon rain, I saw something out of the corner of my right eye. What I saw was so quick, so passing, so momentary, but it made me do a doubletake.

There, under one of those posts that hold up the huge green signs above the freeway, sat a truck. The truck was no ordinary truck. This truck was completely wrapped around the concrete barrier, like paper around a present. It was nearly indiscernible as a truck. I remember my initial thought: that there had been a car accident earlier in the day that they had failed to finish cleaning up. It soon dawned on me that they don't leave car accidents for later. The wreck just happened. Nobody else had come up to it. No one else knew. Except me.

Unsure what to do next, I went into emergency high-adrenaline mode. I pressed on my blinkers, swerved to the side of the road, and got out of my car into the pouring-down rain in my tweed jacket, tie, and shiny teaching shoes. Locking my car with my briefcase inside, I ran to the truck. The run was slow, the way waking up on Saturday morning is slow. Time slowed down. My mind began to race as the rain hit my face in the few yards between me and the giant mass of metal before me. *What would I find in this truck? Who would be in there? Would they be alive? Dear God, don't let there be children!*

From the looks of it as I approached the truck, I couldn't imagine that any human could survive such an accident. Not one part of the vehicle, save the trailer, was recognizable. But I knew someone in there would need my help. I got to the truck. It was so mangled I could barely see inside. Then I heard him. A man, about fifty-five, was trapped inside. I could not believe it. The sound of his voice will never escape me. He saw me, turned his barely moveable head in my general direction, and pleaded with all of his might for me to help him out of the vehicle. Of course, I couldn't do a thing to help him out of the mess of metal, glass, and broken plastic.

No one can prepare you for the powerlessness you feel in situations like that. The sound of his pleas will be with me until the day I can't remember things anymore.

All I could do was pick up my phone to call 911. As I did so with a man yelling at me to help him, I was completely destroyed to find that my phone was dead. No power. *What?* Of all the times for the phone to be dead, why now? Why this moment? How could this happen?

Since there was no one on the road and no exits for a mile or so, I did not have many options. Without having the ability to call anyone, all I could do was be with the man and hope someone else would drive by and see. I crawled onto the vehicle and did just that. Positioning myself where I could reach him, I reached down into the truck, put my hand on his shoulder, and told him I was there with him. There I found myself holding on to a man I never thought I'd be meeting. I could sense that he was calmed by the touch.

By God's grace, someone *did* see us. They stopped and called the emergency line. But there I was, holding on to the shoulder of a stranger. In ten long minutes, a squad of fire trucks, ambulances, and police cars arrived at the scene to assist. I moved away from the truck and just waited. The rain poured off my face onto my tweed jacket. My shoes were doused. But I couldn't leave until I knew the man was out. I watched for the next hour and a half as they worked to pull his mangled body out of the truck with the Jaws of Life. As he was freed, I could see he was still awake.

As I drove home, the rain and my tears seemed the same. Some drops were cold, some were warm. I was in shock at what I'd seen.

I know someone who works at the hospital, and I heard that the man survived. I don't know if he has family; I don't know if he can walk; but I do know he survived.

—⁓—

One of our greatest needs is to be *touched.* God created this need; it isn't accidental. In wandering through life, we need to be touched. And when we aren't touched, we die a slow death. They say that a baby who is not held and touched in the months after birth will eventually die.[6] What if the same were true for those of us who have grown up? When we cease being touched, we lose all hope. I came across a poem by Julia Kasorf about funerals that reminds me of this. It rings so true. "I learned that whatever we say means nothing, / what anyone will remember is that we came."[7]

Touching someone is often our greatest sermon on God's love, a love that has no loophole. It isn't a loud sermon with lots of words, but it is always received by the person who most desperately needs it. Over the last year since the accident, I've thought about that evening time and time again. I had nightmares for some time. I was watching a TV show just after the event, and there was a gunshot. The gunshot completely overwhelmed me. All the blood brought me back. It was horrific.

But as I look back on that event, there is one thing I know was from God: my phone didn't work. I would not know this until later, but my phone being dead was the greatest gift from God imaginable. Had my phone been working, I would not have been able to be present with that man in his suffering. I would have been frantically trying to get someone there to help. What the man needed was someone to be there with him.

I think that has become the human condition. We come upon others in their need. What do we do? We get on our phones. We look to somewhere else. And we wonder why in our own suffering so few people come to our aid.

"Grace and truth *came* through Jesus Christ" (John 1:17, emphasis added). I wonder if the most helpful definition for a contemporary audience of the incarnation of Jesus Christ—of God coming into the world—just might be this: "And God put down his phone."

Having all of one's needs met can actually harm the human soul because it removes us from needing anyone else. I believe we were created to not have everything we desire. One of the most important texts written in the twentieth century on the evolving nature of society is a book called *Habits of the Heart*.[8] In this book Robert Bellah captures the prevailing way Americans are now living their lives. We are, more than ever, individuals first and foremost. For most Americans, our communities, families, and churches all take a backseat to our individualistic impulses. Mostly what the book shed light on was this new reality that Americans increasingly are people who can take care of their own needs and no longer need one another. We have become self-sufficient.

Let me illustrate from my garden again. I didn't realize until I started the process of learning how to grow my own food that gardening isn't easy; you learn this the hard way. It requires a good deal of skill and knowledge to do it properly. What did I do to gain the knowledge necessary to complete my task? I went to Google to find some videos to help me solve the problems. I found an endless stream of websites and videos that showed me how to go about starting the process.

What could be wrong with this? a reader may ask. Well, before the invention of the internet just a few short decades ago, and before one could Google "how to grow strawberries," I would have had to pursue the question relationally—more often than not, I would've had to go to a neighbor or a friend or a family member. Or I would've physically had to go to the store. I would've had to go to *someone*. Insert the ability to Google everything, and those avenues of exploring reality are no longer needed. We have replaced neighbors with Google. We no longer *need* anybody. We can do it all, figure it out, and accomplish everything on our own.

What if needs—and I mean needs *in and of themselves*—are an essential part of the way God has established that humans should live their lives? In other words, needing each other is how God wants us to live. What if God created us to need so that we would have to lean on one another?

Needs are the building blocks of a relationship. Sexual needs in a marriage are how a couple can remain connected and intimate. Any married couple knows that if one of the partners is fulfilling his or her own needs on the side through infidelity, pornography, or masturbation, this can lead to a breakdown of the relationship. Needs are not only created—needs literally bring people together.

I was recently running some errands. I drove to the bank, parked, and walked up to the ATM to make some deposits and get cash. Then I walked across the street to the store to get some stuff for dinner. I went through the self-checkout line and got back into my car. I sat down in my seat and realized that I had managed to make a deposit at the bank, get cash, buy some groceries, and get back into my car not having to talk to one single person.

I think this type of life is the breakdown of what neighborliness is all about. Jesus said that we should love our neighbors as we love ourselves (Matt. 22:39). We are increasingly creating a world in which we don't have to know or interact with our neighbors at all. Soon we won't even have to talk to anybody—we will just walk from place to place seeking out the commodities that we so desire and want, all the while walking past the very thing that we need the most—others.

Being a neighbor becomes increasingly possible if someone is willing to acknowledge a need. Our needs connect us. No wonder it is so hard to make friends. We no longer *need* friends. It was easier to make them in the past when you had absolutely no idea whatsoever how to do something. Once I realized that I had essentially been replacing my friends and neighbors with a computer, I stopped. Then I asked a neighbor to come over and show me some things. It turns out people love being needed. When they are asked to help, friendships are born. After the store and the bank experience, I prayed and felt as though God wanted me to change the way I used both of them. I think it is the Christian thing to do. I no longer use the self-checkout line or the

ATM—neither of them force me to look someone in the eye and see the face of God, the *imago Dei.*

This actually helps us understand a good deal of Jesus's life. Jesus was God. He could do anything. If he wanted to turn the stones into bread, he could have. He did turn water into wine. Yet he asked, and still asks, his followers to help him with his mission. Why was Jesus supported financially by his disciples? Why did he ask to borrow people's boats, donkeys, and homes? He did this not because he is a needy God but because it is in asking us for help that he gets to participate in our lives. Jesus modeled being needy so that he could enter into our lives.

When Jesus encountered the woman at the well, the God who invented water ironically asked a woman for a cup of water (John 4:1–26). Did he do that because he had a water problem? No. He did it because in living as people with created needs we can find the kind of life that necessitates relationships. Relationships end when needs end. That is the best missionary advice in the world—if you need a cup of sugar, don't go to the store. Go to your next-door neighbor. Ask. Seek. Knock. Literally. It requires that we actually have a neighbor or two to do what Jesus said about neighbors. Want neighbors? Start having needs. Stop using your computer to ask the questions. Stop going through the self-checkout line. Stop using ATMs. Stop replacing people with technological devices that are separating each and every one of us.

If being touched is an integral need God has created within us, then it should explain why Jesus is as touchy-feely in the Gospels as he is. Jesus is always touching people. Have you ever noticed that? Jesus touched all kinds of people: he touched a leper (Matt. 8:3), Peter's mother-in-law while she was sick (Matt. 8:15), his disciples (Matt. 17:7), and people with all kinds of diseases (Mark 3:10). The list could go on. He also let other people touch him all the time. He didn't have much of a discernable personal-space bubble. He even let his enemies touch him. And this fact is very important for the way we understand God.

In recent years, a discussion among psychologists has captured my attention. A topic known as "psychology of disgust" has developed to better understand why we do and don't develop relationships with certain people. One article, "Spiritual Pollution: The Dilemma of Sociomoral Disgust and the Ethic of Love," is gripping.[9] The author, a scholar named Richard Beck, was doing pioneering work in the field. He talks about how we psychologically see certain people and things as "disgusting," hence the psychology of disgust. He pointed out that in normal, everyday interactions, we assume that dirty things make clean things dirty. For example, if I were to take a piece of sourdough bread and dip it into a bowl of toilet water, the bread would become dirty. The toilet isn't made clean by the bread. In our world, dirty things make clean things dirty.

A perfect illustration of the psychology of disgust can be seen in Victorian literature. One of the marks of Victorian romance writings is some kind of love affair between a person of one social class and someone of another. The formula often goes as follows. An upper-class statesman falls in love with a lower-class peasant woman. In such a case, particularly during the Victorian age, the upper-class romantic was made dirty, or lowered, by such a love affair. Never in Victorian literature is the lower-class person made upper-class by falling in love with a statesman. In just about every case, the noble is brought down the social ladder by his or her love of the peasant.

This similar scenario plays itself out quite often in our social relationships. From the perspective of the psychology of disgust, socially abnormal and dirty people make clean people dirty. This plays itself out in myriad ways. For instance, if a person in a community is known to be morally and ethically strong but hangs out with a stripper, it brings the clean person down to the level of the dirty person.

Such a psychology of disgust is prevalent among many Christ followers. We increasingly believe in guilt by association rather than mercy by association. Guilt by association was one of the key arguments against Jesus during his life. People hated him, alas, because he hung out with all the wrong people.

Of course, this view of association fails to take into account the whole vision of Christianity and the purposes of Christ. The gospel story is one of a perfect, spotless, gracious God who comes to touch, love, and help—even wash the feet of—dirty, imperfect, narcissistic sinners like ourselves. In such a context, it is not God who is made dirty by us. Rather, in entering into a relationship of trust with God, we are made clean by him. Theologians speak of the impartation of God's holiness in people when they believe in the gospel.

This is in stark contrast to the way we normally think of things. For in our world, clean things are made dirty by dirty things. In the gospel story of Jesus, however, dirty things are made clean by a holy God. The fact that Jesus, the spotless Son of God, is constantly touching sick sinners and disease-ridden people is telling as to this fact. We should be reminded that their dirt didn't get Jesus dirty; rather, his life made them alive. The normal way of things was reversed. Life was given to the dead, not death to the living. N. T. Wright, again, perceptively offers a powerful description of these healing stories where cleanliness is given to the disgusting: "Here is Jesus touching a leper: now you just don't do that, or if you do you become ritually unclean yourself, and quite possibly contract the disease into the bargain. But somehow Jesus' cleanness and wholeness *infect* the leper, instead of his being infected by the leper."[10]

In Jesus's world, the path of infection is reversed: a sick world is infected with grace.

—✺—

Jesus touched even his enemies.

Judas has always been a fascinating character to me. His story of rejecting Jesus and selling the information that would lead to Jesus's arrest does not fascinate me as much as Jesus's eternal love of Judas despite the fact that Jesus knows what he is about to do. For on the night of Jesus's arrest, Judas will bring a mob of soldiers to his whereabouts. Notice that when Judas comes to Jesus, he doesn't approach Jesus with a sword. Judas approaches Jesus and kisses him. What rips this story open is that Jesus knew Judas had betrayed him. And yet Jesus allows Judas to touch him.

There is a prophetic line in Isaiah that describes a people who would "come near to me with their mouth and honor me with their lips, but their hearts are far from me" (Isa. 29:13). This could not have been more clearly fulfilled than it was in Judas. Judas kissed Jesus with his lips but murdered him with his heart. Judas's lip service, as it were, was a dark sign of humans' ability to pretend to love others while hating them in their hearts—something we've become masters at. Jesus knew this would happen. Yet Jesus still served Judas. In the end, Jesus spent the last evening of his life washing the feet of his would-be betrayer. Even knowing his impending death was upon him, Jesus made himself available to, opened himself up to, those who would hurt him.

Name one other god who washes the feet of his enemies.

It got me thinking about Judas. Jesus washed Judas's feet. He did that knowing whose feet it was he was washing. Jesus wasn't made dirty by serving Judas. Rather, Jesus was enacting his eternal love toward Judas.

We always assume that to serve someone means that we endorse that person. Some churches would get in trouble for serving a local organization that supports questionable endeavors because it is often assumed, in our way of thinking about things, that touching it makes us dirty like them. We assume service is an endorsement. It isn't, at least not in the kingdom of Jesus. Even Jesus served the one who was against him. In the kingdom of Jesus, through serving, touching, and being present, we embody the sanctifying life of Jesus Christ. This frees us to serve, in love, anyone as the Spirit of God enables us. Foot washing, of course, was not an endorsement of Judas's way of life. Rather, it was a final act of love before he went off the deep end of destruction.

A Wanderer's Rest

Some wandered in desert wastelands,
    finding no way to a city where they could settle.
They were hungry and thirsty,
    and their lives ebbed away.

Psalm 107:4–5

Every Wednesday, my son, my wife, and our chickens take a break—it is called a Sabbath. The challenges to taking a Sabbath day of rest are endless. Perhaps the hardest part of Sabbathing is that it completely undermines my American sense of personal economic value. On the Sabbath, I become basically useless to the system of our world; our family stops shopping, buying, driving, and working in total. We don't even have to make our beds on the Sabbath. Keeping a Sabbath goes entirely against the kind of good, American values I was raised to believe in. In the end, the real enemy of free-market, profit-driven capitalism is Sabbath—it undoes one's deeply held ideas about what success and value really are all about. Too often we have assumed that our value is economic, a quiet assumption that basically equates capitalism with the kingdom of Jesus. But shame on us whenever we equate God's kingdom with capitalism. They are far from the same thing. This idea of resting, of ceasing—Sabbath—is that time-honored tradition drawn from the Jewish vision of life that was lived out by Jesus and that is rarely received with praise in our Western, capitalistic life. Since we literally live to make money, a Sabbath is interpreted as a kind of cultural heresy. The idea is that we rest in who God is and not in anything else—we don't rest in our work, in how many people follow us on Twitter, in our economic state, in how well things are going at the studio. Sabbath keeping is living in God's love for us one day a week and refusing to find ourselves in anything else.

The most common objection I hear about Sabbath keeping is that people don't have time to do it. I can understand the disruption one may feel being told one of the days of their week is God's and God's alone. I sympathize greatly. Obedience rarely fits perfectly into our current work schedule. Obedience to the ways that God has created us to exist never fit into the time God allows for us to live within. Sabbath is a hard thing to keep, ironically. The Jews were well aware of this fact and would take an entire day—the "day of Preparation"—to get ready for the Sabbath day. On that day all the work would be done to prepare for Sabbath rest.

It turns out rest requires a lot of work and intentionality. Rest never "just happens."

Anyone who attempts to keep a Sabbath will run into some personal crises. For me, the greatest challenge on the Sabbath is my phone. It is, without question, the hardest thing to let go of on the Sabbath. Turning it off is like coming down from an addiction. Fingers trembling, my rest truly begins when I am no longer of value to the world through that little device that never rests. On occasion, I forget to turn my phone off. At some point in the day, I'll glance to see a swarm of messages that need my attention, crises that need me, and cool little stories I'd like to read. I've learned that when I know others are waiting for me, I can't rest. And so whenever that happens, my rest tends to cease. Sabbath is saying to the world that you are of no value to it for that day. You find your value solely in your Creator.

We never truly rest, do we? Some of us try to take a day off. But a "day off" is generally just a day that we are at home thinking about work, preparing for work, and answering emails. Eugene Peterson has a word for these kinds of "days off," those days in which we are supposed to rest but instead restlessly think about how we are planning on working and getting stuff done on the day we are back to work—he calls it a "bastard Sabbath."[1] A "day off" is not the same thing as a Sabbath. It is a day we *look* as though we are at rest, but in reality we are inwardly toiling, preparing, and thinking about what we are going to accomplish once we get all this silly "resting" business done. Sure, we say we rest in Jesus, but it is really just a bastard Sabbath rest.

I have already written about the positive side of wandering—that we wander with God through dry places and find ourselves in him. But wandering can be a very negative thing as well. And it becomes increasingly a problem when we refuse to enter into the rest that God has given to us. When we never fully enter in, we wander. Our souls wander. Our hearts wander. Our thoughts wander. And we never really just *are*.

We are perpetually in a state of "bastard Sabbath."

—⟨⟨⟨—

The Jewish wandering experience didn't happen overnight. Rather, it lasted a long time. For nearly forty years, the Jewish people wandered in circles through the desert as they waited for God to deliver them into the land he had promised. What a long, dusty, arduous path—a path requiring a good deal of hard-nosed perseverance. God's people continue on that dusty, dangerous road so that they might press forward to realize the goal. As I've discussed, Paul's language almost seems reminiscent of this theme: "I press on toward the goal to win the prize for which God has called me heavenward in Christ Jesus" (Phil. 3:14).

He speaks as one who is on the journey and awaits that final place Christ had called him. Ours is a journey toward the promised land, a distant place where final rest and peace and solace will be discovered. It is a place they talked about for generations and quietly longed for. The place of rest would be a place of their own.

One can still hear the little Israelite children during the desert wanderings in the back asking, "Are we there yet? Are we there yet?" to the elders around every turn. "Just around the next corner," they might say. But, of course, they didn't have the slightest idea how long it would take. The length alone would have been disappointing. That's probably why God never told them in advance it would be forty years. Wandering is an odd place to be. The prospect of wandering is most uncomfortable precisely at the moment you are wandering because you have no idea when it will end. With dust in your eyes, there is a constant mix of excitement and trepidation swirling in the desert air as you await the place God has called you. But you aren't there yet, are you? You still look. Wandering takes time. It doesn't end overnight. For Israel, it would take the space of some forty years. For you, who knows?

This may stir up some impatience in us as it did in Israel. For a people who have just been rescued miraculously from Egypt, walked through the Red Sea, eaten manna off the desert floor, and seen miracle after miracle before their very eyes, impatience is an ever-present possibility. In short, impatience happens when we begin to have an entitled sense of ownership over God's sovereignty. Having seen the miracles of God, we expect them to be around every corner and to be done *when* we want them to be done. Impatience is loving God's sovereignty but hating his timing. In knowing that God can do anything God wants to whomever he wants, we often grow entitled, thinking he should use his powers to do for us whatever we want and whenever we want it. The people of Israel grow impatient over and over again for this very reason—why aren't we in the promised land yet? It is as if they are constantly wondering, "If God can do the Red Sea and the manna and the miracle, why can't he get us to the promised land a little quicker?"

We are a people who have been miraculously saved from our sin; no wonder we are impatient people. We wonder how, after years of being on the journey with God, we can still struggle with the same old sins that held us down at our conversion. How can we struggle with the same old junk years after the fact? Why doesn't God deliver us quicker than he does? I mean, he's all-powerful, right? Can't he get me out of this mess?

Of course he could. But that would get us out of the whole "growing up" thing. I've held close the words of my theological hero Colin Gunton: "God works the long-term."[2] We aren't taken to the promised land overnight. Patience is the attitude of wanderers because they know that God often takes a very long time accomplishing in our lives what he desired to accomplish when he created us in the first place. Patience involves holding dearly not only to God's sovereign plan but also to his sovereign *timing*. When we recognize that God works the long term in our lives, we can come to rest in the idea that all of life isn't about getting some*where* as much as it is about God making us into some*one*.

As Israel wanders through the desert for forty years, one of the things God insists on over and over is their need for Sabbath. There are some challenging stories about this commandment. For instance, there is an episode in the book of Numbers where God orders a man to be killed for picking up some sticks in the desert on the Sabbath day (Num. 15:32–36). Why would God be so incredibly harsh about this commandment?

Consider for a moment where Israel had just come from: Egypt. In Egypt, Israel was enslaved by an oppressive economic system that was propped up by their slavery. Israel was valuable to Egypt for their work alone. Their work was their identity. And so when they came out of Egypt, one would think that they could easily slip into their old Egyptian ways of thinking: that they were merely their work. This is exactly why learning Sabbath is so important for new Christians: for the longest time, non-Christians have had the wrong ideas about where their value lies. When they become freed, emancipated Christians, their value no longer resides in their relationships, money, or work. They have a new center of being: God.

There is no evidence that the Egyptians had a word for freedom. It was work, work, work all the time. The God of Israel and the God of Jesus is the God of freedom. Freedom, the kind envisioned in Christian faith, is always like that dusty, wandering road to the promised land that takes as long as it does. Freedom is not merely something you receive; it is something that must be lived. Freedom is established in a heartbeat but lived out and entered into over the course of a lifetime. For example, consider the Emancipation Proclamation. Of course, the Emancipation Proclamation was signed and made into law by the president. Then what happened? Scholar Michelle Alexander accurately writes, "President Abraham Lincoln issued a declaration purporting to free slaves held in Southern Confederate states, but not a single black slave was actually free to walk away from a master in those states as a result. A civil war had to be won first, hundreds of thousands of lives lost, and then—only then—were slaves across the South set free."[3]

Freedom on paper is one thing—freedom in reality is another. Israel perhaps is free on paper, but it takes years, decades, and centuries for their freedom to be lived out and made a reality throughout the land. Declaring freedom and having freedom are different things. Israel could be in the desert "free," as it were, but it would take some forty years for them to actually enter into the space of freedom God had desired. Maybe that is precisely why God got so angry with the guy picking up sticks on the Sabbath—God is not joking about being a God of freedom. He really means it.

Humans are created with the need to rest. Writers and readers both know that rest is a necessity. A paragraph break, for example, exists for one singular purpose: to give the reader a little break. Without paragraphs, we have no place to stop and think about whatever we have just read. A book without paragraphs is a life with no naps, no sleep. We were created to rest.

A life of faith without rest isn't bearable or even all that good. God provides paragraph breaks in life so that we can enter into life. Even the journey of seeking freedom is one that requires a break here and there. The text of Numbers 10:33–36 provides a picture of this: "So they set out from the mountain of the LORD and traveled for three days. The ark of the covenant of the LORD went before them during those three days *to find them a place to rest.* The cloud of the LORD was over them by day when they set out from the camp" (emphasis added). One might quickly move past this particular story and pay no attention to how Moses—the stutterer, the insecure, the one who doesn't believe in himself one bit—responds: "Whenever the ark set out, Moses said, 'Rise up, LORD! May your enemies be scattered; may your foes flee before you.' Whenever it came to rest, he said, 'Return, LORD, to the countless thousands of Israel.'"

Our translations of the Bible, I think, get it wrong here. Moses, I suspect, didn't "say" these little stanzas of Hebrew poetry. It is more likely to me that Moses sang them. It is likely these were originally a song. And Moses sang them boldly, like a solo in a vaudeville show. As with other songs in the Bible, it appears as though these are little songs that Moses belted out loud in the desert. Now, for a man of such insecurity, the singing of a song must indicate that something cool must have just happened. What made Moses so excited? He caught a glimpse of Yahweh Shabuoth, Lord of the Sabbath.

Moses saw a side of God's character that simply made him sing as the Israelites came out of Egypt. He sang because his God was the provider of rest. God was going ahead of him to "find rest" on his behalf.

What kind of God does this?

—⚉—

Rest is hard to come by, isn't it?

The prophet Jeremiah describes us in very stark terms—as sheep who have lost their shepherd. He writes, "My people have been lost sheep; their shepherds have led them astray and caused them to roam the mountains. They wandered over mountain and hill and forgot their own resting place" (Jer. 50:6). Ezekiel records the same kind of words on the lips of God: "My sheep wandered over all the mountains on every high hill. They were scattered over the whole earth, and no one searched or looked for them" (Ezek. 34:6). Rest is hard to come by, even when we have entered into the dimensions of salvation that he has brought us into.

In many ways, the world does Sabbath better than the church. Consider for a moment the idea of a sabbatical, which is directly derived from this ancient principle. A friend of mine just got done with a three-month sabbatical in which she stopped all work and enjoyed life. She told me afterward how rested she was. But she also said it was terrorizing upon her soul because she worried whether she would be loved and welcomed when she got back. I think one of the reasons we don't take sabbaticals, or rests, is the same reason Moses wouldn't want to go back up the mountain after finding God's people worshiping a golden calf. It's probably the reason I'm scared to take a sabbatical. Because if I go up the mountain and come down to find God's people worshiping a golden calf, I'm a bad leader. Worse yet, if I go up the mountain to come down and find them worshiping God, I'm no longer needed. A sabbatical is a hard thing to come by. And it is hard to do because we have a lot of fear wrapped up in it. On the sabbatical, our normal sense of self becomes shaken.

Sadly, when and if we think about rest, we often think of it in ways that are out of sync with (if not opposite from) the way the Bible thinks and speaks of rest. For example, we assume that rest is the same thing as getting enough sleep at night, doing enough yoga, having enough downtime to gather our thoughts, or getting away from it all. As Americans, we see rest as largely environmental and emotional. We see rest as something that's fundamentally self-created, self-initiated, and self-made.

The Bible takes no such individualistic perspective on the topic of rest. Nor is rest something that comes with getting our lives in order, necessarily. Rest, as we come to find in the story of Moses in the desert, is something God finds on our behalf. "The Lord went before them . . . to *find them* a place to rest." What kind of God does this? What kind of God has time, let alone a passion, for finding rest?

You see, the God in the Bible is the one who *creates* rest, who *finds* rest, who *makes* rest for his people. God is always looking for a place where his people might rest. This is not a theme of God's character isolated just to the book of Numbers. When one compares the biblical story of creation to other ancient creation narratives such as the *Enuma Elish*, one is surprised that over and over one stark difference appears between them. Of all the deities in the religious creation stories, the God of the Old Testament is the only one who—time and time again, more than any other—mandates, who commands, who creates a day of rest for people. While other gods may demand seven days of work with no rest whatsoever, this God is different. The gods of contemporary society rebel against this kind of Sabbath insistence. Get to work, they say; never rest. Or you'll get the pink slip.

True rest simply isn't self-created. It isn't self-made. Rest isn't self-attained. Rest is provided. It is built in. In fact, it is in the creation account that God makes the Sabbath day *kadosh*, or "holy." Not even humanity gets such a demarcation. The first thing in the Bible that God makes holy is a day, the Sabbath day. And when Sabbath isn't honored, all of God's creation begins to break down. In the same way that God invented the sun for our plants to make chlorophyll, God invented rest that we might live and enjoy living. God has made it since the foundation of the world. To not honor the Sabbath and wonder why we are so exhausted is to cut off the oxygen valve in the world and wonder why people are dying. Sabbath is a dimension of holy living that we are invited to enter *into*. This is precisely why one can only "enter [God's] rest" (Heb. 4:3) according to the book of Hebrews. Rest is a place that is made, created for us. It is not a geography we create for ourselves. The author of Hebrews writes, "There remains, then, a Sabbath-rest for the people of God; for anyone who enters God's rest also rests from their works, just as God did from his. Let us, therefore, make every effort to *enter that rest*, so that no one will perish by following their example of disobedience" (4:9–11, emphasis added).

The Jews were an interesting people. They washed their hands a certain way, celebrated certain holidays, wore certain clothes, had certain views of marriage and sexuality. But perhaps most important, the Jews all celebrated a day called the "Sabbath." The word comes from the Hebrew word *shabbat*, meaning "to cease," "to rest," or "to end." The Sabbath was a day in the week when the Jews would stay home, eat good food, sing some songs, and just be God's people. Again, this is why the Jews spoke of "keeping" the Sabbath. Nowhere in the Bible do you "create" or "make" Sabbath. You protect it, you enter it, and you keep it like you would keep or protect something that isn't yours and someone has asked you to take care of. In this way, the Jews understood Sabbath as a gift, not a rule or a law.[4] They also understood the Sabbath as a bride. It is the thing you think of, wait for, and constantly dream of.[5]

In fact, it is this gift, this bride, of Sabbath that reminds us who we are as human beings. The Sabbath is our weekly reminder that we are not God. To take a day a week and simply enjoy God is to give a double-barrel "no" to the world for a day. It is to say to the world that the world does not complete me—only God can and does. As Mark Buchanan has written, "We mimic God in order to remember we're not God. In fact, that is a good definition of Sabbath: *imitating God so that we stop trying to be God.*"[6] To Sabbath is to remind yourself who you are: imperfect, fallible, dependent, and not omnipresent.

Sabbath keeping pulls the carpet out from under all our self-worship.

It is idolatry, those invisible drives in our heart, to say that humans are the most important thing in God's creation. The world isn't about humans—the world is about God, its Creator. I can remember being told that human beings were the "pinnacle" of God's creation, the most important part. This is, I believe, the cornerstone thought of human self-centered idolatry. Again, Moltmann writes, "If we look at the biblical traditions that have to do with the belief in creation, we discover that the Sabbath is not a day of rest following six working days. On the contrary: the whole work of creation was performed *for the sake of the Sabbath.*"[7]

Rabbi Abraham Joshua Heschel once said that Sabbath was a sneak preview of heaven.[8]

—ᴍ—

Sabbath was about ceasing. Two things take place on this day of "ceasing" called the Sabbath. One, called *zakhor shabbat*, was a call to remember who one is, who God is, and who God is for your people. One would cease forgetting who they were and who God was in the world. There was also the *shamor shabbat*. This was a "ceasing" of all work. All striving and all work would cease for one day. What would a Sabbath look like for a Jew?

All candles would be extinguished.

They would cook their food the day before so they didn't have to on Saturday.

They would sweep the whole house of yeast so that it could not work by "growing" on the Sabbath.

Even if they were building their tabernacle, they would stop, for rest was more important than their holy buildings.[9]

They would not take anything from their animals. Even the pets got the day off.

There were many more things. So, clearly, as you can tell, this was hard to do. For this reason, they had a whole day, the day of Preparation, to get ready for the Sabbath. Rest, true rest, is really hard work. It doesn't just happen.

And the penalty of not obeying was a bit harsh: death (Exod. 31:12–17; 35:1–3). All of this was something that the enemies of the Jews would be aware of. Some of the Jewish enemies knew that if they attacked on one certain day, Saturday, they would face a group of fighters that would be at home with their families.

This was a very hard day to live, especially when you couldn't afford it, or if you were at war, or if you were a workaholic. But if Sabbath happened, the world would be reconciled to God. Some Jewish rabbis, it turns out, taught that if everyone in the world rested, that is, Sabbathed, then the Messiah would come back. God would come back to rescue the world.[10]

—ᴍ—

137

A wanderer has to learn how to rest. It doesn't come all that naturally. We used to *have* to rest. In America we used to have the blue laws. Stores would shut down, we would go to church, and we would stop for a day. Now, we have lights on all the time that allow us to work constantly and never take a break. We live in a 24/7 world. We are overworked, overscheduled, and overlived. There are no time protections for us to just be human beings.

And we love it—secretly. When someone says "I am busy" with a very forlorn face, what they are really saying is, "Look at me, I am busy." Being busy is a trophy today.

Blessed are the busy, for they will inherit the earth. That is our new motto.

That's our American gospel. Because of our commitment to this gospel of never-ending busyness, distraction has become our liturgy. We envision ourselves as omnipresent. We think we can be here, there, and everywhere all at once. And it is killing us. Our stress has increased, our attention spans have shrunk, and our willingness to be *anywhere* for a long period of time has diminished.

And I think we love it.

As I mentioned, on the Sabbath the hardest thing to do is turn off my phone. My fingers tremble. It is scary. Not only does being distracted make us feel as though we are worth something; it simultaneously distracts us from what we feel about our lives. Every one of us has a low-grade hum of disappointment about our lives.

Being a Christian does not permit us to think in such destructive ways.

Sabbath living is contented living. Fact: non-Portlanders think Portlanders do nothing more than sit around watching *Portlandia* and eating Voodoo doughnuts. That's our reputation. Bacon maple bars and Fred Armisen. What stereotyping, one bemoans. But stereotypes are often based in reality. In all truthfulness, I'm one of those narcissistic, self-centered Portlanders who *does* watch a show about his city, laughing cynically at himself. And for the record, if I weren't dieting, a bacon maple bar probably *would* be in my hand.

Stereotypes are almost always well earned.

Portlanders are a proud, envious people. One *Portlandia* episode depicts two Portlanders sitting at a coffee-shop table. One looks up and asks if the other has read a certain article in *The New Yorker*. The person has, of course, and the question is asked back about another article. The first person has read that one too. The banter ping-pongs forever. As a piece of social commentary, of course, a slice of Portland culture is dissected: intellectual envy. That conversation *actually* happens, all the time. And it drives me to be well read. As a result, I'm continuously surprised at how much reading I do—not out of love or desire to learn but out of raging envy over everyone else's reading and the hope of looking knowledgeable to everyone I meet. I *want* to keep up, *want* to look well read. I want to have thoughts on that editorial exposé.

The altar of my literary envy is Powell's City of Books.

Envy fuels so much of our lives. The same principle recently came into play when my friend returned from a month in Africa. Recounting her wild missionary travels, I found myself seething with jealousy over all she experienced, leaving me to question if I was living a life crazy enough for God. Hearing her tales of adventure made my tales of mundane life feel so puny and boring.

Why do I read so much? Why am I jealous of my friend's travels? I suspect because internally—right or wrong—I believe there's some sort of narrative hierarchy in the world. In this mythic hierarchy I've emotionally constructed, the one with the biggest and craziest stories wins. This is why we try to one-up everyone's stories. The most well-read person is triumphant.

It's what I call *narrative envy*—the envy to have the best story out there.

To satiate our narrative envy, we hoard narratives. We go overboard trying to create crazy stories to make other people jealous just like we have been. We commit the sin of narrative gluttony. We turn stories into merit badges: Did you read? Did you go? Have you heard? Have you been?

But I wonder if God is inviting us to participate in a new economy of stories—an economy where the ancient biblical secret of "contentment in all things" rules (Phil. 4:11). At this table, I'm given permission to freely engage and rub shoulders with others in a great exchange of rich narratives and experiences without presumptively and lustfully being driven to need, own, and conquer others' stories. At this table, my boring old life is okay. Life's redundancy and normalcy, which so often mark my experience, are gleefully sanctified and welcomed just as they are as the guiding gifts of God's love to me before the creation of the world.

In this new economy, I am fulfilled by my boring little story that God has given me. Thus, the only way to fix that humming depression is to stop incessantly looking at Facebook, get off the computer, and invite a friend to coffee. That'll set you straight. People always look great on Facebook but are really screwed up in real life. I promise.

I think God invites us to bring our boring old selves to the kingdom of God. We can have narrative contentment—practicing thankfulness for every story God has given us as a gift from above.

But that'll never make it onto *Portlandia*.

—◊◊◊—

As a Christian, it's actually in the terrible context of tragedy that I find my sense of rest.

For any Jew, Saturday is understood as the most holy, sacred day of the week. On the first Saturday, God himself had rested. Saturday is the high point of the Jewish calendar. And for the Christian, it is to be equally holy and sacred. A general survey, if I dared to take one, would reveal that it is very common for a Christian nominally aware of the story of the life of Jesus to know what happened on Good Friday. Of course, on Good Friday, Jesus died on a cross. Similarly, it would be clear that most, if not all, are aware of what happened on Easter Sunday. On Easter Sunday, Jesus was resurrected from the dusty grave. But—and I don't think this is a stretch—few if any of us spend much time talking about (let alone celebrating) what happened on what church tradition has called Holy Saturday.

What happened on Holy Saturday?

Not much. On Saturday, Jesus lay in a tomb in the earth. The place was paltry, unexciting, and out of the way. Pay attention to that. Jesus, who was with the Father in the beginning, who is God through whom all things were made, including the earth, lay in the earth. The Creator *lay* dead in his own creation—ironically, I might add, on the same day God rested in the creation story. As God rested on the seventh day of creation, Jesus lay in the ground on the seventh day. Only this time, he lay there dead—doing what you do when you are dead. Rotting. Ceasing. Lying.

Holy Saturday is the first earth day.[11]

Of course, I've taken the liberty of looking at Holy Saturday from the angle of God's perspective. The same God who rested at creation is again resting on the seventh day because of the hatred and anger of the world. But to take it a step further, what was Holy Saturday like from the angle of those fearful, shaking, scared disciples who had just lost their Lord? What did *they* do on the Sabbath? Well, they didn't do all that much either. As their Lord rested, *they* rested. We are left with one fairly ambiguous story describing for us, two millennia after the fact, what happened on that most holy of Saturdays.

The account is found in Luke 23:55–56: "The women who had come with Jesus from Galilee followed Joseph and saw the tomb and how his body had been laid in it. Then they went home and prepared spices and perfumes. *But they rested* on the Sabbath in obedience to the commandment" (emphasis added). Now, the first Christians were Jews. And as Jews, they were faithful to a number of religious commandments. That is why the earliest Christians did not gather together to worship on Saturdays. For the earliest Christians, as Jews, Saturday was their day of rest. Sunday became their day of resurrection.

How can we describe this? A close friend of mine, a man I've had the chance to do a good deal of meaningful work alongside, used to be one of the top emergency-room physicians in the United States. His name is Dr. Matthew Sleeth. Matthew worked as the head doctor in the emergency room at a gigantic hospital in Maine. By his own account, he made exorbitant sums of money, received accolades, was a local superstar, and was well liked by his coworkers. He had, I think, what most of us would consider to be a good life.

As Matthew tells me, his soul became more and more empty, the way a well with no water sounds when you drop a coin down its hole. This—compounded by a season of life when his family experienced a series of personal tragedies (including a family member drowning in front of him and his children)—was making him ask big questions about life. On top of this, he was seeing sicker and sicker people come into his emergency room.

One day Dr. Sleeth, exhausted, bewildered, and frustrated at all the struggles of the world, was at his wit's end. As he walked through the waiting room, he saw a little orange book. He picked it up and read it.

The little orange book was a Bible. Dr. Sleeth became a Christian.

Everything changed. With his newfound faith, he began to ask deep, life-altering questions about what he was to do with the rest of his life. He tells me of one evening when he and his wife were sitting and talking. She turned to him and asked, "What's wrong with the world, Matthew?" He paused, then said with such deft clarity, "The world is dying." I think he meant it literally.

As Matthew read his Bible, he began to take note of one of the commandments that he observed Christians weren't living: the commandment to "Sabbath," to rest, to take a day to let God be God.

Matthew believed that this was to be the calling of his new life. He and his family sold their massive home and began spending their life teaching Christians how to observe the Sabbath. He has spent every waking hour of his life since then teaching people how to take a Sabbath, how to rest. Lots of people didn't like him for it. But he has dedicated his life to running around the world speaking, writing, and teaching people that without rest we are not fully alive.

I was with Matthew recently, and he told me that there has been one day in our contemporary society when we have Sabbathed, when we have truly rested. There has been one day when we've put off our jobs, gone home, and just *been*.

September 11, 2001.

On that day, all of us who could, went home. We stopped flying. We left our work. Our whole society rested. We called people we were at odds with and reconciled. Imagine what it would be like if we rested for something good: because we are reconciled people. It is like the famous *Yom HaShoa* festival in the nation of Israel. For one day each year in Israel, the entire nation stops what they are doing to remember the Holocaust and its victims. Cars stop driving, people stop working, gas stations stop pumping gas. Everything stops.

In a weird way, it required a tragedy to cause us to rest. A *horrible* tragedy. But that tragedy caused us all to go home and tell people we love them, to stop working, and to just *be* for a day. Like September 11, Holy Saturday was rest that was brought about by tragedy. And we rest because of Holy Saturday. The Jewish rabbis said that if everyone rested on Sabbath, the Messiah would come back. The Christian story twists that. For in the Christian story, when the Messiah comes back, *everyone* can rest from their toil. We no longer have to strive to become something before God and can, for once, rest in his love.

A Christian lives the Sabbath rest of Jesus.

The day before Holy Saturday, the disciples' leader, friend, and mentor was put up on a cross and killed. Jesus's being raised on the cross was similar to the towers being felled on 9/11: annihilation, loss, sadness, sheer tragedy. What exactly did the disciples of Jesus do on that fateful Saturday after the pain and toil of the day before? They rested. They Sabbathed. They went home.

Just the way, I might add, a good group of Jews would.

But I think there is more at play here. The Jewish people rested for a very big reason. In the Jewish tradition, the day after Passover was an important day. The day following was always a Sabbath day. It was a day to rest and celebrate and party and find joy in the forgiveness that you had just experienced. Nobody would work on that day. The tragedy of sin was followed by a party of rest.

What did they do the day after the tragedy of Jesus's death? They "rested." Why? Because, as Jesus had said on the cross, "it is finished."

143

A Christian does not see a Sabbath as a period of time. Sabbath, for a Christian, is a way of life. All of life for a Christ wanderer is a Sabbath. All of life is one big period of rest—not rest from the day job or rest from responsibilities, but rest from striving. From saving ourselves. From all of that.

The Christian life is a life of Sabbath. It truly is a powerful insight to reflect upon that we worship the God who invented rest, cares for it, and demands his freed people live it and extend it as a gift to others. And we can, with that, take heart that God is always seeking out a rest for us. As C. S. Lewis would remind us, "Our Father refreshes us on the journey with some pleasant inns."[12] There is always vacancy in the Sabbath inn.

DISPLACEMENT

As citizens, Christians share all things with others, and yet endure all things as foreigners. Every foreign land is to them as their native country and every land of their birth as a land of strangers. . . . They pass their days on earth, but they are citizens of heaven. They obey the prescribed laws, and at the same time surpass the laws by their lives.

Epistle of Mathetes to Diognetus

Everything has its rightful place.

There's an Old Testament command concerning what one is to do if one stumbles across the lost animal of another person. "If you come across your enemy's ox or donkey wandering off," the book of Exodus commands, "be sure to *return* it" (23:4, emphasis added). If a person misplaced his or her sheep, for instance, the finder was the one who was to return it to its rightful owner. This was a commandment of great importance in a culture where there were no police or FBI—people had to follow a moral code or else everything in all of society would fall apart. Of course, the Bible pushes it even further than most of us would be comfortable with. Not only was the finder to return a friend's lost sheep; they were expected to return an *enemy's* sheep also.

"Finders keepers, losers weepers" is an American theme. It is nowhere in the biblical text.

A similar commandment is the Jubilee. During the year of Jubilee, everyone would release people of their debts, free slaves, and return land to the original owner. Everyone would be off the hook for their debts. Of course, historians would be quick to point out that the Jubilee was probably never actually done (that they know of). And mostly, it was never done because had it actually taken place, the entire economy of the nation at the time would have collapsed. It turns out that God's kingdom often puts a wrench in *our* ways of doing economics. But the whole Jubilee commandment implied one thing: if everyone was giving back land to the original owner, then nobody would own any land. The land was God's. *He* owned the land, not us. And Jubilee would be a scheduled reminder that we were to return to the Creator what was originally his.

As organizational theory tells us, everything should have its right place. The same goes for God's kingdom and the world God created. A person after the heart of God knows that everything has its place, even the sheep of an enemy. And our role is helping put things in their proper place. Jesus's entire ministry was based on this very principle: reconciling himself to his enemies. Jesus went after sheep, even sheep that were once enemies.

When something is displaced, it is not where it naturally belongs. If one were to put eggs in a washing machine, those eggs would be very displaced. A block of ice in the desert is displaced. Displacement is largely the result of some kind of abnormality—of something being in a place it is not naturally supposed to be. This theme of displacement is intertwined with God's people in the Bible and in the history of Christianity. By that I mean that Christians are a displaced people. For example, some time ago I stumbled across the fascinating story of a Christian woman by the name of Fabiola.[1] During the tumultuous years of the fourth century in which Fabiola lived, the Christian church, just four centuries old, was beginning to find its sense of communal identity. During this time, contemplation and reflection became very important. In fact, whole schools and communities of Christians began to form so that they might explore what the Christian faith would look like. Many of these Christians were called monastics, or monks. Mostly, they were known for living off the grid, in the hills and the mountains and deserts, to seek the face of Jesus. In seeking Jesus and living in community, many of them wrote music and copied Scripture, and later, some of them even began brewing beer. They were well liked.

Then there were monastics like Fabiola, known to church history as "wandering monks." Fabiola's form of Christian faith inspired her to constantly be on the move, going and finding the place God was taking her. Unlike those who lived in the hills and the mountains and the deserts, there was a whole class of monastics and nuns and hermits and wanderers who chose to spend their time traveling the world to share the gospel, love the poor, and serve those along the way. Their itinerant pilgrimage, marked by constant movement, became a kind of sign of their identity. They were not of this world; thus, they could not get comfortable in this world.

Of course, a Christian is never really fully at home in the world. What Fabiola illustrates for us, and what her tradition sought to witness to the world, is that there is a kind of "homelessness" in the context of one's Christian identity. "Our citizenship is in heaven," writes Paul. "And we eagerly await a Savior from there" (Phil. 3:20). In short, Fabiola would remind us that a Christian's life is itinerant, out of place, and temporal. In a very real way, Christians exist in a kind of perpetual exile until their death. We are simply passing through. We are a pilgrim people. And we have a leader who paved the way: Jesus was constantly on the move and going from one place to another. It is of great importance to the story of Jesus that it was when he went back to his own hometown that he was most starkly rejected. The Gospels plainly put it that "he did not do many miracles there" (Matt. 13:58). The saying rings true. A prophet has no honor in his hometown. Maybe that is why Jesus lived on the road so much. The people who knew him in his childhood would make no room for him. Others felt threatened by him. He didn't, as he once said, have a place to put his head. Jesus spent almost his entire ministry going from place to place. If you are from heaven, then this isn't the place you were meant for, nor will you be welcomed. Jesus even told his disciples that, like him, they would be hated and persecuted and treated as outsiders and that they should expect nothing less. We shouldn't be all that dismayed at being disliked by the world. For wondering why the world doesn't like the church is like asking why Judas didn't wash the feet of Jesus.

By no means does this mean that whenever and however the church is hated and maligned, it is doing good things: pain and suffering don't make the martyr, the cause does. Sometimes we are hated for all the wrong things. But the kind of displacement that people of Jesus should expect is not just the result of happenstance—it should be expected. Pilgrim thinking like this saturated the early church and ultimately became the basis for the wandering monks and those who were like them. Being on the move, going places, and traveling became the sign of one's true citizenship, which was elsewhere. One scholar brilliantly draws the connection between constant travel among the wandering monks and seeing oneself as being from somewhere else: "Travel was viewed as an imitation of the life of Christ, a literal rendering of the life of a Christian, a life only 'temporarily on this earth.' One was a wanderer until death, and with death eternal life in the Christian's true homeland, heavenly Jerusalem."[2] The importance of physical displacement—of being "on the go"—was that it caused one to believe constant movement was an imitation of Christ. Such radical travelers and ascetics, in the words of one religious scholar, seemed like they were on the "edge of the world."[3] Wandering became a way to express their homeless nature before the world and God. It was as if to say they wouldn't settle down because they weren't from around here. We aren't from here, so we should not need to be anywhere.

In a way, Christians never really find their rightful place outside of God.

—\m—

I've often thought back to Fabiola and with a sense of jealousy for what she got to do, in the same way I have a secret jealousy toward people who are always on the road speaking, playing shows, and doing all the gigs. Part of me longs for a life on the road. For more of us than we might imagine, there's almost a seductive lust in our hearts to be wandering monks—living a life of constant travel, of going here and there, of being whisked away to exciting places. And some of that lust is probably not all that good. We all have a kind of wanderlust—a desire to go anywhere and be anywhere but *here*. For sinners, any *other* place is always better than where we are.

And I suppose that one could take the texts we've looked at and quickly draw the conclusion that a life on the road is the ideal Christian life because we really aren't even from around here anyway. But, as there often is in Scripture, there is another side to the tale. For while we are wanderers and exiles and pilgrims, we are simultaneously called to be rooted and sent by God to some place. A Christ follower is paradoxically exiled and rooted, simultaneously pilgrim and settler. While Paul did believe that our true citizenship was in heaven, he was as quick to point out the importance of being responsible members of the world. "Make it your ambition," Paul writes, "to lead a quiet life: You should mind your own business and work with your hands, just as we told you, so that your daily life may win the respect of outsiders and so that you will not be dependent on anybody" (1 Thess. 4:11–12). Paul is saying, get a job, be in a neighborhood, be respectable, and take good care of yourself.

So, there is a pilgrim nature and a settler nature to every Christian. We are called to responsibility to a place *and* to never be fully at home here. There is a balance to be lived out that I admit is awkward at best. All of this is not to say that Christians shouldn't travel or should only be homebodies. Some people, such as Christian missionaries overseas, are often called to a life of travel. Christian history is sprinkled with people who were *both* on the road *and* rooted in a given place. In fact, historically, there's strong evidence in the early church that there were "wandering" Christians—those called to live on the road as traveling missionaries—who existed alongside more localized and rooted Christians who lived in a given place over a longer period of time.[4] And there is abundant evidence that these two types of Christians worked alongside one another and respected one another's calling. They didn't look down on one another. Christianity needs both. We need people to go overseas and people to stay in a local community just as we are citizens of heaven who are called to be Christ followers in our neighborhood.

But I think today the greatest need is for those bold and intrepid Christians who are willing to settle down and be in a neighborhood for a long time. In short, we need more Christians who garden. A long time ago, the Jewish people were destroyed by a nation called Babylon, who picked them up and carried them off to a foreign land. This is called "the exile." And during the exile, God speaks to his people through the prophet Jeremiah. Through the prophet, God gives them some rather odd commands. He tells them to "plant gardens" (Jer. 29:5). Why? Because exile was complete displacement. It was knowing your home still existed but that you were miles and miles away from it.

Exile is real to many of us. We experience it every day; we are displaced, uprooted, and all over the place. Seeing ourselves as exiles helps clarify the role of the church in our lives. As exiles, we always need to have a safe place to share life with other exiles who are not from this world. In his book *Longing for Heaven*, Peter Toon masterfully reminds us that, as foreigners to this world, the church becomes our embassy.[5] I love that image: the church is an embassy in a foreign land. It is within the church that we share our identity, values, culture, and dreams. Although in the world we may seem out of place, the church, suggests Toon, is where we share our Jesus-made identity with others. If we are foreigners in this world, then the church is an embassy.

Yet exile can be painful. Tamara Eskenazi offers a brilliant definition of the kind of exile I am referring to: "Exile. It is not simply being homeless. Rather, it is knowing that you do have a home, but that your home has been taken over by enemies. Exile. It is not being without roots. On the contrary, it is having deep roots, which have now been plucked up, and there you are, with roots dangling, writhing in pain, exposed to a cold and jeering world, longing to be restored to native and nurturing soil. Exile is knowing precisely where you belong, but knowing you can't go back, not yet."[6] And in this complete displacement, what does God invite his people to do? Garden. Gardening is, in a way, a protest of our life of displacement. It is to look at a world that is constantly on the move and to say, "No, not today." I think that is why I like my garden. It places me somewhere. It keeps me somewhere. I have to keep my eye on it. A garden is a protest against our efforts at being omnipresent. A garden is a protest against placelessness. A garden is our boycott of being displaced.

Like the Good Book says, gardening is our primal human vocation as an exiled people.

I've traveled and spoken all over the world. And something funny happens when you're on the road. You become a little glitzier, a little shinier. You become a celebrity, or, at least, a celebrity in your own mind (in my case). One who travels a lot will admit that it is much easier to lie when you're on the road. Or it's easier to make your stories seem a bit more inflated, mostly because people don't know the truth. They don't live with you. I think that is probably why I have an unhealthy love of traveling to different places when I'm asked to speak.

I get to travel every once in a while, and it is fun indeed—to a point. And there are benefits that come from speaking and sharing stories with one another. But it can also be destructive. When I travel and speak, people seem to like me more than the people at home. My jokes are new to them and thus still funny. I am exciting. I can preach my best sermons, and people think I am the best preacher they've heard in a long time. My stories are way more indulged than when I am at home because nobody knows the difference. I can stretch the truth when I'm on the road because there is nobody who was there when the story actually happened. This is way different than when I am home. At home, it's hard. My church knows me all too well. They have heard my best stuff three times over, they know my best lines, and they know what makes me tick. And at home, my wife doesn't laugh at me anymore. She knows my jokes all too well.

Again, physical wandering—always moving from place to place—isn't always good. In constant displacement, constant movement, in physical wandering, our soul can be lost. In wandering, we lose something. We lose the joy of roots. We lose the joy of years. We lose so much. Being on the road can become our drug. It helps us numb the pain of what we perceive to be a boring life.

We all lust a little to be like Fabiola. We all have a lust, a desire, a longing to be anywhere but *here*.

"Come as you are"—one of those catchy, shallow, saccharine church marketing phrases we preach to ourselves and use with great regularity but in the end don't really mean. Or at least we don't in practice. None of us wants people to come as they are. We want people to come as we want them to come and become what we want them to become. Really, it's our sales pitch to get people in the door. I don't like saying "come as you are" if by saying that we are falsely advertising that through these doors you are not expected to change. Jesus's kingdom is not about remaining the same. Jesus's kingdom will wreck us. It's fine if we say "come as you are" as long as we extend the same hospitality toward God as we do the neighbor. If we come as we are, and God comes as he is, I have a suspicion that only one of the two needs to change.

It doesn't surprise me that people are having a hard time doing the church thing. A trend has begun to take shape in the church that is both troubling and telling. Christians are either not choosing to be a part of a church or, perhaps worse, wandering from church to church in an endless search, looking for something that they don't seem to be finding. But what are we looking for that we aren't finding? Why do we wander from church to church?

I saw this for myself. At our church, we have "Welcome to Theophilus" dinners. At the two-hour gathering, we begin with a big meal in our living room. Then, after dinner, we open up a dialogue for about one hour where we share a little about the church and hear the stories of those who are new to the church. The first couple of times were hard. We didn't know what we were getting ourselves into. During those times, new people came and shared openly how hurt they were by their last church. The stories were bitter and cold and heartbreaking. And on almost every occasion, people indicated they wanted to be a part of something that was different, something that wouldn't hurt them. The expectation was, latently, that this new church would not hurt them.

Language reveals everything about the pain. I noticed that when people talked about the church they had left, they would always speak about it with a good deal of distance. It was always "that" church. They removed themselves even linguistically from the church they came out of. It was as though there was shame by even associating with it. After two dinners, I realized I needed to change the way we talked about church. Now the first thing I do is tell everyone that I brought them to the dinner to tell them that our church will not be a good fit for them. It will hurt them. It will disappoint them. They will be let down. And I need to do that because too few Christians are aware that they are looking for something that does not exist—a perfect community of worshipers.

I've come to really respect Roman Catholics. A lot of Catholics stay with their local church parish for a whole lifetime, even if they grow bored. Pain, death, boredom—few things can tear them away from their community. I love the way Catholics talk about being Catholic. They are typically not scared to identify with their broken family. It is *their* church. It isn't *that* church.

In watching people come in and out of community, it never ceases to shock me how little hardship it requires for someone to want to leave their church. Our covenants with a local church are as deep as our *feeling* like it is a good fit. We leave a church when our feelings are hurt. This, of course, makes it challenging for any of us to have honest, painful dialogue about the things in our lives that need to change. For if we leave when we are hurt, we don't say anything in order to not alienate someone.

I hear that occasionally someone will marry another person for his or her money. You'll hear about some twenty-year-old marrying some older wealthy widow or widower. Years later, everyone is hurt. That is anything but a relationship. We do that to the church of God all the time. We don't marry the church because we love God. We marry the church for the "money." We love it as long as it gives us *x*, *y*, and *z*. And so we, in essence, give the church a prenuptial agreement—we'll stick around as long as all demands are met.

That is not a covenant. It's a prenuptial agreement. I'm in as long as my wants are fulfilled. And the minute they aren't, I'm out of here.

All of this, of course, is not to minimize the pain many of us have had in Christian communities. There are times when we need to leave, particularly in cases of abuse—emotional, physical, or any other kind. Sometimes we need to part ways. But the opposite of that is equally true. We leave a church over the silliest stuff—whether we like the music, whether it feels right, whether they do this or that program.

So we go from church to church. We shop for churches. We hop churches. We have church wanderlust.

But what are we looking for?

We look for another place that will fit our needs.

We search for something.

We are looking for something else that makes sense.

But we will never stop looking as long as we are looking for something that does not exist. And we will pay quite the cost. The church in America has almost the same experience as a military child who moves from city to city every few months, developing shallow friendships on the go that are not given the time to flourish into real, life-giving friendships that make life worth living. A military child and an American Christian have almost identical psychologies.

But the question on my mind is, what are we looking for? What would cause us to stay? What are we not finding?

—⟋⟋⟍—

Wherever we are displaced, there is something we are in deep need of. "Wherever there is a distance," once wrote the ever-wise John O'Donahue, "there is a *longing*."[7] His point was that any distance from one another, from God, or from the church is the result of a longing. There is something *else* we are looking for that we are not finding.

So much of our culture's literature is about the distance that our false longings create and about escaping. I was reading *Eat, Pray, Love*. It is about a woman who goes to find herself by traveling the world. I found myself wanting to leave my family, my church, and the people I know to escape to the world out there and find myself. It is not a shock to me that a handful of divorces have had the same story: someone reading *Fifty Shades of Grey*. It is a book about escaping from the mundane of real life. It is not a book about lifelong fidelity. It is a book about escaping reality and creating a new one that feels better than the old, less exciting one.

Still, a life of displacement isn't manifested just in physical displacement. Sometimes we are displaced internally as well. For me and many in my generation, we constantly find ourselves being displaced by our commitment to busyness. And our way of worshiping busyness is primarily through incessant, thoughtless, disembodied multitasking. We do everything all the time at the same time, particularly as it plays itself out on social media and an online world that disrupts our presence in a given place.

Busyness is sexy. It makes you look good. It makes you feel like you are something. It props you up. It's a cultural merit badge. But we have become busy to the point of having no time to do anything of real meaning. This fabricated, artificial busyness gives us an out to say no to things, and it simultaneously feels good as a constant reminder that we are "worthy" in what we do. We have equated worth and value with a schedule. A person with nothing scheduled clearly has a problem.

An artificially busy schedule says to everyone that we are productive, that we are doing well in life, that we have important things to do.

An antidote to multitasking, it seems, is a life of constant prayer. Paul's words on prayer can be misinterpreted. When he said "Pray without ceasing," one could wrongly read that as a call to stay in a church confessional all day long and only come out for meals (which you eat silently in prayer). A life of prayer without ceasing has been confused with a life of solitude. Prayer doesn't just happen in silence or when our heads are bowed. A life of prayer is a life directed toward God at all times. Prayer isn't narcissistic—it isn't a place where we baptize our own plans in the dirty water of our selfish desires. Prayer is mostly joyous death.

The Jewish vision of prayer is inspirational for me in this way. Abraham Joshua Heschel spoke of the "scattered forces of the self." Writing just previous to our age of incessant multitasking, Heschel knew in a small part what we experience. We are a wandering people because we are scattered. Heschel and other Jewish theologians advocated for a kind of prayer they called *kavanah*.

Kavanah is a constant internal gravitation toward God. Heschel writes, "*Kavanah* is direction to God and requires the involvement and redirection of the whole person. It is the act of bringing together the scattered forces of the self; it means the participation of heart *and* soul, not only of will and mind."[8] I would suggest this is what Paul is after. It is a life oriented toward God in all we do. When I eat, I *kavanah* toward God. When I work, I *kavanah* toward Jesus. When I love my family, I *kavanah* toward the Holy Spirit. Prayer is a life oriented toward God. All things become intentional. Action becomes thoughtful. Breath becomes memorable. Things are no longer just clicks and presses of the button from world to world.

The problem with multitasking is not only that it isn't effective. Its major problem is that it leads to a life lacking intentionality and presence. It's hard to be here if I am everywhere else all the time.

—❦—

I often see people looking at their phones while sitting together. There's a brilliant book on the topic of what social media and technology are doing to our relationships that aptly describes the kind of relational disconnectedness we find ourselves in: the book is called *Alone Together.*[9] That sums it up. The sickness of our age is that we have all the proximity minus the intimacy. We are *around* one another. We are present with each other physically but in no other way. Our phones have become our sacrament of placelessness. They permit us to be everywhere but where we are. One time I nearly broke my iPhone during the second point of my sermon to try to get the Christians in our church to turn off their phones.

That week's sermon, out of Mark 1:14–20, was about *kairos* time— about how, in our American hubris, we're constantly tempted to believe we can cram into our little earthly lives way more than God really desires for us to. Omnipresence, we assume, is a characteristic of human beings. I talked about how the Bible frequently dismisses such arrogance and how God, in the creation narratives, is a multitasker, creating multiple beings and entities in one day all while sustaining that which he had already made. On the other hand, humanity had a much simpler task: garden, eat, and make love. Rinse and repeat. Mix up the order if you like. But that was Adam and Eve's simple task. Simple and uncomplicated. Humanity is intrinsically bounded by divine boundaries, I argued—boundaries not to be transcended. We aren't God. Multitasking is God's job; "singletasking" is ours.

But our desire to be like God was in our bones. So we ate the apple.[10]

I reminded the congregation that the first apple represented a fundamental breakdown and disrespect for these intentional boundaries. Humanity, I suggested, sinned by transcending the moral boundaries of Eden by eating *whatever* they wanted. Humanity hasn't evolved. Railing against our addiction to multitasking, I pulled out my Apple iPhone in front of the congregation. And with a homiletical anger I've rarely experienced, I yelled,

The first one was an apple that led us astray. And, once again, we find ourselves in a similar position. An apple [my iPhone] has deceived us, causing us to believe we can transcend the boundaries of humanity. We can't! God made the boundaries. Your phone is not an escape from human limitations. It doesn't make you a god. You can't be everywhere! So, friends, put your phone away, for heaven's sake. Sit in God's presence. Enjoy the garden he's already given you. Be present. Repent of your supposed omnipresence.

By sermon's end, I was steaming, sweating with anger, and just about ready for the floor to cave in and reveal the pits of hades as it mythically did during Jonathan Edwards's "Sinners in the Hands of an Angry God." I pulled out my phone, reached it out before the congregation, and went to break it in half. Luckily I didn't. Had it been a flip phone, it would have been quite the memorable moment.

The opposite of displacement is not being in the same physical place for years, ceasing all travel or any other physical requirement. The true opposite of displacement is prayer. Prayer is truly that place where we are placed squarely by the Holy Spirit wherever he has placed us. And in prayer, we are reminded that any place can be a holy place. Prayer reminds us that if God can show up in a burning bush, then any place may be sacred. A life of prayer is one where the thing being done, the task, the job, isn't of ultimate importance. Rather, every event becomes what Martin Buber called "God-oriented intent."[11] I found this idea beautifully portrayed in the works of Brother Lawrence, who famously invited Christians to follow God in daily, everyday tasks like washing dishes and cleaning the house. Brother Lawrence, who worked for much of his life in a monastery kitchen, wrote a book called *The Practice of the Presence of God*. In it he speaks eloquently of the "God of pots and pans and things."[12]

But this approach to the sacred everyday doesn't play well to an adrenaline-induced church. Christians seem to have almost become allergic to rooting ourselves in one place for a long time. We have become travelers, wanderers, movers and shakers, abandoning the simple and mundane places where we have been placed. This is precisely the kind of life I've seen made popular in American Christianity in recent years. For many Christians, the only way to express one's love of Jesus Christ is to do radical things that take us to *other* parts of the world. Our faith can only be expressed in doing insane things for Jesus. In our radicalness, we define faith as that which takes us to anywhere but here. And with such grandiose ideas, we try to change the world. Christians have begun to worship "changing the world." Changing the world can often mean abandoning the simplicity of worship around here.

I find it interesting that I don't hear people saying they feel like Jesus is calling them to a low-paying job, or a job at a grocery store, or a job at the bank. We only say Jesus is calling us to something if it is radical and daring. What about the call of Jesus to the mundane? Honestly, it has to be a sign that the Spirit is up to something when a janitor says they do what they do because Jesus told them to do it. Be assured: a Christ that dies on a cross and calls it success isn't a Christ who invites people only to things that are successful in our eyes.

Trust me.

—⁓—

A Christian culture is afoot that discourages Christians from being the simple, rooted, local, neighborly types who consider a life well lived to be a holy calling. Christians today are talking too much, I think, about being radical in the sense that we have to go somewhere else to be doing the work of Jesus. For many of us, Christianity has become a religious form of *Fear Factor*—who can do the next crazy and insane thing for God? But what of the person to whom God says, "Hey, stay put. Be a dad. Keep the job. Pay your taxes. And do PTA." Is there room for that person in the gospel? I would hope so. And more power to those who feel led by God to go overseas—don't misread me. But what if selling all one's possessions and moving overseas isn't what Jesus wants someone to do? What if Jesus is actually asking someone to keep the house, start a college fund, and be in one place for a long time? Can that be an option too? What if God wants someone to plant a garden and water it?

There are two problems with this *Fear Factor* Christianity, which suggests someone has to continuously enact insane things to follow the path of Jesus. First, it cuts out a lot of people from the work of God. *Fear Factor* Christianity doesn't create much of an opportunity for the stay-at-home mother or the person sitting in a wheelchair or the six-year-old child to be a disciple of Jesus Christ. My friend Joshua Butler tells a story of a stay-at-home mom in his church who asked him how she was to live out Matthew 25, where Jesus says we are to feed the hungry and thirsty, clothe the naked, and visit people in prison. Joshua's answer to this woman was beautiful. Joshua comforted the woman and agreed that while she couldn't spend her time at homeless shelters feeding the poor, she could fulfill Jesus's command. Joshua told her that feeding and giving drink to those little ones crying out to be fed and nourished and cared for still counted. We all have people we care for—we all have someone to feed. Not everyone can spend their days at the homeless shelter.

We must resist, and eventually reject, the idea that Christianity cannot be lived out in the everyday. It can be lived out in the everyday; in fact, I think that is where it is best lived out. Christianity is to be lived out in the mundane and everyday realities of our lives. Or you might just say that mundane, everyday Christianity is the *most radical* form of Christianity at its core. Of course, part of our draw to *Fear Factor* Christianity is that we live in a culture that is increasingly intolerant of people who do normal things. To be special around here, you have to be "different." So nobody wants to be ordinary. It's as if we've become allergic to the ordinary. We must resist this shift. G. K. Chesterton was right—the path to radical Christianity shouldn't require us to always go do crazy tasks. Sometimes, Jesus asks us to just be ordinary. "The most extraordinary thing in the world," wrote Chesterton, "is an ordinary man and an ordinary woman and their ordinary children."[13] Ordinary, in God's kingdom, is the new radical.

The second problem with *Fear Factor* Christianity is that someone is always paying the price for this drive to constantly be on the move. I was talking about this very topic to a group of Christians. I was telling them that perhaps my own greatest temptation is not of a sexual or physical nature. I think perhaps my greatest temptation is to be one of those famous Christians who travels all over and speaks. I want it because it makes me feel incredibly loved. I can go to some church, preach my best sermon, and afterward during coffee hour be showered with accolades about how incredible my sermon was. People on the road tell me I am funny. They laugh at all my material. I am so tempted by it.

But after one event, a man came up to me, threw down a gold, million-mile frequent flier card, and said, "Don't do it. That little card cost me my entire family."

His words pricked my heart like a pin on a balloon. Being on the road can easily become my way to escape the holiness of whatever Jesus has already put in front of me to do. And no, I'm not jumping on people who travel for work. For some, that is a way of life, and I am not questioning that it can work. But I am saying that when we are constantly going everywhere, I think we do so to get away from that place we have been placed.

It is nearly impossible to "love your neighbor as yourself" if we don't give ourselves time and space to actually have one.

The price of constantly going elsewhere to do ministry is that our neighbors don't connect with us, our children don't see us, and our friends don't know us. Count the cost. Some are called to a kind of *Fear Factor* Christianity—just count the cost! Don't buy into the lie that a spiritual journey must be a physical journey. Remember, we can grow where we are stuck. It is possible to be spiritual right here. Because we are discontent with our tiny, seemingly insignificant lives, we want to escape and go where the action is. The road becomes our drug to escape our life. Or running away to travel becomes a way to be free of responsibility. Or unhealthy and dangerous sexual practices become our way to escape the holiness of the mundane.

We do everything we can to satiate our longing. But at the end of the day, what are we longing for as we wander through this world? What are we after that we are not finding?

—⁓—

One of the greatest paradoxes in this life is how those who have everything they've ever wanted are often the least joyful. Shopaholics are often radically depressed people who never have enough. John D. Rockefeller, one of the richest men ever to live, responded with the phrase "one more dollar" when he was asked what it would take for him to find happiness.[14] That doesn't surprise me. Nor is it out of the ordinary for people who go from exciting world traveling experience to exciting world traveling experience to be dissatisfied with their lives. I'm no longer caught off guard to find that people who've had sexual encounter after encounter in an attempt to fulfill their wild, boundaryless fantasies have found little to no lasting joy. Nor does it perplex me that those who seek happiness itself above all else end up being completely disappointed in the results. Haven't we learned? Will we ever? We wander around seeking to secure life in all the wrong places. Until we learn, we'll continue to wander from thing to thing, having shallow, lifeless experience after experience.

In his *Confessions*, Augustine wrote, "You have made us for yourself, and our hearts are restless until they find rest in you."[15] This theme plays itself out over and over again in Augustine's writings: without God we are unshakably incomplete. Until we rest in the gentle arms of our Maker, we will long for anything else. God, Augustine believed, actually made us to *need* him. God creates us as his dependents in order that we will wander about until we discover this fact.

This groaning and longing that Augustine gave voice to is similar to how C. S. Lewis described the human longings each of us have. Lewis spoke often and vividly of *Sehnsucht*, a visceral human longing for something else. For Lewis, *Sehnsucht* was a kind of yearning purposefully placed in the hearts of all people to want to find something outside this created realm. *Sehnsucht* is feeling as though you are constantly out of touch or out of reach of something. Lewis describes this as follows: "Our lifelong nostalgia, our longing to be reunited with something in the universe from which we now feel cut off, to be on the inside of some door which we have always seen from the outside, is . . . the truest index of our real situation."[16] Lewis and Augustine are on the same page. We are discontent with our mundane lives for a reason. We are longing for a purpose. Life, *real* life, isn't in all the shallow waters we think it is. There are deeper waters—the waters of God. When we recognize this, we can be free from thinking we must wander to that next marriage, that next church, that next friendship, that next place we think will have what we are looking for.

Your heart doesn't truly long for those things. The one thing that our hearts wander around for is the love and grace of God. Stop wandering, wanderer. You can stop looking *elsewhere* to find what you seek. Look no further. Proverbs 17:24 could save us some time: "A fool's eyes *wander* to the ends of the earth" (emphasis added).

A fool keeps looking. The wise one centers on the truth. Whenever we find true joy and retrace our steps to when that joy began, I would suspect it begins when we find true satisfaction and identity in Jesus, and Jesus alone. This brings up a crucial point. It isn't that happiness is wrong, or sex is bad, or money is evil. These things are good things that God gives to us. The point is that they are awful things to worship. The minute we center on them, we lose our very selves. That is why the Bible calls us to repent. *Repentance* is a funny word in the Bible. It means *return*. But sometimes we get repentance all wrong. We often think repentance is returning from doing bad things to doing good things, like we're switching sides. But repentance isn't turning from bad things to good things. Repentance is turning from bad things to Jesus Christ. This means, at times, we even turn from good things to Jesus.[17] Repentance requires that we be willing to forsake doing good things so that we might return to Jesus.

In the end, true repentance is placing our longing, our wandering, our desires, our dreams, in the arms of God, whose arms are outstretched. That is repentance. And until we do that, we will find everything to be a little dull.

Losing Jesus

Either I determine the place in which I will find God, or I allow God to determine the place where He will be found.

Dietrich Bonhoeffer, letter to Dr. Rudiger Scheicher

When I was a junior in high school—shortly after my conversion to Christianity—a young man in my circle of friends became a Christian (we'll call him Stu for the purposes of anonymity). Long story short, Stu and I had been sharing a long conversation about faith and Christianity, a conversation he had shown more and more interest in as time went on. While initially hesitant, over the course of a year Stu grew in his interest in faith as we talked about some of his preconceived notions of what faith was all about. I had no idea what I was talking about; it was all very new to me. But what I lacked in knowledge I made up for in zeal. One evening, after a long walk through the suburbs of our hometown under the luminescent hum of the streetlights, Stu became

164

a Christian. It was the first time I led someone in what is called the "sinner's prayer"—although I'm pretty sure I did it all wrong. There may have been some cuss words in there. I basically winged it.

Soon enough, Stu started attending church with me with the zeal of a young convert. He started reading his Bible. He confessed his sins. He even tried fasting. In the mornings before school, we would pray together in front of my locker. Of course, whether Stu converted to Christianity because I annoyed him or wouldn't let the issue go, I still can't answer. Regardless of my words or works in his life, Stu said it was so real for him. He described for me what I've seen so many other people describe when they claim to have a personal encounter with the living God—he said he could *feel* God so near and close to him. The experience, with all its overwhelming emotions, was understandably powerful.

After graduating from high school, I didn't see Stu for nearly a decade. It wasn't that we didn't want to talk; it just became harder and harder to stay friends after high school. Then I saw him. One afternoon, after years of distance, we got to talking. He caught me up on the last ten years, and I did the same. Then he told me that he was no longer a Christian. Furthermore, he showed almost no interest in the topic of faith. It turns out, Stu said, that he stopped feeling God after I had left to go to college. I wasn't there to talk to him about faith; I wasn't there to read the Bible with him; I wasn't there to pray with him. When I left, so did his faith. Stu came to believe that those feelings of faith were really just that: mere feelings. And that those feelings were not reality. He concluded it was not God that he felt but mere emotions. Stu believed those feelings were little more than the result of being a young, pimple-faced teenager who was overly emotional because of an overly excited pituitary gland.

What I couldn't understand was the disparity between his feelings from the past and his experience now. I couldn't conceive that he had such a real, personal, enlivening experience back when we were in high school, and now he had rejected it all.

I still think about Stu. I wonder if I did something wrong.

—⁂—

Feelings are a fickle business. And many of us live in our feelings as though they are a constant source of good direction. Feelings aren't good or bad; they are just fickle. More often than not, we put feelings at the center of our lives to such a degree that we eventually come to believe our lives are literally defined by *how I feel* my life is going. So, if we're feeling happy about our future, then our future is good in our minds. If we're feeling disappointed about our performance at work, then we are a disappointment at work. If we constantly feel shameful and guilty about our mistakes, then we're guilty and shameful people who must be locked in the cell of our shame. Largely, we have allowed our feelings to be our identity—we are what we feel about ourselves. We base our identity and self-worth on how our careers are going, how we feel our marriages are, how good we think our children are doing, whether we have gained some popularity or not, and if we have garnered respect from those around us. When we feel things are bad, then things are bad. When we feel things are good, they are good. But such a way of living creates a cycle of life that is both destructive and unsustainable. When we are our feelings, our fickle feelings betray us.

The gospel of Jesus—the love of God in Christ—is not based on feelings by any stretch of the imagination. There is a danger in constantly giving our feelings a place of sovereignty in our lives. When we give our feelings all the power they wish to have, we can safely assume we will eventually find ourselves in a kind of spiritual paralysis. Feelings are not always good barometers of reality. I might *feel* as though Pluto is a planet, but my feelings don't have any bearing on what is or what isn't. Reality is not shaped by our feelings about it. Likewise, Christian faith is not the sum of our feelings on the topic. We may not *feel* as though God loves us, but our feelings on the subject have no bearing on the reality. Emotions do not change truth, no matter how strong they may be.

I catch myself sinking into this trap all the time. It's incredible how much you learn about yourself after a while. I know *me* really well.

Although I didn't recognize it for the longest time, I have a habit of asking people who are close to me in age how old they are, particularly those who have experienced success. I almost obsess about it. After reflecting on it, I have learned that the pathology behind this is that I am sizing myself up to them. If I know how old they are and what they've done up to this point in their life, I have a safe indicator of how I am doing in life. If they are older and have accomplished less, I am doing okay. If they are younger and have done more, then I become a train wreck. I *am* how I feel about my life. Of course, such an outlook on life is just plain silly. For even the Son of God, the Savior of the world, was a thirty-year-old woodworker; it seems that there were no notable accomplishments before he entered the final three years of his career. (Those three years, I admit, were incredible.) The older I become, the more successful younger people are. And the cycle could continue. But I have decided that youthful success is overrated and that life isn't a competition.

What would it look like if we didn't bow in worship toward our feelings?

Someone will raise the point that feelings are good and should be respected. Unquestionably. Feelings are a gift from God. Feelings help us know and sense, and they lead us to realize problems and blessings in our life. Feelings are the internal nerve endings of the soul. They help us know when something may be off. I am not suggesting we discount our feelings as though they don't matter. Sometimes, entering into our feelings is of great importance. The best counselors (the ones I've worked with, at least) who help people sift through life's problems are masters at this. They don't try to get you *out* of what you are feeling. They ask you to sit *in* the feelings. Play in the dirt of your feelings. Just be there. But—and I think there is a balance here—a Christian has to learn the lesson of simultaneously being aware of his or her feelings but not worshiping or bowing before them.

While feelings are a gift from God, I am concered that we give way too much credence to something Jesus didn't really seem to discuss or even care all that much about. The "feelings" and "emotions" of the disciples are not mentioned once. Jesus had very little, if any, teaching on how people were feeling about his ministry. Feelings are not a central concern of the Bible. In fact, I would go so far as to say that at times our emotions and feelings about reality actually undermine our sense of identity before God. Do you know why that is? Because human feelings are not the main moderator of truth. We can feel one thing, and reality can be something completely different. "The Spirit gives life," Jesus said, "the flesh counts for *nothing*" (John 6:63, emphasis added). Feelings (while being gifts from God) can lie to us. And they often do.

Feelings can actually lead us astray when we bow to them. Joseph Campbell, the famed anthropologist who wrote *Hero with a Thousand Faces*, rejected the narrative of Jesus as the Son of God and Savior of the world. Belief in that way had no meaning for Campbell. At one point, Campbell said that he had no need for doctrine because he had experience.[1] When we live by experience alone, then we have no need to think of, consider, or worship Jesus. The Christian narrative says life is not made up merely of experience and emotions; rather, it is experience mixed with doctrine that makes it all worth living.

We wander about life thinking and believing that our feelings are reality. They aren't reality. Are they important? Yes. Can they help us come to reality? Yes. But are our feelings always right? No. Our feelings can betray us.

I'm a wreck at parties. I become inflexible, like the tin man after a rainstorm. I just never know what to do. Sometimes I can't move. The problem is I never know what to do with my hands. When I put my hands behind me, I feel like I'm scaring people, as though I'm hiding something behind my back. Then again, when I cross my arms, it seems like I'm defensive. And then there is the hand-in-the-pocket thing. That's proven to be the best. (What doesn't work is when I take my hands out and there is lint or candy wrappers stuck to them.)

Quinn tells me it is because I don't know what to do in a social situation where I don't have an assigned role. She says it's because I don't have a job to be doing. I think this is true. I do great at church because I know what my job is. I do great at home because I know I'm supposed to be a father and a husband. I do great at a pastoral care meeting because I know my role. But when I don't know what to *do*, then I don't know how to *be*.

A Pharisee is basically someone who has to be doing something. A Pharisee can't just *be*; they have to *do*. A Pharisee is one who doesn't know what to do with his or her hands when there is no job to do. That is, in the end, the root of *all* legalism and human religion. And most of all, it is the root of what is wrong with most of us. Legalism means one can't exist without an assigned role, a task, a job. Legalism involves having to do something with your hands at all moments in order to be valuable. It is having to be doing something to feel like you are something.

Paul said that the Christian should be drunk on the Spirit but not wine (Eph. 5:18). It's funny how sometimes at parties people—especially the introverts—don't normally dance until they've had something to drink. I don't drink anymore. But I've seen that people who normally don't dance do like to dance when they've had a few drinks in their system. The benefit of drunkenness (the sin of drunkenness) is that when you are drunk, you lose all inhibitions. And one of those inhibitions is paying attention to yourself. You stop living with self-consideration. You stop being all about you.

Drunk people, above all, are exceptional risk takers.

Drunk people stop looking at themselves and thinking about themselves and focusing on what others are thinking about them. I think living our lives in the power of the Holy Spirit involves becoming people who don't spend all of our time thinking about ourselves. In short, the Holy Spirit helps us dance. When Paul wrote, "Do not get drunk on wine, which leads to debauchery. Instead, be filled with the Spirit" (Eph. 5:18), I wonder if he said that as someone who had been to a couple parties. He'd seen what happens when people have a few. They stop thinking about themselves. People today say they are trying to find themselves. Everyone is. We all seem to have lost ourselves. Christianity has *nothing* to do with finding yourself. In fact, it is entirely about losing yourself. Jesus said that it is entirely possible to find yourself and lose him. That is the scariest idea, isn't it?

A Pharisee can't be someone unless they are doing something.

A Christian can be someone even when they are doing nothing.

—∿—

Can God be felt?

My immediate response is yes. There are countless episodes in the Bible where someone experiences an emotional response in their encounter with God. These can and do happen. But *must* God be felt in order for God to be true? I don't believe so.

This question, I think, raises quite a few problems for the life of the Christian. If God can be felt—and I believe that God can—what is the feeling of God like? When we equate God's presence with a certain feeling, then we will most likely believe that is the sign of God being near. For instance, if God feels like joy, then I can know that God is near as long as I am joyful. While I do believe that God can bring about great joy, I have overwhelming discomfort with the idea that God can only be felt when we are joyful. Or excited. Or sad. Or lamenting. Because when those particular feelings end, the assumption is that God's presence has ceased. If God is felt through joy, the minute we experience pain or sadness, God must be dead. And in that case, we become like my friend Stu, who stopped believing in God the minute the feelings of God ended.

Because we have had real, tangible experiences with God in the past, we spend so much time, energy, and emotion doing whatever we can to get back to those experiences. We are so focused on past experiences that we can't enter into today with grace and love. God was so close when we first became Christians, but now things are just, well, different. God feels a little further away. Or perhaps we used to belong to a church that really was being the church. And now we have to settle for something else. Our faith becomes nostalgic. We live in the past. Everything we are doing is not nearly as good as what it used to be.

Can God be felt? Certainly. But I'm not sure that we *want* to experience God the way the people in the Bible did. We should not forget that in the Bible God is invisible. John says, "No one has ever seen God, but the one and only Son . . . has made him known" (John 1:18). The same writer goes on to say that "God is Spirit, and his worshipers must worship in the Spirit and in truth" (John 4:24). God's invisibility is going to raise a ruckus among two groups of people. First, it will cause problems with those who have a hard time believing in anything that can't be tested, tried, and evaluated with scientific precision. Those who can't test something before believing it will struggle with God. Alas, God can't fit into a test tube. But more commonly, the people who will struggle with God's invisibility in the Bible are going to be God's own people. There are countless times in the Old Testament when the Jews rail against God because he does not show up or reveal himself the way that the gods of other religions do. God's people wish he were more *visible*.

And so God is invisible. But God still shows up. He reveals himself in physical ways. For instance, on one particular occasion, Moses was walking through the desert when he stumbled upon a burning bush that talked to him. It turns out the bush was not only talking to him but that God was in the bush. The experience was of such great importance that God revealed his own name to Moses—the first time in the Bible. The God in the bush was *Ehyeh-asher-ehyeh*—"I AM WHO I AM" (Exod. 3:14). I heard a Jewish rabbi once say that Moses wasn't all that special. He said that there is an ancient teaching that lots of other people had walked by the bush but did not have the gumption to lower themselves to talk to a bush. Moses, he concluded, was unique in that he was willing to stop, take off his shoes, and talk to God in a bush. Consider also that moment three visitors came to Abraham in Genesis 18—many have argued that he was visited by the divine Trinity. Or consider that moment when God comes to Elijah in the wind. We could go on and on. The point is that God comes down to people where they are, on their level, and reveals himself in ways they can handle.

171

All of these revelations are of the invisible becoming visible. Theologians call these physical manifestations *theophanies*—physical revelations of an invisible God. And while God does at many points in the Bible appear in a theophany, there is an explicit point made over and over again: "You cannot see my face and live." God will show part of himself but not his face. One of my favorite old-time preachers, Dr. Martyn Lloyd-Jones, argued that God will show us his glory, but God will not show us his face. Moses later learns this. In Exodus 33, he goes into the "tent of meeting" to talk to God. The text even says that he spoke to God "as one speaks to a friend" (v. 11). Then, in the same episode, Moses asks God if he can see him in his fullness. God says no. Instead, he says, "You cannot see my face, for no one may see me and live" (v. 20).

The Bible is after something: we *cannot* see God's face. And the reason is simple. You see, Jack Nicholson was right in *A Few Good Men*: you can't handle the truth. At all. We can't see God's face because if we did, we would die.

This gives the picture of heaven much more depth. John, the same one who talked about God's invisibility, says that we *will* see God's face in the future. For it is there, in glory, that we will "see him as he is" (1 John 3:2).

This brings me back to Stu. We all want to feel God. We want to *see* his face for what it is. But there is a kind of hiddenness to God. He can't show us everything because if he did, we couldn't handle it. We can feel God and still in the end betray him.

The only mother in the world who could worship her child and not be committing idolatry is Mary. Her story as a mother has continued to fascinate me. A few years ago, I wrote a book about my ongoing fascination with the idea that the Bible opts to portray our heroes—David, Mary, Peter—in such an honest, forthcoming light. The Bible doesn't Photoshop out our heroes' imperfections. Rather, it gives them to us blow by blow. One such story of honesty that has long captured my attention is that of Jesus's childhood, a story unlike any other. In Luke, the only story about Jesus's childhood is told from the time around his fourteenth birthday. At that point, his parents—Joseph and Mary—take him to the temple in Jerusalem to be dedicated to God. Leaving their small town of Nazareth, they head to the big city to give their child to God.

After their time in Jerusalem, the family begins to head home. Some of the finer points are murky, but the biblical text tells us that on the journey home, Jesus is lost. He is gone. Mary and Joseph likely think they are horrible parents. *How could we do this? What were we thinking?*

We all are susceptible to doing this. Mary and Joseph's response to having done this has always stuck with me. Luke tells us they do three things. First, they look for Jesus among their relatives (Luke 2:44). And if any parent lost a child, this would be the first thing they would do. What is the significance of their action? It is precisely what we often need to do when we sense that we have lost Jesus—look for Jesus among the people who know what he looks like. In a first-century world without smartphones and photography, the only people who would have known what Jesus looked like were those who knew him before he was lost. Mary and Joseph's action is of great importance for us today as wanderers, for often we find ourselves having gone down this or that road without Jesus, or at least without sensing his presence. This is why we need church. This is why we need community. This is why we need others around us who know Jesus. Because when Jesus has been lost, we will have given ourselves a community of people who know precisely what Jesus looks like and how we might find him.

When they didn't find Jesus among the relatives, Luke tells us they "went back to Jerusalem to look for him" (Luke 2:45). This action, like the first, is of great help to those who sense they have lost Jesus. Sometimes, when we sense a loss in our spiritual lives, the best thing we can do is to return to the last place we saw him. Was it in the reading of Scripture? Was it in prayer? Was it in serving the poor? Was it in singing to him?

Finally, but certainly not of least importance, they looked for him for three days (Luke 2:46). Three days. That is a long time to look for your child who is lost in a distant, foreign city. This speaks, I believe, to the great perseverance and long-suffering of Jesus's parents to locate him. They didn't stop looking until they found him after three days.

Jesus was eventually found.

And Jesus can still be found. It was three days after Jesus was left in the temple that he would be found by his parents, who returned to find him. It was three days after Jesus was left in the grave that he would be found by his disciples, who returned to find him. And he is still able to be found. Inverted Christianity, as I've heard it described by Mark Batterson, is when we ask Jesus to follow us, when we invite him to come along with us for the ride.[2] That is *backward* Christianity. We are invited on the wild chase of following Jesus. We are all like Mary in a way. I am. Stu is. We can have Jesus in our midst. But just because we have him with us does not make him our possession. Faith isn't a one-time deal. It is seeking, asking, and knocking every day. Jesus is still found by those who endlessly seek. If I were sitting with Stu now, I would tell him that even Mary and Joseph lost Jesus. Even *they*, the parents of the Son of God, knew what it was like to feel out of touch with their child. When we feel as though Jesus is gone, our response is critical. Will we take that feeling of loss as a reason to search him out, or use it as proof that we have been fooled by faith?

PERCEIVED FAMINE

Open your mouth and eat what I give you.

Ezekiel 2:8

It isn't without rationale that the medieval poet Dante described being middle-aged as "a dark wood."[1] Dante, like many others who went before him or followed behind, uses less than flattering language to describe one's middle age, a time that can consist of great crisis and personal anguish. Generally speaking, middle age is much older today than it used to be. Because of medicine, ample food, and hygiene, we live longer lives now. But long ago, in the times of Dante, making it to thirty was a big deal. Thirty, in the ancient world, was basically late middle age.

But worse things can happen during one's middle age than growing disgruntled with work, being underwhelmed by one's love life, or growing burdened with some lust to buy a completely unnecessary red Corvette with leather interior. Ours are often crises of occupation and place, and little more. Jesus's midlife crisis was the *crucis*, the cross. Around his thirty-third year of life, Jesus would carry the very "dark wood" of a Roman cross for the sins of the world. The cross was the end of a very busy three-year period. Just three years before his gruesome death on the cross, Jesus was baptized at the age of thirty in the river Jordan by the prophet John the Baptist. It was then, we're told, that Jesus entered his public ministry. Clearly, that water baptism marks a critical moment in Christ's earthly life and identity. Given the fact that the Gospels speak almost nothing of his life before baptism (minus a few excerpts concerning his infancy, childhood, and early adolescence), the sheer space given to his post-baptism life makes clear that everything changes the moment Jesus comes up out of the waters of the Jordan.

Without question, the overarching story of his earthly life takes a dramatic turn following the baptismal event. We observed that immediately following the descent of the Holy Spirit upon him in his water baptism, Jesus is "led by the Spirit" (Matt. 4:1) into the dusty desert just outside Jerusalem. There in the scary, unpredictable, wilderness place, Jesus is tempted by the devil after not having eaten for forty days. The cumulative result of the story is that Jesus comes out unharmed and unscathed, but tempted nonetheless. It reveals the self-control and security of Christ in times of spiritual battle. After overcoming the temptations of the devil, the text says that he was "with the wild animals, and angels attended him" (Mark 1:13). Consider, if you will, the unparalleled self-control of Jesus in the desert. Jesus was comforted by the wild animals.

Most of us, in the same situation, would almost certainly have eaten them.

—⁓—

Jesus was tempted while he had an empty stomach. Generally, people make funny decisions when they're hungry. I read a story in the newspaper a few years back about a study on parole board judges.

The research tracked eight judges in over 1,100 parole-board hearings over ten months. What they discovered was mind-boggling: a prisoner had a better chance of being granted parole depending on the time of day he or she sat before the judge. In the end, a prisoner's odds of receiving parole from the judge spiked after lunchtime. At that time, the study said, 65 percent of the prisoners were granted a parole. Before lunch, however, the chances of getting a favorable parole hearing plummeted. Prisoners' chances of parole leapt up to 65 percent at one other time: right after the judge's mid-morning snack.[2]

People change after they've eaten.

And this is important for married people. I don't have much better advice for married people than this: eat regularly. Married people know this well. There are four rules to getting into the most petty, silly fight about things that don't matter at all. Do these four things, and you are promised a fight about something meaningless:

1. Be driving.
2. Be hungry.
3. Be late to something.
4. Be tired.

I've often said, and I still believe, the secret to a good marriage mostly has to do with blood sugar. Divorce rates would plummet if we ate three to five healthy meals a day.

—*m*—

For Satan, timing is everything.

Notice, for a moment, *when* the devil tempts Jesus, because it was anything but accidental. The devil tempts Jesus when he's tired, lonely, and very hungry in the desert. It's as if the devil knows this would be the best time to get under Jesus's skin. As an old theology colleague used to say to me, the devil is, above all, a brilliant anthropologist. Satan knows human nature well, and he knows when to come to us with his alluring offers of power and glory.

The devil comes to us in nearly the same way as he did with Jesus. He comes to us at that moment that we are most hungry, most lonely, most tired. Perhaps one of the most helpful books on the temptation narrative is Henri Nouwen's *In the Name of Jesus*.[3] Nouwen says that the three temptations Jesus faced were about very specific things. Jesus, like us, will be tempted by relevance (being somebody), by being spectacular, and by being powerful in the world's eyes. All of these temptations are more apt to come to us when we are tired, hungry, and alone.

Of course, the kingdom Jesus brought about was anything but the kind of kingdom people were looking for. Jesus didn't use armies—he used disciples and truth and the allure of heavenly grace. He didn't utilize force—he used love. Shusaku Endo theorized that Jesus was actually being tempted *through* an Essene who would have lived near the desert just outside the river Jordan in a place known today as Qumran. He also suggests that the Essene came to Jesus trying to tempt him to abandon his plan to establish his kingdom in the way of God and instead do so in the way of the Essenes, through military and force.[4] In essence, Endo's theory is that temptation comes *through* someone or something. It doesn't just pop up out of nowhere. Few of us can claim to have gone out to the wilderness to have it out with the devil. Few of us, hopefully, talk to the devil. But temptation does come through *something*.

And so Jesus didn't turn rocks into bread. Could he have? Yes. Given that he turned water into wine, it doesn't seem to me he would have had a hard time pulling off a rocks-into-bread miracle. But in refusing to turn stones into bread, Jesus was refusing to go about his work in the way of the power structures of his time. Jesus did it differently. It should be noted that God never once told Jesus that he was not to turn rocks into bread. Nor is there any biblical injunction against that rare moment when we might actually turn rocks into bread. It's not like it would have broken any rules had Jesus actually done so. It's that the way and the means of how his kingdom was conducted were as important as the fact that it was being established. In that moment, turning rocks into bread represented the temptation of power and control in the way that was not fitting of Jesus's ministry. And Jesus refused to do it that way. Jesus always did victory a different way.

—ᴍᴡ—

The fact that Jesus was "sent" into the desert suggests a powerful message from the life of Jesus—namely, that being in the desert is not the same as being deserted. Jesus was in the desert, but he was not deserted. As with Jesus, the desert is exactly where God wants us to be from time to time. The difference between Jesus and us is that Jesus has the power and will to withstand the ways of the devil. This story of Christ in the desert can be so misread. We do a great disservice to this story to imagine that it is a series of "how to" tips on dealing with the devil. In the end, this story has nothing to do with how we might withstand the devil. Rather, it is about how only Christ himself can withstand the devil. Set in its context, what Jesus did was deeply moving because he undid the same story of Israel when they were in the desert. Just like Israel, following *their* baptism in the Red Sea, Jesus ventured into the desert after being baptized in the river Jordan. Just as Israel did for forty years, Jesus went into the desert for forty days. And just like Israel who had the cloud and fire, Jesus went by the leading of the Spirit. But unlike Israel, Jesus worshiped his Father alone. There are no golden cows in the story of Jesus going into the desert.

The stories of Israel in the desert and Jesus in the desert become even more illuminated when we contrast Jesus in the desert and Adam and Eve in the garden of Eden. In essence, Jesus in the desert *reverses* the whole garden of Eden story. In creation's paradise, Adam and Eve had everything they needed—food, friendship, drink, relationship, and peace. They were all set; the environment was perfect. Yet in that idyllic state, they still managed to fall into temptation and sin. Adam had a wife. Jesus was single. Adam had food. Jesus's stomach rumbled. Adam had shade in the garden. Jesus was in the blazing heat. Yet despite the drastic environmental differences, Jesus had the ability to reverse the destructive narrative of the garden of Eden, which is why we call him the second Adam—he undid what the first one did.

And so this story is anything but a story about how *we* can face our temptations with valor and glory. This story is actually about how we *can't* and how we *haven't* faced our temptations with faithfulness. It is a story about the only one who could face them. The key to the desert temptations is not having a stronger spirit or soul—it is to recognize that we simply cannot defeat temptation by any strength we might be able to muster.

—⁓—

In the desert, Jesus said we can't live on bread alone. We need God. His point was that we could have full stomachs and empty hearts.

But we've certainly done our best to be sustained by food alone. A good deal of research has been undertaken on the famous da Vinci painting of the Last Supper. Some have looked at the food on the table, scrutinizing it to discover what the food represents. Along with the many studies, there have been a great many replicas of the famous piece. People through history have sought to rework, reinterpret, and reproduce the painting. It is one of the most copied paintings in human history. It is often pointed out that one thing is certain: as there have been more and more replicas of the painting, something has changed on the table. The further we go on in history, more and more food is on the table. The latest replicas have way more food than the original done centuries earlier.[5]

It is human nature, I suppose, to always want more than we have. And we have tricked ourselves into thinking that the key to our own happiness is more and more food. But we don't live on bread alone. We also live by the words of God. If our physical needs are met but not our spiritual needs, then we are not truly human. We were created to live on both.

—⁓—

When Israel was in the desert wandering their way to the promised land, God gave them a kind of food called *manna*. The best description we have of it is a kind of Wheat Thin covered in coriander seed.

180

But even that is hard to be sure of. The word *manna*, this bread-like substance, literally means "What is it?" You always know that a food is interesting when it is named a sentence. In short, manna is like the I Can't Believe It's Not Butter of the Old Testament.

The food was intended by God to sustain the hungry people on their journey. It is interesting to consider the image this role of God would have had on the people. The role of being a maker of bread was, in the ancient world, that of a tender, motherly figure. As the provider of manna, God would have been imagined by the people in the desert as a caring mother.[6] As their caring mother, God instituted some rather clear guidelines surrounding the collection and ingestion of the "What is it?" We find these laid out in Exodus 16. For instance, we learn that God would provide the bread in the morning for the people to collect for the day's needs. Also, there were stipulations regarding how much bread was to be collected: if one was collecting for a big clan, they were to take more bread. If they were collecting for a small clan, they were to take less. The size of the need was to be reflected by the size of the collection. People were to collect only enough for their needs, not their wants. And finally, they were to put some of the bread into a jar that they would carry around with them everywhere they went. This was to be a reminder of the provision of God in future days.

I have heard this social arrangement called a "manna society."[7] In such a society, all of the needs of the people could be met, nobody would go hungry, and all would be provided for.

The only problem was that they were on the road. And being on the road, they became selfish and greedy.

One of the things that most tempts people in the Bible is food. Over and over again. And that is no different in this story. One of the problems of being on the road is that our instincts often take over. It's really hard to eat well when you are on the road. A health coach told me that my body was storing up food in case I didn't find a restaurant soon. Whenever I do travel, I find that, first, the options are horrible, and second, my tastes lean toward all the not-so-good foods. There is a physical dimension to this. When you are on the road, you subconsciously eat not knowing if you will have food tomorrow. I call it a *perceived famine*; you know in the back of your head that you need to be storing up food for tomorrow. A perceived famine can easily lead to practical greed because you start taking more than you need. Whenever we *think* there isn't enough to go around, we tend to hoard, collect, and save way more than we would ever need. This is sad. Others go without because we think so shallowly.

God is teaching his people to be on the road with him and still trust that tomorrow he will have traveled with them to the new spot they find themselves in. God cares so much about this idea of the manna society that one chapter later—at the end of Exodus 16—God's people disobey his boundaries and stipulations surrounding the manna. Early one morning as the people go out, some of them take way too much food, leaving some to go without. As promised, the food goes bad, rotting by the next morning.

The lesson of the manna society is that God *always* provides enough for everyone. That isn't the problem. The problem is that those who are being provided for are selfish hoarders keeping manna from others who need it.

—◊—

A bumper sticker in my neighborhood reads, "God is all powerful. God is good. There is evil in the world. Pick two."

One of the most widely used arguments against the existence of God (or, at least, a *good* God) is summed up in a question: if God were truly all-powerful and all-benevolent, why would he allow so many people to die of hunger and thirst? This question has rightly disturbed people who think through their faith. A number of years ago, a man by the name of Charles Templeton had a radical conversion to Christianity. At the time of his experience, Templeton was one of Canada's most famed illustrators and cartoonists, widely respected in the general culture. Soon after his conversion to Christianity, he began to work as an evangelist with the famed Billy Graham, traveling the world to tell the story of Jesus and how it had transformed his life. There is a story about him that goes like this. One day Templeton was reading *Time* magazine. On the cover was a picture of an African mother and her child both starving due to lack of food and water. Templeton couldn't escape that picture. He pondered it. He was disturbed. *How could a sovereign God let people die of thirst or hunger?* Templeton wondered.

The question didn't go away. In fact, it went deeper and deeper. Years later, Templeton would reject Christianity and become an agnostic. In the end, he simply couldn't resolve the question. Of course, this is a troubling thought. How *could* God allow hunger and thirst to happen?

For me, this theological and practical conundrum is resolved by looking at the manna society in the Old Testament. It is there that we find a clue to our question. When we look at the story of the manna and how God provided enough for everyone every day, the issue isn't that God doesn't provide enough for people, including the woman and child on the cover of *Time* magazine. The issue becomes our selfishness: there are selfish people around them who are not letting them receive the food and water that God is sending. The problem isn't God's ability to provide; it's our sinful tendency to hoard and keep from others who need it. We oppress one another by stealing from one another. God is a good provider. And God always provides enough for everyone to be sustained. It just so happens that there are always going to be hoarders who take more than their allotted amount and in so doing steal from others.

Dorothy Day, the famed founder of the Catholic Workers Union, once said that if we have two coats, we have stolen one from the poor. That illustrates the manna-society idea quite clearly. Christ invites us to live in a manna society where we have to learn to share with one another. And it turns out that when God's economy is respected, there are always leftovers (as the stories of all the multiplied loaves reveals). I know someone will wonder: Does this lead us to believe that everyone's task is to give away everything they have? And the truth is, I can't answer that for you. In fact, the easy way out is to say no. Jesus *did* say to one person, the rich young ruler, that he was to give away all of his possessions and come and follow him (Matt. 19:16–22). But he allowed others to have possessions. We must remember that some of Jesus's disciples had houses, possessions, and even boats. What was key was that when Jesus asked his disciples for their possessions, they lived open-handedly.

Greed is never a good thing. At the end of his book *The Abolition of Man*, C. S. Lewis speaks of what he calls the *Tao*. Lewis, of course, spoke early on of having investigated God before becoming a Christian. Before his conversion, he spent years studying all the religions of the world. What he found was that while religions didn't agree, they all talked about God. This disturbed him. He was famous for saying that if there was no water, then why are we all so thirsty? In his study of the religions, Lewis discovered something. He said the idea of the *Tao* was that if you took all the religions of the world and compared them, they would all basically say the same thing. Certainly, Lewis saw in Christianity something unique. But at the end of the book, he takes all the major teachings of all the major religions and compares them. They largely agree that murder is bad, stealing isn't good, and honoring parents is positive.

When we compare all the religions of the world, we find that *not one of them* argues that greed is good.

Eating was one of the first commandments in the Bible, alongside having sex. It should not surprise us that eating and sex are often the first things that are attacked by the enemy when we are in the desert. We overeat. And by doing so, people are going hungry.

Malnutrition and starvation are rooted in overnutrition and overeating.

Which brings up an important point for our discussion. Every good, every blessing, every gift from God has the tremendous capability to be used in malicious ways. The more sacred something is, the more powerfully it can be used by evil. For instance, look at sex in the Bible. Sex, the act of human intercourse, is used in two different ways. First, in the Song of Solomon, a long, nearly fourteen-chapter love scene is played out in graphic detail between two lovers on their honeymoon night.

The thing is unbelievably graphic. There is a reason that the Jewish people wouldn't let young boys read the text until they were older and married. But the Bible doesn't include this erotic imagery for just any reason. The rabbis would tell us that, undeniably, the erotic interlude is a graphic image of the love of God for his people Israel. Thus, sex has the beautiful capability to be a picture of God's love. But second, as James will tell us, the image of sex is an image of human sinfulness.

—⁂—

Years ago, there was one particular month that was very difficult financially. Quinn and I had given extra money away to a ministry that we particularly believed in. I think that in writing that check, I was hoping that what seems to happen to everyone else would have happened to me. You seem to hear, when you are in the church long enough, story after story of someone being generous and giving and, at the end of the month when they are just about to bounce all their checks and not be able to pay their mortgage, they get a check *for the exact* amount they needed that month. It's always the same. An anonymous check shows up and is just the right amount. I think that when we wrote that check, I secretly was banking on that happening.

And does it happen? Absolutely, it happens. The God of providence does stuff like that. God works wonders, I have seen it.

It just didn't happen this time.

No check came. No cash came. Nothing. We lost money that month. It was tough.

Sometimes you give and you just don't get back. That is the hard fact of gospel living. Sometimes you give and give and give and no check comes in the mail. It would be easy to think in those times that God lets us down. But I look back on that month and remember that while we may have not done well financially, we learned an even more important lesson: we have friends, and family, and brothers and sisters in Jesus who love us dearly. I lost money but gained friends. And sometimes God's kingdom may work like that. Often we lose where we thought we would win but win an even more precious prize.

THE QUIET OF THE WALK

I have discovered that all the unhappiness of men arises from one single
fact, that they are unable to stay quietly in their own room.

Blaise Pascal

One of my favorite nuns (if I'm permitted to have a favorite nun) in the
history of the church is a woman by the name of Hildegard of Bingen
(1098–1179). Hildegard is known to history by the name "the green
nun." This moniker derives, most assuredly, from her years of living
in the bogs, forests, and fields of Germany. Hildegard loved being
outside. She is kind of the church's first ecofeminist for Jesus. Unlike
other contemporary mystics of her time, Hildegard preferred the forest to the hard, disciplined, often grueling life of the monastery. Her
story stands out above the rest. Hildegard was one of ten children in
a Christian family devoted to the church. One year, her parents, who
were known as generous givers, were unable to give financially to

the church. So, in place of giving money to the church, they offered Hildegard (their daughter!) *as a tithe* out of their utter poverty before God. Hildegard was an act of piety and sacrifice by two parents who couldn't afford to give money. Hildegard was a tithe. And her life would be devoted to the ways of Jesus.

Hildegard had an unforgettable mark on the history of Christianity. Even the pope was overwhelmed by her story and message. Pope Eugene III was so impressed that he'd eventually make every one of her visions and writings official church teaching; quite the feat for a church enmeshed in a rather patriarchal time. Writings that come to us from the life of Hildegard are breathtaking. From being one of Christianity's first playwrights to writing music and even preaching, Hildegard had a spirit marked by creativity, holiness, and a unique style of humor. Her best-known work is called the *Scivias*. Consisting of some twenty-six visions, it spans nearly ten years of Hildegard's life.

Hildegard's experience of Jesus bleeds through her writings. But it was an experience that many other people did not know how to deal with. I recently came across these words in her *Scivias*:

> Heaven was opened and a fiery light of exceeding brilliance came and permeated my whole brain, and inflamed my whole heart and my whole breast, not like a burning but like a warming flame, as the sun warms anything its rays touch. And immediately I knew the meaning of the exposition of the Scriptures. . . . But I had sensed in myself wonderfully the power and mystery of secret and admirable visions from my childhood—that is, from the age of 5—up to that time, as I do now. This, however, I showed to no one except a few religious persons who were living in the same manner as I; but meanwhile, until the time when God by His grace wished it to be manifested, *I concealed it in quiet silence.*[1]

An attentive reader of the *Scivias* will find an interesting detail in the text. Hildegard, the mystic, poet, and revolutionary, received her first vision from Jesus at five years old. That's right. Five. One of the remarkable observations from the life of the mystics is how many of them claimed to have seen Jesus at a young age. Some, like Hildegard, had this experience before they were ten years old. Few if any of the mystics felt as though they had permission to tell people about it.

Hildegard's words echo down through the history of the church to our own hearts: "I concealed it *in quiet silence.*"

Of course, she kept her vision in "quiet silence" because she lived in an age when people would respond to such experiences by cutting them off from the church community. Today, we would give them an antipsychotic. This trips me up. Our culture and our churches have no outlet for children to proclaim God's words to us. Why can't God speak to children? Why should we stop them from listening?

In all seriousness, how would you respond to a child, either yours or a friend's, who claimed to have received a vision from God? And why do you think that *couldn't* be a possibility? We often isolate ourselves from children and their visions because, I would argue, we think that their visions and perspectives are inferior to our adult ways of thinking about God, particularly, I might add, in how we do church. We have systemically cut children off from worship. It is a general practice in churches to separate the ages. You put the adults in the big sanctuary, the middle and high school kids in a gym, and the children in the children's ministry down in the basement. Now, in a way that doesn't surprise me. I understand why we do this. I think it is partly a need for a break. But there is a cost to this. When you remove children, particularly the littlest and most inquisitive ones, you remove the best questions from a community's life of faith.

It continues to shock me how much grief I get from other Christians that children in our church can come forward and take communion. Children can believe in Jesus, can they not? They *do* believe in Jesus— the way a child would believe in Jesus. Jesus instructed us very clearly: "Let the little children come to me" (Matt. 19:14).

A child's gift to the church is his or her curiosity about Jesus. Curiosity isn't a fruit of the Spirit, to be sure, but if I had the power, I kind of wish it were added as an amendment or something. Curiosity, the kind that children embody, is so integral to a healthy Christian life. People don't like curiosity because, as with Curious George, it always creates trouble. Curiosity disrupts. Curiosity prevents us from doing something just because we always have. Curiosity asks questions. But without that disruption, there is no solution. Without curiosity, you don't have problems. But you also never move forward into maturity. Adults shed their curiosity over the years, sort of like their hair. Remove the kids and you remove the curious questions about God. Our children's pastor tells me that kids ask the most challenging questions about God; more challenging than the ones adults ask.

But they are the most beautiful.

May they never sit there in *quiet silence*. The best stuff comes out of the mouths of babes.

—ᴍ—

A gentile mother—unnamed as gentile mothers in the Bible often are—approaches both Jesus and his disciple groupies in the gentile district of Tyre and Sidon. Her trek has been about one thing: she hopes that he might heal her daughter, whom she believes is "demon-possessed" (Matt. 15:22). I empathize with this unknown, gentile, road-weary mother. All parents harbor—at least *all* parents in our household—hold similar sentiments about their children. Her issues must have been different, however, from the general parental headaches one incurs from time to time. Quite clearly this woman understands her situation to be unique; this isn't a troubled child, this is a *possessed* child. And she lacks the motherly power to overcome her child's problem.

Jesus's response (or lack thereof) remains as troubling today as it most likely was in its original setting:

> Jesus did not answer a word. So his disciples came to him and urged him, "Send her away, for she keeps crying out after us."
> He answered, "I was sent only to the lost sheep of Israel."
> The woman came and knelt before him. "Lord, help me!" she said.
> He replied, "It is not right to take the children's bread and toss it to the dogs."

189

"Yes it is, Lord," she said. "Even the dogs eat the crumbs that fall from their master's table."

Then Jesus said to her, "Woman, you have great faith! Your request is granted." And her daughter was healed at that moment. (Matt. 15:23–28)

One commentator has appropriately, I believe, rendered this story a "troubling embarrassment" for Jesus and the church.[2] For here we witness Jesus engaging in a few actions that seem at the onset quite uncharacteristic for an all-loving, gracious Savior who would die "for the world." To mention a few, take note of the social faux pas riddled through this brief dialogue: Jesus responds to a lowly woman in great need with a kind of ambivalence, evidenced by an immediate silence. Jesus also exhibits a kind of nationalistic pride and exclusivity in telling her that he only came to help his own people. And Jesus calls the woman a female dog.

To boot, Jesus's disciples are equally unhelpful, by requesting she be sent away. At first look, here we appear to have a racist, closed-minded, nationalistic Jesus and his thoughtless men quickly coming behind. If it feels uncomfortable to you to have Jesus, the Son of God, calling people female dogs in public and coming across as racist and indifferent, then you're like the rest of us. This is a troubling story to any reader. For such reasons Christians in the contemporary world typically like to sidestep this story.

But we needn't be afraid of this story—it has a gem of a lesson. For the church, it was such an important story that not only would it be relayed, but so also would a parable that almost seems to be the same story. In the parable of the persistent widow, Jesus tells of a judge who keeps getting bothered by a widow who is asking for justice. The judge, tired of being bothered, gives her what she has asked for. Jesus compares God to the bothered judge (Luke 18:1–8).

To understand the story of the woman in its correct way, we must momentarily be willing to remove our own cultural glasses to read this text in its original light. In other words, we mustn't read this story as twenty-first-century Americans. Of course, the never-ending problem with reading the Bible is that all people inevitably read it as though the Bible were written for them in their own time. But the Bible wasn't originally written with twenty-first-century Americans in mind. The Bible was written for ancient Jews and Christians.

That does not mean that we are asked to stop being whoever we are when we read the sacred Scriptures. Nor can we escape importing into the Bible our own assumptions, beliefs, and cultural mores. But we must resist the urge to tell the Bible what we want it to say to us. In any reading of the Bible, we will always read it and bring into it our own at times unhealthy assumptions. My three-year-old boy illustrates for us the problem of reading the Bible in the twenty-first century as Americans. In the middle of dinner, he regularly grabs my glass of fresh, clean water. Often, he gets to it before I do. And as he drinks, I can see large chunks of food from his mouth intermix with my fresh, clean water. It's called backwash. For whoever reads the Bible, there will always be a kind of textual backwash, as it were, diluting the message that is intended. I call it hermeneutical backwash. I would go so far as to say the younger the reader, the more the backwash. As we read, our stuff will taint the purity of Scripture. Sometimes we can't tell what is Bible and what is us.

And so we must return to our text with fresh eyes. First, notice that Jesus is silent in his response to the woman's plea. The request seems simple enough. Jesus has healed plenty of people before. So it stops us in our tracks when we read the Gospel's account of his response: "Jesus did not answer a word." Jesus responds to a bold act of faith *with silence*. Of course, Jewish men, especially respected Jewish rabbis like Jesus, don't talk to women in public under the threat of grave punishment. So it would be normal for a man to respond in silence. And the woman's efforts are again rebuffed by the disciples, who don't like the fact that she has been yelling at them. The woman comes back again, this time kneeling and shouting all the more for the Lord to have mercy on her daughter.

Immediately we have a problem with this story because we are reading it as Americans. Westerners naturally interpret Christ's silence as indifference or apathy or a lack of an answer. We view silence as a nonresponse. We see it as though something were wrong. But if Jesus is seeking to teach both the woman and the disciples, I imagine that the silence has some learning value. Why didn't one of the disciples stand up and make a statement? Why didn't one of them say, "Hey, Jesus, it is good for you to be silent"? Here is why. Disciples are bent toward seeing their way as the special way. A disciple will often respond to God's silence as the same thing as God's rejection. "Send her away," they say.

Such a shallow perspective about the way God relates and speaks to us comes to a halt in the story of Jesus in the garden of Gethsemane. Jesus, about to die, tells his disciples to go and pray. Instead, they fall asleep. Alone, tired, afraid, and anxious, Jesus is in the garden praying. He asks the Father to remove the cup. That means he asks to not have to be crucified. That was his prayer.

If I were to ask an American if Jesus's prayer was answered, almost everyone would say that it wasn't. But Jesus's prayer *was* answered. It just so happens that it wasn't the way he wanted it to be answered.

This idea may be awkward for many Christians, for we rarely understand God in silence. But I am more and more committed to calling into question the idea that silence is some kind of nonanswer in our dialogue with God. God isn't a vending machine. God created sound *and* silence. And silence can be as much an answer as anything else. It often is the answer. Most of the time we consider our prayers answered only when we get what we want. That isn't prayer for Jesus. And thank God Jesus's prayer in the garden wasn't answered in the way Jesus wanted it to be. Jesus asked to have his cup of suffering removed. It wasn't removed. The world, as such, was saved through a prayer that wasn't answered as requested.

Second, Jesus calls the woman a "dog" and suggests that he was sent only to the lost sheep of Israel. In what appears to be blatant racism and indifference, Jesus initially responds in a troubling way. Jesus comes off as a racist.[3] Was he? Consider that Tyre and Sidon (where the story takes place) were essentially gentile lands. Jesus had entered the world of the gentiles. And, I might add, Jesus had taken his disciples to gentile spaces many times before, and he would many times after. I would ask, *If* Jesus were a racist, would he have ventured into this region with his disciples? *If* Jesus were a racist, would he have spoken to a gentile woman in public? *If* Jesus were a racist, would he have said she had great faith, far before he ever lends such accolades to his disciples?

No, he wouldn't.

Jesus wasn't a racist by any means. When we look at this story in light of the first century, Jesus is openly breaking through two major cultural boundaries. A man speaks to a woman in public, and a Jew speaks to a gentile in public. Here we see Jesus breaking all the rules. The ones who weren't breaking the rules were the disciples. They upheld both cultural boundaries: refusing to talk to a woman and a gentile. We can see their latent racism and bigotry dripping from the text.

Jesus exposes them. Frankly, the only way to expose sin is to do it to the extreme. Jesus is using satire here. Isn't it interesting that when Jesus does call the woman a dog and remains silent, his disciples don't speak up in defense of her? It is possible to hang out with the Lord of the earth and still not understand the scope of God's love. If Jesus were a racist, he would not have talked to her, helped her, and said she had such great faith.

The best person to read this story is a doctor. A good kind of backwash comes to us in the form of a Christian of the eleventh century named Ibn al-Tayyib. He was both a doctor and a theologian. When he comments on this story, he notes some things that a nondoctor might miss. First, al-Tayyib says that the woman does not say, "Have mercy on *my daughter.*" Rather, she says, "Have mercy on me."[4] Only a doctor like Luke, who is writing this story, would make seemingly unnecessary observations like this story. Then, Jesus responds not by saying that her daughter will be healed. Rather, he says, "Let it be as you desire." It is a physician who notices that it is the caregiver who has the greatest need. The healer needs healing first.

Commentators are quick to point out that when Jesus did this, he did so with a "double interaction." That is, Jesus wasn't seeking to help *just* the woman—he had other people in mind as well. He was also seeking to teach his disciples, who were sitting in the front row, watching what was going on.

The racism of the disciples is one of the reasons I am a Christian. What other religion would include this story in its sacred scripture? Every other tradition would want to get that stuff out of the text. The Bible outs the disciples, exposes them, calls them what they are: racist sinners. Ignoring a problem is never the Bible's answer to a problem. This story is so embarrassing for the church. As a Christian, Jesus is constantly exposing my racism and indifference. And as a Christ follower I am not invited to hide it. I am invited to deal with it, confess it, and overcome it.

We need others. Community is a house of accurate mirrors where we can really see our own sinfulness. Perhaps the hardest conversation I've ever had with my wife was when she called me a racist. She pointed out some of the ways in which I look at people that are not Christlike. I hated it. But I needed it.

We see our own prejudice when we see it lived out in others toward us. At the end of this story, the disciples are going to see Jesus celebrate the woman and not them. I wonder if it woke them up.

Jesus was seeking to teach his disciples about his worldwide mission. But he was also seeking to heal this woman's child. I think the most uncomfortable thing about this story is the perceived indifference that Jesus embodies. When she asks, Jesus is silent. Jesus tells her that he came for the house of Israel, the Jews, not her. It seems that he doesn't have time or energy to waste on such a person. But Jesus is anything but indifferent.

An interesting observation arises from a number of the healing stories. Jesus, on many occasions, puts up what I want to call a "wall" before eventually healing someone.

For instance, a man who couldn't walk for thirty-eight years begs Jesus to heal him. Jesus's response was, "Do you want to get well?" (John 5:6). Who would ask such a question? Clearly the man wants to be healed. But Jesus wants to hear it out of the horse's mouth. Jesus puts up a wall to be climbed. Outside of Jericho, he says something similar to a gentile widow who has a needy child. Jesus puts up a wall. Why does Jesus put up a wall to climb for such healings?

If I were a coach and had the chance to give my time and attention to the best downhill skier in the world, the worst thing I could do is have them practice on the little snow hill in my backyard. The best thing I could do for that person would be to take them to the toughest track in the world. Only hard things bring out the best of us.

A wall is Jesus's way of clarifying whether we really want something. Every writer will hit the wall. Every doctor will hit the wall. Every disciple will hit the wall.

The gift of God to us is silence. The silence speaks louder than words. Silence helps us press in.

Sometimes, our talking *at* God is our way of sidestepping the holiness of silence.

—〰—

There are a few walls one will have to overcome in our pursuit of Jesus.

There is the wall of offense. Jesus is offensive. He has basically called this woman a female dog. We are all aware of what this would equate to in our culture today. Jesus is offensive. And this raises an even bigger point that is found throughout the biblical narrative. Everyone—outsiders, religious people, kings, soldiers, even the disciples—will hear or see Jesus do something that is not politically correct, kind, or even all that helpful.

The Bible should offend *everyone* who reads it. If it doesn't offend you—if Jesus doesn't offend you here and there—then you aren't reading the Bible honestly. And the offensive thing here, of course, is that we have God calling a woman a dog. God is calling someone something that is powerfully uncomfortable.

The woman's response bears rereading. "Yes it is, Lord. . . . Even the dogs eat the crumbs that fall from their master's table." Look at that. She does two things. First, she acknowledges her "dogness," if I may.

And none of us should expect to be heard by God without accepting our "dogness." We are *all* dogs before Jesus. Ibn al-Tayyib wrote that the woman's humility is embodied in her willingness to "lower herself to the place of a dog."[5]

We should not for a moment assume that Jesus called someone a name only in this instance. In fact, Jesus called people names all the time. Peter himself was, at one point, called the voice of Satan.

If we are politically correct, we will never be able to fully enter into the brash but honest narrative of God. God doesn't care all that much for political etiquette. He stands for truth telling. And truth is offensive.

Jesus's response is probably the most troubling response in all of the written Gospels. He says, "It is not right to take the children's bread and toss it to the dogs." He is, of course, referencing his very laser-like mission. Jesus was sent to those of Israel who were lost. Jesus is God sent to his own people. And if I were an outsider, a Canaanite as this woman was, my response would have been to pack up my bags, count the loss, deal with the embarrassment, and just go home.

She refuses to give in to Jesus's no. She presses in. And if I were Jesus, I would have been rather annoyed. She is blessed for *not* taking Jesus at his first word. She doesn't relegate herself to his first word. She is persistent.

—⁓—

The lesson of persistence plays itself out in parables and in history in the life of Jesus. That makes it a very important lesson. And a difficult one indeed.

I was taught a long time ago to not just live in the Bible. Get out. Spend time with people. Walk the streets. Lay your hands on the sick. Go to hospitals. Walk and pray.

I take Fridays to pray. I should say, I try to take Fridays to pray. There is no event during the entire rhythm of the week that is more challenging to enter into than walking and praying on Fridays. It's rather anticlimactic. I will often walk up Division Street past the shops and the ice-cream parlors and the upscale grocery stores. There's a Catholic church I like to creep into. They leave the front doors unlocked. I like the Catholics for that—their doors are almost always open.

The building is simple but breathtaking.

As you walk up the aisle, you can catch a glimpse of a binder to the right side of the altar next to the candles. I like to light the candles, but I never have cash. I admit that it would look funky to put a credit card machine next to the candles, but it would at least give me a way to pay.

One time, I opened the prayer book.

I admit, reading other people's prayers is awkward at best, voyeuristic at worst. (Often, after everyone leaves church on Sunday and we are cleaning up, I will find that someone has left behind their journal. I am often tempted to read it to see what they got out of the message. I don't look. I fear what I would find.)

Filled from front to back with nameless requests—prayer for healing, for provision, for general help—the book meanders. As I read, something caught my eye. Every Thursday, at the same exact time, every week, was the same name and the same request. I looked to see how far back it reached. A good three years.

"Jesus, in mercy, I pray for a job."

"Jesus, in your love, I pray for a job."

"Father, I ask you for a job that I might work."

While there were minor variations, it was the same request every single week. Then it ended. One day a few months ago, it just stopped. I wonder if Jesus finally just got annoyed by the person praying for a job. I wonder if that was the lesson about persistence. I wonder if that is what prayer is all about.

Persistence in prayer is refusing to take the first word as the final word. It is pressing on against all odds.

Persistence is the discipline of annoying Jesus.

But Jesus, it turns out, isn't annoyed. It is telling that "ask," "seek," and "knock," Jesus's commands to his disciples (Matt. 7:7), are expressed in what is called *present imperative*. It is a command to continue doing it until it is fulfilled.

—∽—

It's believed that Blaise Pascal said that all of people's miseries derive from not being able to sit in a quiet room alone. Nobody wants to be a quiet listener. And nobody wants to be a listener because nobody ever got famous for being a good listener. Good listeners are recognized only at their funeral. And nobody ever becomes famous at their funeral.

Nobody wants to be a listener, and nobody ever expects to actually be listened to. We're almost shocked or alarmed when someone else listens to us. "Being heard is so close to being loved," once wrote David Augsburger, "that for the average person, they are almost indistinguishable."[6] When someone actually listens to us, we want to ask, "Hey, wait, you are actually paying attention to me?"

To be listened to is a daring act. We almost fear being listened to because in being listened to we enter into something real and substantive. Fear always causes us to run to those who don't really listen. These ruthless rebel fears ruin the garden and peace of my heart. Like gangrene, they spread like rot and death on my dreams, my desires, and my hopes. *You aren't a good enough writer.* My friend Dan told me that we never really get rid of our fears, we just learn to live with them. He said we have to learn to love and be hospitable toward our fears. Like a good Samaritan, we must make room for, care for, and learn to live alongside our greatest and darkest fears. Shivering on a plank over the abyss of the raging waves of my fears, I can always see the hope of God in the periphery. Looking at the waters makes it hard to see that hope. Our greatest fears cause us to run from being heard because then we are shown for who we really are.

Listening to others has a similar effect to foot washing in the first century. Listening is a kind of twenty-first-century foot washing. It involves placing ourselves squarely at the feet of someone's stinky story and hearing what they have to say.

All good listening has its starting place in learning to listen to God—something, I might add, most of us are horrible at. Prayer isn't primarily about rhetoric or oratory brilliance. It is about silence. About listening. W. H. Auden once said that to pray was to pay attention to someone or something other than oneself.[7]

Smack-dab at the beginning of Numbers 3, I recently found myself introduced to two characters of the Bible I knew nearly nothing about: Nadab and Abihu, the two priestly sons of Aaron. Perhaps you've never heard of them either. I'd be shocked to find that either character remains a household name in even the most pious of Jewish or Christian homes. With their subtle obscurity, they are given a brief introduction and a rather dreary conclusion. One verse is devoted to their demise: "Nadab and Abihu . . . died before the LORD when they made an offering with unauthorized fire before him in the Desert of Sinai" (Num. 3:4). They were priests who died before the Lord. Leviticus offers a little more explanation, but not much (Lev. 10:1–2). What became of both remains shrouded in a good deal of mystery. Of course, we could go into the normal historical, cultural, or even biblical contextual rigmarole to explain away *why* they died, but that would eventually let the reader off the hook. Such incidents happen quite often in the Bible. That is, God does rather mysterious things like letting people fall dead in service to him. There's Uzzah and Ananias and Sapphira, among others.

What surprises me, and even instructs me, as I think about the writings of the Bible from the perspective of a writer, is that the literary genius behind the whole book didn't pause, think, and add a footnote as to why Nadab and Abihu died.

No explanation.

No rationale.

No footnote.

And, it should be said, such ambiguity comes with much of the mystery of the Almighty. God's mystery isn't cleared up with explanatory citations all the time. Sometimes the stories just don't have explanations. Sometimes it just is what it is, end of story. For a moment, I want to give a little attention to that little emotional reaction one might have to such a "hard saying," as it is often called. Pay attention to your soul as you hear about such stories.

Do you want to *explain* the story away?

I certainly want to explain the story away. That lurking desire to explain mystery can lead to some comical explanations. For example, I read some time ago of a scientist named Immanuel Velikovsky who theorized that Nadab and Abihu had found some oil and put it in their censer. Unaware of what it was, they lit it on fire only to experience a massive explosion that was interpreted as fire from heaven.[8] And that brings up the difference between a mystery and a secret. Christianity is not a movement of secrets. It is a movement of mysteries. A secret is knowledge withheld from others. A mystery is knowledge imparted to others; it just so happens that the knowledge is beyond our finite minds to fully comprehend.

God is a mystery.

Resurrection isn't logical. Grace isn't rational. Love isn't reasonable. I cherish how much mystery I'm invited into every day.

And God's mystery has a terrible beauty.

People are no different. The human person is a complex, high-touch, nuanced being who is created in the image of God. As God is mysterious, so is God's creation. At times, I stand before people hearing their stories and wondering why it is that they are who they are. What makes them tick? Why do they continue to do the same silly, mysterious things over and over again?

As a preacher, I am learning that one of the greatest skills of the best preachers is that they refuse to iron out the "unironables" in the Bible. They don't seek to explain away the story of Nadab and Abihu—they just let it be. I think that the same goes for the people in my life who have loved me with Christlike persistence. These are people who, like the best preachers, don't try to iron out all of me on their own.

When I was in my doctoral program, a New Testament PhD student told me something I've held on to. He said that an oppressed Bible oppresses people.

In other words, when we malign, quiet, or manipulate the holy words of the Bible, we can use it for whatever ends we want. Frankly, and I want to stress this, I think the same stands for our relationships with other people. Oppressed people oppress people.

At the very place we ourselves are not loved *as we are*, when and wherever we find ourselves, we will refuse to do the same for others.

I increasingly hear Christians, when facing such stories in the Bible, say things like, "I couldn't follow a God who could do that!" Of course, at the core of such a sentiment toward God is the same sentiment toward others. We refuse to love God for who God is on God's own terms. We welcome embracing a God that fits logically, culturally, and sensibly into our own sensitivities. But the minute God colors outside those lines, we bounce.

We are as guilty of this in our love toward others.

Jesus's words were actually true. "'Love the Lord your God with all your heart and with all your soul and with all your mind and with all your strength.' . . . 'Love your neighbor as yourself'" (Mark 12:30–31). Our love of neighbor is a shadow of our love for God, and vice versa.

Just as a Christian is invited to love God on God's terms, a neighbor is invited to love their neighbor on their neighbor's turf.

Two weeks ago, I had the chance to spend two hours with a famous New Testament scholar. I planned on spending the time asking this person question after question. But she would have none of it. For two hours, this internationally acknowledged scholar spent time asking *me* questions about my family, my studies, and my ministry.

The professor entered into the mystery that was *me*!

I want to be that way. I think Jesus wants me to be that way, to live a pathology of irrational listening. Of sitting in *others'* stories and just letting them be what they are. C. S. Lewis, in his science fiction novel *Perelandra*, portrays the devil as one who hands us a mirror. The enemy of our souls finds his greatest pleasure in getting us to look at ourselves. The prophet Ezekiel depicts the fall to earth of an angelic being who is presumably Satan. The angel fell because he saw and fell in love with his own beauty.

Ron Frost once wrote about the mirror and our obsession with it. He said,

The contemporary obsessions of the Western civilization suggest that the "gift" of a mirror may well be the best metaphor for sin—as in the apparent account of the satanic fall in Ezekiel 28:17—"Your heart was proud because of your beauty; you corrupted your wisdom for the sake of your splendor." The gaze of faith can only be on one who exists as our eternal "other"—on Jesus, the author and finisher of our faith—so that the solution to the Fall is found not in a mirror but in magnifying the Other, who in turn reveals his Father to us; and all of this by the presence of the Spirit, who is our life and love.[9]

The devil's gift to us is a mirror to get us to focus on ourselves. Jesus's gift to us is a window so that we can pay attention to others. Jesus followers can see outside themselves. God is a mystery, and so are others.

—◊◊◊—

The desert is lonely.

A friend of mine went to Haiti after the big earthquake. Rescuers were still looking for people who were trapped in the rubble. The only way they could find people was for everyone else to be silent. And in the silence, they could hear the sound of those in the rubble crying out for help.

Picturing that image has helped me learn how to talk to God again.

In the desert, the wanderer that you come to face isn't the other. It is often yourself. Silence allows the real you to poke its head out.

Dan Rather interviewed Mother Teresa before her death. Rather was caught off guard by her answers:

Rather: "When you pray, what do you say to God?"
Teresa: "I don't say anything. I listen."
Rather: "Well, okay . . . when God speaks to you, then, what does He say?"
Teresa: "He doesn't say anything. He listens. And if you don't understand that, I can't explain it to you."[10]

When I think of Teresa's explanation of prayer, I am reminded of David's words: "Rest in the Lord" (Ps. 37:7 KJV). Resting prayer isn't a free-flowing exchange of intellectual ideas. Resting prayer is just being there.

JESUS THE STRANGE WANDERER

What do you think? If a man owns a hundred sheep, and one of them wanders away, will he not leave the ninety-nine on the hills and go to look for the one that wandered off? And if he finds it, truly I tell you, he is happier about that one sheep than about the ninety-nine that did not wander off. In the same way your Father in heaven is not willing that any of these little ones should perish.

Matthew 18:12–14

In the early part of the summer of 2011, I went to Britain to defend my PhD dissertation at the University of Birmingham under the supervision of Dr. Mark Cartledge. It would be, if all went according to plan, my final trip in order to graduate. After what felt like an endless (yet very fruitful) three and a half years of study, I packed my bags, kissed my *very* pregnant wife good-bye, and flew to defend my work. My flight, after a few slight delays, arrived at Birmingham International Airport. My doctoral adviser's wife, Joan, picked me up at baggage claim. The epitome of hospitality, Joan warmly greeted me and wished me well on my defense, which would take place the next day. After dropping me off at my lodging, Joan said to me, in my somewhat comatose state, "We'd love to have you come to church tonight. It's in two hours. Get showered. Let's go." Not wanting to be a poor guest or a delinquent worshiper, I obliged.

St. John's Anglican Church was a warm and hospitable worshiping community I'd visited many times during my studies in England. On one occasion, I even had the opportunity to preach there. I always enjoyed the chance to return.

After being refreshed by a much-needed shower and ravenously taking in a little food, I waited outside my hostel for Joan and Dr. Cartledge to pick me up to go to church. When their little British car pulled up, I was pleasantly surprised to find a kindly young woman of dark complexion and a bright countenance sitting in the back of the car with me. I'd never met her. She was a quiet, young, Muslim girl the Cartledges had met weeks earlier, and she had expressed interest in joining them for a church service one Sunday. During the ride, and struggling through the language barriers, we exchanged a modicum of pleasantries. Her English and my Arabic were unpolished at best. After the church service finished, I noticed my new Muslim friend sitting quietly by herself in what looked like deep reflection about the sermon. Quite honestly, I wasn't entirely certain she understood the message that evening. But it appeared she'd been moved. I thought it would be kind to engage in some conversation about how she was doing, so we began to talk.

She told me she'd come to Britain earlier that year to escape an abusive home life and eventually settled in Birmingham. I've known well enough for some time that ministry among Muslim people is very challenging work. I'd once heard of a missionary to a Muslim country who spent fifty years there and led three people to Christ. I knew the cards were stacked against us. This young woman told me that earlier that week she'd been alone and had a vision in which she believed Allah, her God, had told her to go to church. Faithfully, she did. Without raising questions about her faith, I simply listened. The moment was beautiful. I had the opportunity to hear her story, cry with her, and share the message of a loving Jesus as best I could, despite the language barriers. Our conversation ended, we parted ways, and I never saw her again.

After passing my doctoral defense, completing my work, and packing to go home, I got on the return flight. I thought of the young woman all the way home. I thought about how it felt that she'd been placed squarely in my life for that moment in time and that God had set up something that neither I nor anyone else could ever have set up. I began to get the sense that I was looking over the shoulder of the Spirit as he did something profound, rather than him looking over mine. The Spirit doesn't follow me, I concluded. I follow the Spirit. Because only the Spirit can set up stuff like that.

Once home, I received an email. The young Muslim woman had, that week, become a Christian. I got a picture of her ascending from the waters of baptism. In truth, I'm convinced those four years of doctoral work were probably about that young woman. One could wrongly think it was all about the studies. But God had more up his sleeve than school for me.

God was scheming to save this human being.

Being a Christian is to be truly hospitable above all. Most Christians are hospitable to others; to be a Christian is to first and foremost make room for Jesus. This is why Jesus comes to us as a wandering stranger. Hospitality is a major biblical theme. In the wandering account of Abraham and Sarah in Genesis, Abraham welcomes and serves some strangers who are passing through (18:1–15). After a short discussion, Abraham offers them a meal and some rest while they wash their feet. The text implies that Abraham did not know who his company was: three angelic beings. Some commentators have even suggested this is an image of the Trinity. Abraham's hospitality is praised as a model for the person open to God. The New Testament, furthermore, offers a plethora of images of hospitality, perhaps no more than in Luke-Acts.[1] In Luke, Jesus welcomes and dines with outsiders and foreigners to the dismay of the religiously pious. He brought "good news" to the poor, the destitute, and the blind (Luke 4:18–19). Whereas Aristotle taught that friends had to be moral equals,[2] Jesus had friends who were certainly not his moral equals (John 15:15).[3] Jesus could do this because he inhabited the Holy Spirit (Luke 4:1, 14).

While Jesus extended hospitality to others, he also *received* hospitality and even depended on it for his kingdom message to spread. The Emmaus Road story reminds us of this (Luke 24). Two disciples walk down the road just after Jesus's resurrection. They have an inkling that Jesus has been resurrected, but they are unaware that Jesus is standing in their midst. A stranger comes up to them and begins to ask them questions. After a brief interchange, the two disciples invite this stranger—again, unaware it is Jesus—to their home to eat a meal. It is there in the middle of breaking bread that their eyes are opened. It is Jesus, the resurrected one!

It is in welcoming the wandering stranger that these two disciples see Jesus. The book of Hebrews says when we welcome strangers, we may be entertaining angels (13:2). Both stories (of Abraham and of the disciples) are so important and give us the impetus to constantly welcome in the wandering stranger we know nothing of—it may be an angel. Or better yet, in welcoming the stranger, we may be welcoming Jesus Christ himself.

That is why we should treat everyone like an angel, just in case. We don't know who we may be inviting in. The whole "don't talk to strangers" thing we were taught as kids may be necessary, but over time it becomes a surefire way to keep Jesus out of our midst. Jesus comes to us as a stranger. "I stand at the door and knock," Jesus says. "If anyone hears my voice and opens the door, I will come in and eat with that person, and they with me" (Rev. 3:20). That young Muslim woman invited Jesus in to dine, and it changed her life. Those two unknown disciples invited Jesus in, and their eyes were opened.

Will we be so hospitable toward the God who comes as a stranger?

—⟋⟍—

We will always wander, we will always long, and we will always be hungry until we find what we were created for. Until then, we will wander from place to place looking and searching, never finding and never being fulfilled. Heaven is, above all, the end or our wanderings.

Until then, we are all a little like Tom Hanks's character in the movie *Cast Away*. Chuck Noland, an executive in a multinational delivery service, is in a plane crash over the ocean. He survives only to swim to an island where he will spend the next few years in desperate isolation. His life is gone. He has lost everything. Even his clothing has been lost. The only friend he has is a volleyball that he calls Wilson. But he has one possession that he did not lose—a small pocket watch with a picture of his fiancée in it. Every night, he looks at that picture and dreams of going home. That picture is his hope. If he keeps his eyes on her, he has a reason to get up in the morning.

We all have something that gets us up in the morning—a lost hope. We can only hope that someday we will find what we long for. There is, of course, a difference between having a picture of God and having God. More often than not, we have a picture of God. And having a picture of God gives us hope. We should constantly look at our picture of God. But we should also know that God doesn't just desire for us to have a picture of him. God wants us to know him. And the hope of Christianity is that we will experience him in all his glory. "But we know that when Christ appears," writes John, "we shall be like him, for we shall see him as he is. All who have this hope in him purify themselves, just as he is pure" (1 John 3:2–3). We look at Jesus, thinking of him, dreaming of him, and hoping for him.

—⟋⟍—

We arrive at an ending.

The ending of a book is a challenging thing to complete. I never know how to end a book. I like authors who don't finish their books all nice and tidy, perfectly wrapped up with a bow on top. Books with

rough endings are my kind of thing because life often has rough endings. Life isn't always a series of nice-and-tidy endings. "And everyone
lived happily ever after" is a farce, a lie used by marketers to give us
a momentary flush of butterflies in our bellies. But life doesn't work
that way.

The endings of so many of the books and stories of the Bible, and
the stories of Jesus, are anything but "everyone lived happily ever
after." Bible scholars have long believed that many of the parables,
for instance, were told in such a way that the ending would cause the
hearers to want to respond. For instance, at the end of the parable of
the prodigal son, the younger son has returned from his years of par-
tying and squandering in a distant land. He has returned home only
to find the older son completely dissatisfied by the father's love and
acceptance of the younger sinner. The older brother grows angry and
pleads with his father, saying *he* should get the love and acceptance
of the father because he never left in the first place. The end of the
story goes like this: "'My son,' the father said, 'you are always with me,
and everything I have is yours. But we had to celebrate and be glad
because this younger brother of yours was dead and is alive again; he
was lost and is found'" (Luke 15:31–32).

Of course, this ending is so unresolved—it is not a "happily ever
after" moment. The older brother is left standing there, being lectured
by his father about accepting the younger brother. It seems that Jesus
left the story so unfinished as if to say to the reader, what are *you* going
to do with the younger brothers who come home? What are *you* going
to do with the fact that God loves sinners and welcomes them home?
A moviemaker would call this a breaking of the fourth wall; it is that
moment when the actor in the movie turns toward the camera and
says to the audience, "What are you going to do about this?"

Or consider the way Mark ends his story of the resurrection. Mark
has what has been called a "long ending," a section that was clearly
not part of the original manuscripts of the New Testament. The long
ending has some teachings of Jesus, but the original ending is abrupt
and rather abrasive. In the original ending, the women come to the

tomb to see that it is empty. The ending of Mark's Gospel would have originally read, "Trembling and bewildered, the women went out and fled from the tomb. They said nothing to anyone, because they were afraid" (Mark 16:8). Mark ends his Gospel with the women running in fear away from the empty tomb. Not a "happily ever after" ending. Or finally, look at the book of Acts. Acts is the story of the Holy Spirit working through the early church. In the tale of Acts, Paul, Barnabas, and Peter travel the world to preach the message of Jesus, whom they served and loved. And as the gospel spread through the world, Paul got into quite the trouble. In fact, that is where the book of Acts ends. Paul, in the final chapter of Acts, is in prison in Rome and ready to be executed for his work as a preacher of the message of Jesus. But of course the ending of the chapter is followed by what happened in history afterward—namely, the message of Jesus spread through the world for centuries, capturing the hearts and minds of millions upon millions of people. Why, then, would Acts end with Paul in prison preparing to die? It does so to accomplish a literary device that an ancient reader would have understood. It is like Acts is saying, "Hey, you can tie up our messengers, you can put us in prison, you can put us in chains, but you *cannot* put this message in chains. It will go forth."

Such endings are really a kind of beginning. For as the story ends, it is like the one behind the Bible turns to us, the readers, and says, "What are you going to do with this?" New Testament scholar Conrad Gempf wrote prolifically on this idea and said that Jesus's parables and riddles—and likewise all such endings—are like wedges that "seem to be poking at you, forcing you to take one side or another."[4] Such endings are intended to get us off the fence.

I came across a theologian who described Jesus as a migrant.[5] And it is true—Jesus is from another land, takes the lowly job no one else takes, speaks a different language, and never gets the benefit of the laws of the land. Jesus isn't always welcomed, is he? But the message of Scripture is that we are given a chance to welcome him, to make space for him, to hear what he has to say.

Will we?

209

The gospel *is* a wanderer. It wanders like a pilgrim—road weary and resilient—through the hearts, minds, and souls of people in history. As it touches our hearts, it changes us. But we must first let it in. This wandering gospel has gone through countless generations to come into my heart. It has cost lives, families, jobs, and homes for it to make it into this little mind. How many roads has the gospel walked before it came to me? Countless.

And let me tell you, I didn't create it. I didn't make it. I have no control over it. All I can really do, like you, is receive it.

Welcoming in that wanderer, strangely, is our only way home.

NOTES

Preface

1. E. B. White, *Essays of E. B. White* (New York: Harper Colophon, 1977), vii.

2. Quoted in Diogenes Allen, *Spiritual Theology: The Theology of Yesterday for Spiritual Help Today* (Lanham, MD: Rowman & Littlefield, 1997), 23.

Chapter 1 Wandering and Lamaze

1. Quoted in Thomas Long, *The Witness of Preaching*, 2nd ed. (Louisville: Westminster John Knox, 2005), 11.

2. Louis Jacobs, *Jewish Preaching: Homilies and Sermons* (Portland, OR: Valentine Mitchell, 2004), 13.

3. Rodney Reeves, *Spirituality according to Paul: Imitating the Apostle of Christ* (Downers Grove, IL: InterVarsity, 2011), 47.

4. At the same time, it is also true that there is no better place to be than in Christ and in the hands of a gracious God (cf. Matt. 11:28–30).

5. Quoted in David J. Bosch, *A Spirituality of the Road* (Scottdale, PA: Herald, 1979), 32.

6. Quoted in J. E. Norris-Bernal, *Forgiving Others and Trusting God: A Handbook for Survivors of Child Abuse* (Maitland, FL: Xulon, 2011), 88.

7. Vincent of Lérins, *Commonitory*, 22.27, quoted in Thomas C. Oden, "The Faith Once Delivered," in *Evangelicals and the Nicene Creed: Reclaiming the Apostolic Witness*, ed. Timothy George (Grand Rapids: Baker Academic, 2011), 18.

Chapter 2 Mom's Gazpacho

1. Quoted in Robert K. Johnston, *God's Wider Presence: Reconsidering General Revelation* (Grand Rapids: Baker Academic, 2014), 1.

2. Helmut Thielicke, *A Little Exercise for Young Theologians* (Grand Rapids: Eerdmans, 1962), 36.

3. A. W. Tozer, *Of God and Men* (Harrisburg, PA: Christian Publications, 1960), 26–27.

4. Marianne Moore, *Complete Poems* (New York: Penguin, 1994), 36.

5. Quoted in Stephen Gaukroger and Nick Mercer, eds., *A–Z Sparkling Illustrations* (Grand Rapids: Baker, 1997), 76–77.

6. This idea has become so fundamental to me that I included it in my first book, *Messy* (Grand Rapids: Kregel, 2012). The idea was first introduced to me by Andrew Goodwin, an elder in my church community at Theophilus.

Chapter 3 Banished

1. For an example of architectural reflections on the creation account, see Nicholas Choy, "The Architectural Witness of Salvation History," *Cultural Encounters* 5, no. 2 (2009): 25–40.

2. Dietrich Bonhoeffer, *Letters and Papers from Prison* (London: SCM, 2002), 77.

3. I am not the only one to suggest something like this. Anne Lamott is reported to have said, "My deepest belief is that living as if you are dying sets us free."

4. Sigmund Freud, quoted in Brian Anthony Farrell, *Philosophy and Psychoanalysis* (New York: MacMillan College Publishing, 1994), 163 (emphasis added).

5. Howard Snyder, *Salvation Means Creation Healed: The Ecology of Sin and Grace; Overcoming the Divorce between Earth and Heaven* (Eugene, OR: Wipf & Stock, 2011), 102.

6. K. A. Mathews, *Genesis 1–11:26* (Nashville: Broadman & Holman, 1996), 1A:278–79.

7. H. D. M. Spence-Jones, ed., *Genesis* (London: Funk & Wagnalls, 1909), 81.

8. Sheldon Vanauken, *A Severe Mercy* (1980; repr., San Francisco: HarperSanFrancisco, 1987), 38.

Chapter 4 Deserts

1. Ellen Davis, *Getting Involved with God: Rediscovering the Old Testament* (Lanham, MD: Rowman & Littlefield, 2001), 4.

2. Andrew E. Hill, *1 and 2 Chronicles*, NIV Application Commentary (Grand Rapids: Zondervan, 2010), 23.

3. Leonard Shlain, *The Alphabet versus the Goddess: The Conflict between Word and Image* (New York: Penguin, 1998), 64–65.

4. John Bright, *A History of Israel* (Louisville: Westminster John Knox, 2000), 82.

5. Donald Sharpes, *Lord of the Scrolls: Literary Traditions in the Bible and the Gospels* (New York: Peter Lang, 2007), 172–74.

6. John Calvin, *Institutes of the Christian Religion*, trans. Ford Lewis Battles, ed. John T. McNeill, Library of Christian Classics (Philadelphia: Westminster, 1960), I.xi.8, 1:180.

7. Richard Keyes, "The Idol Factory," in *No God but God: Breaking with the Idols of Our Age*, ed. Os Guinness and John Seel (Chicago: Moody, 1992), 31.

Chapter 5 Invisible Loves

1. James K. A. Smith, *Desiring the Kingdom: Worship, Worldview, and Cultural Formation* (Grand Rapids: Baker Academic, 2009), 40.

2. Augustine's maxim, for example, comes to mind: "Thou hast made us for Thyself and our hearts are restless till they rest in Thee." *Confessions*, trans. F. J. Sheed (Indianapolis: Hackett, 1993), 3.

3. Quoted in Emile Cammaerts, *The Laughing Prophet* (London: Methuen, 1937), n.p. (emphasis added).

4. Jean Paul Sartre, *To Freedom Condemned* (New York: Philosophical Library, 1960), 18.

5. Flannery O'Connor to Louise Abbot, Milledgeville, Sat. [n.d.], in *Collected Works*, Library of America (New York: Library of America, 1988), 1110.

6. Robert Jay Lifton, *Nazi Doctors: Medical Killing and the Psychology of Genocide* (New York: Basic Books, 1986), 46.

7. This is illustrated in the jaw-dropping account by Christopher Browning, *Ordinary Men: Reserve Police Battalion*

101 and the Final Solution in Poland (New York: Harper Collins, 1998).

8. Howard Snyder, *Salvation Means Creation Healed: The Ecology of Sin and Grace; Overcoming the Divorce between Earth and Heaven* (Eugene, OR: Wipf & Stock, 2011), 102.

9. Simon Shama, *Landscape and Memory* (New York: Knopf, 1995), 119.

10. Quoted by the renowned Will Willimon, "Good News! You're a Sinner and Lent Is Here," OnFaith, March 2, 2014, http://www.faithstreet.com/on faith/2014/03/02/good-news-you-are-a -sinner-and-lent-is-here/31125.

11. Madeleine L'Engle, *Walking on Water: Reflections on Faith and Art* (New York: Random House, 1982), 25.

12. See the brilliant work done by F. F. Bruce on wordplay in his *The New Testament Development of Old Testament Themes* (Eugene, OR: Wipf & Stock, 2004), 20.

Chapter 6 Walking

1. A theme throughout Thomas Schmidt's brilliant *Trying to Be Good: A Book on Doing for Thinking People* (Grand Rapids: Zondervan, 1990).

2. N. T. Wright, *Reflecting the Glory: Meditations for Living Christ's Life in the World* (Minneapolis: Augsburg, 1998).

3. Clark H. Pinnock, "A Pilgrim on the Way," *Christianity Today* 42, no. 2 (February 9, 1998): 43.

4. Jürgen Moltmann, *The Spirit of Life: A Universal Affirmation* (Minneapolis: Fortress, 1992), 51.

5. See Louis Jacobs, *Jewish Preaching: Homilies and Sermons* (Portland, OR: Vallentine Mitchell, 2004), 17.

6. Karl Barth, *Church Dogmatics* I/1, ed. and trans. T. F. Torrance and G. W. Bromiley (London: T&T Clark, 1962), 283.

7. Manfred F. R. Kets de Vries, *Leaders, Fools, Imposters: Essays on the Psychology of Leadership* (Lincoln, NE: iUniverse, 2003), 30.

8. Parker Palmer, *The Active Life: A Spirituality of Work, Creativity, and Caring* (San Francisco: Jossey Bass, 1990), 142.

9. Moltmann, *Spirit of Life*, 26 (emphasis added).

10. As tweeted by Miroslav Volf, January 29, 2015, https://twitter.com/mi roslavvolf/status/560755285296693248.

11. R. P. Lightner, "Philippians," in J. F. Walvoord and R. B. Zuck, eds., *The Bible Knowledge Commentary: An Exposition of the Scriptures* (Wheaton: Victor, 1985), 2:650.

Chapter 7 Our Need for Needs

1. Augustine, *On Free Choice of the Will*, trans. Thomas Williams (Indianapolis: Hackett, 1993), 80.

2. This becomes a real problem—God had asked them to "speak" to the rock. My colleague Jen Butler, with whom I wrote *Introducing Evangelical Ecotheology*, points out that this is the closest thing in the Bible we have to fracking—hitting of natural rock structures to procure oil. God would eventually not allow Moses and Aaron to enter the promised land because they hit the rock rather than speaking to the rock.

3. James Jones, "The Secret State of North Korea," *Frontline*, accessed September 15, 2015, http://www.pbs.org /wgbh/pages/frontline/foreign-affairs -defense/secret-state-of-north-korea/tran script-55/.

4. "All-Time Golf Scoring Record Goes with Death of Kim Jong il," Cybergolf, http://www.cybergolf.com/golf _news/alltime_golf_scoring_record_goes _with_death_of_kim_jong_il.

5. DJ Gallo, "Kim Jon-Il Was a Dictator Who Went to Great Links," ESPN .com, http://espn.go.com/espn/page2 /index?id=7369649.

6. Maia Szalavitz, "Touching Empathy," *Psychology Today* blog, March 1, 2010, https://www.psychologytoday

.com/blog/born-love/201003/touching
-empathy.

7. Julia Kasdorf, "What I Learned from My Mother," in *A Capella: Mennonite Voices in Poetry*, ed. Ann Elizabeth Hostetler (Iowa City: University of Iowa Press, 2003), 131.

8. Robert Bellah et al., *Habits of the Heart: Individualism and Commitment in American Life* (Berkeley: University of California Press, 1985).

9. Richard Beck, "Spiritual Pollution: The Dilemma of Sociomoral Disgust and the Ethic of Love," *Journal of Psychology and Theology* 34 (Spring 2006): 43–52.

10. N. T. Wright, *The Crown and the Fire: Meditations on the Cross and the Life of the Spirit* (Grand Rapids: Eerdmans, 1992), 19 (emphasis added).

Chapter 8 A Wanderer's Rest

1. Eugene Peterson, *Working the Angles: The Shape of Pastoral Integrity* (Grand Rapids: Eerdmans, 1987), 66.

2. Colin Gunton, *The Theologian as Preacher: Further Sermons from Colin Gunton* (Bloomsbury: T&T Clark, 2007), 63.

3. Michelle Alexander, *The New Jim Crow: Mass Incarceration in the Age of Colorblindness* (New York: New York University Press, 2010), 20.

4. Walter Wessel, "Mark," in *The Expositor's Bible Commentary*, ed. Frank E. Gaebelein (Grand Rapids: Zondervan, 1984), 638.

5. Matthew Sleeth, *The Gospel according to the Earth: Why the Good Book Is a Green Book* (New York: Harper Collins, 2010), 73.

6. Mark Buchanan, *The Rest of God: Restoring Your Soul by Restoring Sabbath* (Grand Rapids: Zondervan, 2006), 87 (emphasis in original).

7. Jürgen Moltmann, *God in Creation* (Minneapolis: Fortress, 1993), 277 (emphasis in original).

8. A theme throughout his book *The Sabbath* (New York: Farrar, Straus and Young, 1951). Heschel sees Sabbath as an appetizer for eternity with God.

9. Rabbi Daniel Aronson, "Parashat Vayakhel—Exodus 35:1–38:20," Temple Beth Sholom website, February 20, 2014, http://www.tbsholom.org/parashat-vaya khel-exodus-351-3820/2826.

10. Larry Hurtado, *Mark*, New International Biblical Commentary (Peabody, MA: Hendrickson, 1995), 47.

11. My friend Len Sweet has said this to me on many occasions in personal conversations.

12. C. S. Lewis, *The Problem of Pain* (New York: Touchstone, 1996), 103.

Chapter 9 Displacement

1. Maribel Dietz, *Wandering Monks, Virgins, and Pilgrims: Ascetic Travel in the Mediterranean World, A.D. 300–800* (University Park: Pennsylvania State University Press, 2005).

2. Ibid., 3.

3. George Frank, *The Memory of Eyes: Pilgrims to Living Saints in Christian Late Antiquity* (Berkeley: University of California Press, 2000), 64.

4. In the early church, there were two groups: those who sold everything to go and do ministry and those who opened their homes to them and the poor. Gerd Theissen has called these two groups the "wandering charismatics" and the "local sympathizers" in *Sociology of Early Palestinian Christianity* (Minneapolis: Fortress, 1978).

5. Peter Toon, *Longing for Heaven: A Devotional Look at Life after Death* (London: Macmillan, 1989), 4–5.

6. Tamara Eskenazi, "Exile and Dreams of Return," *Currents in Theology and Mission* 18 (1990): 192; Iain M. Duguid, *Ezekiel*, NIV Application Commentary (Grand Rapids: Zondervan, 1999).

7. John O'Donahue, *Eternal Echoes: Exploring the Yearning to Belong* (New York: Harper Collins, 1999), xxii.

8. Abraham Joshua Heschel, *God in Search of Man: A Philosophy of Judaism* (New York: Harper & Row, 1955), 316.

9. Sherry Turkle, *Alone Together: Why We Expect More from Technology and Less from Each Other* (New York: Basic Books, 2012).

10. I understand it may or may not have been an apple. The text doesn't specify what the fruit was. But for my illustration, I use an apple. You will see why.

11. Martin Buber, *Mamre* (Melbourne: Melbourne University Press, 1946), 78. I am thankful to Alan Hirsch and Michael Frost for pointing out these ideas in their *The Shaping of Things to Come* (Peabody, MA: Hendrickson, 2003), 129–32.

12. Quoted in Daniel Strand, *The Holy Spirit and the Christian Life: Historical, Interdisciplinary, and Renewal Perspectives* (New York: Palgrave, 2014), 64.

13. Quoted in Stephen Mansfield, *The Search for God and Guinness: A Biography of the Beer That Changed the World* (Nashville: Thomas Nelson, 2009), xvii.

14. Quoted in Jocelyn Castro, *Wealthy Slaves and the Ecclesiastes* (Bloomington, IN: Xlibris, 2010), 173.

15. Augustine, *Confessions*, trans. R. S. Pine-Coffin (New York: Penguin, 1961), 21.

16. C. S. Lewis, *The Weight of Glory* (Grand Rapids: Eerdmans, 1949), 12.

17. My friend Andy Campbell, a professor of Christian spirituality at George Fox University, made this point in one of the best sermons on repentance I've ever heard. Read his work and you will be super blessed.

Chapter 10 Losing Jesus

1. Discussed in Diogenes Allen, *Spiritual Theology: The Theology of Yesterday for Spiritual Help Today* (Lanham, MD: Rowman & Littlefield, 1997), 159.

2. I like how Mark Batterson puts this as he speaks of "inverted Christianity" in his *Wild Goose Chase: Reclaim the Adventure of Pursuing God* (Colorado Springs: Multnomah, 2008), 4.

Chapter 11 Perceived Famine

1. Kurt Neilson, *Urban Iona: Celtic Hospitality in the City* (Harrisburg, PA: Morehouse, 2007), 9.

2. Ashby Jones, "Justice Is Served, but More So after Lunch," *LawBlog*, WSJ .com, April 13, 2011, http://blogs.wsj.com /law/2011/04/13/justice-is-served-but -more-so-after-lunch/.

3. Henri J. Nouwen, *In the Name of Jesus: Reflections on Christian Leadership* (New York: Crossroad, 1989).

4. Shusaku Endo, *A Life of Jesus*, trans. Richard A. Schuchert (New York: Paulist Press, 1973), esp. chap. 2.

5. See Kenneth Bendiner, *Food in Painting: From the Renaissance to the Present* (London: Reaktion, 2004).

6. Alister McGrath, *Christian Theology: An Introduction*, 5th ed. (Malden, MA: Blackwell, 2011), 98.

7. Discussed throughout Daniel Erlander, *Manna and Mercy* (Mercer Island, WA: The Order of Saints Martin & Teresa, 1992).

Chapter 12 The Quiet of the Walk

1. Hildegard of Bingen, *Scivias*, trans. Columba Hart and Jane Bishop, Classics of Western Spirituality (Mahwah, NJ: Paulist Press, 1990), 59–60 (emphasis added).

2. Kenneth Bailey, *Jesus through Middle Eastern Eyes: Cultural Studies in the Gospels* (Downers Grove, IL: InterVarsity, 2008), 217.

3. I should add that the term *racist* is a rather new invention and is not one that should be used in how we look at the Bible. To say that Jesus could be a racist is the same as saying Judas

Iscariot was a Republican, something that didn't exist as a category at the time. In the end, to ask whether Jesus was a racist is anachronistic, and, therefore, a little difficult to consider.

4. Ibn al-Tayyib, *Tafsir al-Mashriqi*, ed. Yusif Manqariyos (Egypt: Al-Tawfiq, 1907), 2:281–82, quoted in Bailey, *Jesus through Middle Eastern Eyes*, 220.

5. Ibn al-Tayyib, *Tafsir al-Mashriqi*, 1:282–83.

6. David Augsburger, *Caring Enough to Hear and Be Heard: How to Hear and How to Be Heard in Equal Communication* (Scottdale, PA: Herald, 1982), 12.

7. Quoted in David James Duncan, *God Laughs and Plays: Churchless Sermons in Response to the Preachments of the Fundamentalist Right* (Great Barrington, MA: Triad, 2006), 146.

8. Immanuel Velikovsky, *Worlds in Collision* (New York: Doubleday, 2009), 72–73.

9. R. N. Frost, "Sin and Grace," in *Trinitarian Soundings in Systematic Theology*, ed. Paul Louis Metzger (New York: T&T Clark, 2005), 110.

10. Quoted in Charles R. Swindoll, *So You Want to Be Like Christ? Eight Essentials to Get You There* (Nashville: Thomas Nelson, 2005).

Chapter 13 Jesus the Strange Wanderer

1. On hospitality throughout the Gospel of Luke, see the following: Amos Yong, *Hospitality and the Other: Pentecost, Christian Practices, and the Neighbor* (Maryknoll, NY: Orbis, 2008); David B. Gowler, *Host, Guest, Enemy, and Friend: Portrait of the Pharisees in Luke and Acts*, vol. 2, Emory Studies in Early Christianity (New York: Peter Lang, 1991); Andrew E. Arterbury, *Entertaining Angels: Early Christian Hospitality in Its Mediterranean Setting*, New Testament Monographs, vol. 8 (Sheffield: Sheffield Phoenix, 2005); Brendan Byrne, *The Hospitality of God: A Reading of Luke's Gospel* (Collegeville, MN: Liturgical Press, 2000).

2. *Nicomachean Ethics* 1157a.

3. Thanks to James W. McClendon for pointing this out in his *Systematic Theology: Ethics*, 3 vols. (Nashville: Abingdon, 2002), 1:178.

4. Conrad Gempf, *Jesus Asked: What He Wanted to Know* (Grand Rapids: Zondervan, 2003), 33.

5. John P. Rossing, "Mestizaje and Marginality: A Hispanic American Theology," *Theology Today* 45, no. 3 (1998): 293–304.

Bibliography

Alexander, Michelle. *The New Jim Crow: Mass Incarceration in the Age of Colorblindness.* New York: New York University Press, 2010.

Allen, Diogenes. *Spiritual Theology: The Theology of Yesterday for Spiritual Help Today.* Lanham, MD: Rowman & Littlefield, 1997.

Arterbury, Andrew E. *Entertaining Angels: Early Christian Hospitality in Its Mediterranean Setting.* New Testament Monographs, vol. 8. Sheffield: Sheffield Phoenix, 2005.

Augsburger, David. *Caring Enough to Hear and Be Heard: How to Hear and How to Be Heard in Equal Communication.* Scottdale, PA: Herald, 1982.

Augustine. *Confessions.* Translated by F. J. Sheed. Indianapolis: Hackett, 1993.

———. *Confessions.* Translated by R. S. Pine-Coffin. New York: Penguin, 1961.

———. *On Free Choice of the Will.* Translated by Thomas Williams. Indianapolis: Hackett, 1993.

Bailey, Kenneth. *Jesus through Middle Eastern Eyes: Cultural Studies in the Gospels.* Downers Grove, IL: InterVarsity, 2008.

Barth, Karl. *Church Dogmatics* I/1. Edited and translated by T. F. Torrance and G. W. Bromiley. London: T&T Clark, 1962.

Batterson, Mark. *Wild Goose Chase: Reclaim the Adventure of Pursuing God.* Colorado Springs: Multnomah, 2008.

Beck, Richard. "Spiritual Pollution: The Dilemma of Sociomoral Disgust and the Ethic of Love." *Journal of Psychology and Theology* 34 (Spring 2006): 43–52.

Bellah, Robert, Richard Madsen, William M. Sullivan, Ann Swindler, and Steven M. Tipton. *Habits of the Heart: Individualism and Commitment in American Life.* Berkeley: University of California Press, 1985.

Bendiner, Kenneth. *Food in Painting: From the Renaissance to the Present.* London: Reaktion, 2004.

Bonhoeffer, Dietrich. *Letters and Papers from Prison.* London: SCM, 2002.

———. *Meditating on the Word.* Nashville: Cowley, 1986.

Bosch, David J. *A Spirituality of the Road.* Scottdale, PA: Herald, 1979.

Bright, John. *A History of Israel.* Louisville: Westminster John Knox, 2000.

Browning, Christopher. *Ordinary Men: Reserve Police Battalion 101 and the Final Solution in Poland.* New York: Harper Collins, 1998.

Bruce, F. F. *The New Testament Development of Old Testament Themes.* Eugene, OR: Wipf & Stock, 2004.

Brunner, Daniel L., Jennifer L. Butler, and A. J. Swoboda. *Introducing Evangelical Ecotheology: Foundations in Scripture, Theology, History, and Praxis.* Grand Rapids: Baker Academic, 2014.

Buber, Martin. *Mamre.* Melbourne: Melbourne University Press, 1946.

Buchanan, Mark. *The Rest of God: Restoring Your Soul by Restoring Sabbath.* Grand Rapids: Zondervan, 2006.

Byrne, Brendan. *The Hospitality of God: A Reading of Luke's Gospel.* Collegeville, MN: Liturgical Press, 2000.

Calvin, John. *Institutes of the Christian Religion.* Translated by Ford Lewis Battles. Edited by John T. McNeill. Library of Christian Classics. Philadelphia: Westminster, 1960.

Cammaerts, Emile. *The Laughing Prophet.* London: Methuen, 1937.

Castro, Jocelyn. *Wealthy Slaves and the Ecclesiastes.* Bloomington, IN: Xlibris, 2010.

Choy, Nicholas. "The Architectural Witness of Salvation History." *Cultural Encounters* 5, no. 2 (2009): 25–40.

Davis, Ellen. *Getting Involved with God: Rediscovering the Old Testament.* Lanham, MD: Rowman & Littlefield, 2001.

Dietz, Maribel. *Wandering Monks, Virgins, and Pilgrims: Ascetic Travel in the Mediterranean World, A.D. 300–800.* University Park: Pennsylvania State University Press, 2005.

Duguid, Iain M. *Ezekiel.* NIV Application Commentary. Grand Rapids: Zondervan, 1999.

Duncan, David James. *God Laughs and Plays: Churchless Sermons in Response to the Preachments of the Fundamentalist Right.* Great Barrington, MA: Triad, 2006.

Endo, Shusaku. *A Life of Jesus.* Translated by Richard A. Schuchert. New York: Paulist Press, 1973.

Erlander, Daniel. *Manna and Mercy.* Mercer Island, WA: The Order of Saints Martin & Teresa, 1992.

Eskenazi, Tamara. "Exile and Dreams of Return." *Currents in Theology and Mission* 18 (1990): 192.

Farrell, Brian Anthony. *Philosophy and Psychoanalysis.* New York: MacMillan College Publishing, 1994.

Frank, George. *The Memory of Eyes: Pilgrims to Living Saints in Christian Late Antiquity.* Berkeley: University of California Press, 2000.

Frost, R. N. "Sin and Grace." In *Trinitarian Soundings in Systematic Theology,* edited by Paul Louis Metzger, 101–12. New York: T&T Clark, 2005.

Gaukroger, Stephen, and Nick Mercer, eds. *A–Z Sparkling Illustrations.* Grand Rapids: Baker, 1997.

Gempf, Conrad. *Jesus Asked: What He Wanted to Know.* Grand Rapids: Zondervan, 2003.

Gowler, David B. *Host, Guest, Enemy, and Friend: Portrait of the Pharisees in Luke and Acts.* Vol. 2. New York: Peter Lang, 1991.

Guinness, Os, and John Seel, eds. *No God but God: Breaking with the Idols of Our Age.* Chicago: Moody, 1992.

Gunton, Colin. *The Theologian as Preacher: Further Sermons from Colin Gunton.* Bloomsbury: T&T Clark, 2007.

Harvey, Barry. *Can These Bones Live? A Catholic Baptist Engagement with Ecclesiology, Hermeneutics, and Social Theory.* Grand Rapids: Brazos, 2008.

Heschel, Abraham Joshua. *God in Search of Man: A Philosophy of Judaism*. New York: Harper & Row, 1955.

———. *The Sabbath*. New York: Farrar, Straus and Young, 1951.

Hildegard of Bingen. *Scivias*. Translated by Columba Hart and Jane Bishop. Classics of Western Spirituality. Mahwah, NJ: Paulist Press, 1990.

Hill, Andrew E. *1 and 2 Chronicles*. NIV Application Commentary. Grand Rapids: Zondervan, 2010.

Hirsch, Alan, and Michael Frost. *The Shaping of Things to Come*. Peabody, MA: Hendrickson, 2003.

Hurtado, Larry. *Mark*. New International Biblical Commentary. Peabody, MA: Hendrickson, 1995.

Ibn al-Tayyib. *Tafsir al-Mashriqi*. Edited by Yusif Manqariyos. Egypt: Al-Tawfiq, 1907.

Jacobs, Louis. *Jewish Preaching: Homilies and Sermons*. Portland, OR: Valentine Mitchell, 2004.

Johnston, Robert K. *God's Wider Presence: Reconsidering General Revelation*. Grand Rapids: Baker Academic, 2014.

Kasdorf, Julia. "What I Learned from My Mother." In *A Capella: Mennonite Voices in Poetry*, edited by Ann Elizabeth Hostetler. Iowa City: University of Iowa Press, 2003.

Kets de Vries, Manfred F. R. *Leaders, Fools, Imposters: Essays on the Psychology of Leadership*. Lincoln, NE: iUniverse, 2003.

Keyes, Richard. "The Idol Factory." In *No God but God: Breaking with the Idols of Our Age*, edited by Os Guinness and John Seel, 29–48. Chicago: Moody, 1992.

L'Engle, Madeleine. *Walking on Water: Reflections on Faith and Art*. New York: Random House, 1982.

Lewis, C. S. *Perelandra*. Scribner Classics. New York: Scribner, 1996.

———. *The Problem of Pain*. New York: Touchstone, 1996.

———. *The Weight of Glory*. Grand Rapids: Eerdmans, 1949.

Lifton, Robert Jay. *Nazi Doctors: Medical Killing and the Psychology of Genocide*. New York: Basic Books, 1986.

Lightner, R. P. "Philippians." In *The Bible Knowledge Commentary: An Exposition of the Scriptures*, edited by J. F. Walvoord and R. B. Zuck, 647–66. Wheaton: Victor, 1985.

Long, Thomas. *The Witness of Preaching*. 2nd ed. Louisville: Westminster John Knox, 2005.

Mansfield, Stephen. *The Search for God and Guinness: A Biography of the Beer That Changed the World*. Nashville: Thomas Nelson, 2009.

Mathews, K. A. *Genesis 1–11:26*. Nashville: Broadman & Holman, 1996.

McClendon, James W. *Systematic Theology: Ethics*. 3 vols. Nashville: Abingdon, 2002.

McGrath, Alister. *Christian Theology: An Introduction*. 5th ed. Malden, MA: Blackwell, 2011.

———. *The Journey: A Pilgrim in the Lands of the Spirit*. New York: Doubleday, 1999.

Moltmann, Jürgen. *God in Creation*. Minneapolis: Fortress, 1993.

———. *The Spirit of Life: A Universal Affirmation*. Minneapolis: Fortress, 1992.

Moore, Marianne. *Complete Poems*. New York: Penguin, 1994.

Neilson, Kurt. *Urban Iona: Celtic Hospitality in the City*. Harrisburg, PA: Morehouse, 2007.

Norris-Bernal, J. E. *Forgiving Others and Trusting God: A Handbook for Survivors of Child Abuse*. Maitland, FL: Xulon, 2011.

Nouwen, Henri J. *In the Name of Jesus: Reflections on Christian Leadership*. New York: Crossroad, 1989.

O'Connor, Flannery. *Collected Works*. Library of America. New York: Library of America, 1988.

Oden, Thomas C. "The Faith Once Delivered." In *Evangelicals and the Nicene Creed: Reclaiming the Apostolic Witness*, edited by Timothy George, 3–19. Grand Rapids: Baker Academic, 2011.

O'Donahue, John. *Eternal Echoes: Exploring the Yearning to Belong*. New York: Harper Collins, 1999.

Palmer, Parker. *The Active Life: A Spirituality of Work, Creativity, and Caring*. San Francisco: Jossey-Bass, 1990.

Peterson, Eugene. *Working the Angles: The Shape of Pastoral Integrity.* Grand Rapids: Eerdmans, 1987.

Pinnock, Clark H. "A Pilgrim on the Way." *Christianity Today* 42, no. 2 (February 9, 1998): 43.

Reeves, Rodney. *Spirituality according to Paul: Imitating the Apostle of Christ.* Downers Grove, IL: InterVarsity, 2011.

Rossing, John P. "Mestizaje and Marginality: A Hispanic American Theology." *Theology Today* 45, no. 3 (1998): 293–304.

Sartre, Jean-Paul. *To Freedom Condemned.* New York: Philosophical Library, 1960.

Schmidt, Thomas. *Trying to Be Good: A Book on Doing for Thinking People.* Grand Rapids: Zondervan, 1990.

Shama, Simon. *Landscape and Memory.* New York: Knopf, 1995.

Sharpes, Donald. *Lord of the Scrolls: Literary Traditions in the Bible and the Gospels.* New York: Peter Lang, 2007.

Shlain, Leonard. *The Alphabet versus the Goddess: The Conflict between Word and Image.* New York: Penguin, 1998.

Sleeth, Matthew. *The Gospel according to the Earth: Why the Good Book Is a Green Book.* New York: Harper Collins, 2010.

Smith, James K. A. *Desiring the Kingdom: Worship, Worldview, and Cultural Formation.* Grand Rapids: Baker Academic, 2009.

Snyder, Howard. *Salvation Means Creation Healed: The Ecology of Sin and Grace; Overcoming the Divorce between Earth and Heaven.* Eugene, OR: Wipf & Stock, 2011.

Spence-Jones, H. D. M., ed. *Genesis.* London: Funk & Wagnalls, 1909.

Spurgeon, C. H. *Our Own Hymn Book: A Collection of Psalms and Hymns for Public, Social and Private Worship.* London: Passmore & Alabaster, 1883.

Strand, Daniel. *The Holy Spirit and the Christian Life: Historical, Interdisciplinary, and Renewal Perspectives.* New York: Palgrave, 2014.

Swindoll, Charles R. *So You Want to Be Like Christ? Eight Essentials to Get You There.* Nashville: Thomas Nelson, 2005.

Swoboda, A. J. *A Glorious Dark: Finding Hope in the Tension between Belief and Experience.* Grand Rapids: Baker Books, 2014.

————. *Messy*. Grand Rapids: Kregel, 2012.

Theissen, Gerd. *Sociology of Early Palestinian Christianity*. Minneapolis: Fortress, 1978.

Thielicke, Helmut. *A Little Exercise for Young Theologians*. Grand Rapids: Eerdmans, 1962.

Toon, Peter. *Longing for Heaven: A Devotional Look at Life after Death*. London: Macmillan, 1989.

Tozer, A. W. *Of God and Men*. Harrisburg, PA: Christian Publications, 1960.

Turkle, Sherry. *Alone Together: Why We Expect More from Technology and Less from Each Other*. New York: Basic Books, 2012.

Vanauken, Sheldon. *A Severe Mercy*. 1980. Reprint, San Francisco: HarperSanFrancisco, 1987.

Velikovsky, Immanuel. *Worlds in Collision*. New York: Doubleday, 2009.

Volf, Miroslav. "Allegiance and Rebellion." *The Christian Century* 114 (1997): 633.

Wessel, Walter. "Mark." In *The Expositor's Bible Commentary*, edited by Frank E. Gaebelein, 8:601–793. Grand Rapids: Zondervan, 1984.

White, E. B. *Essays of E. B. White*. New York: Harper Colophon, 1977.

Wright, N. T. *The Crown and the Fire: Meditations on the Cross and the Life of the Spirit*. Grand Rapids: Eerdmans, 1992.

————. *Reflecting the Glory: Meditations for Living Christ's Life in the World*. Minneapolis: Augsburg, 1998.

Yong, Amos. *Hospitality and the Other: Pentecost, Christian Practices, and the Neighbor*. Maryknoll, NY: Orbis, 2008.

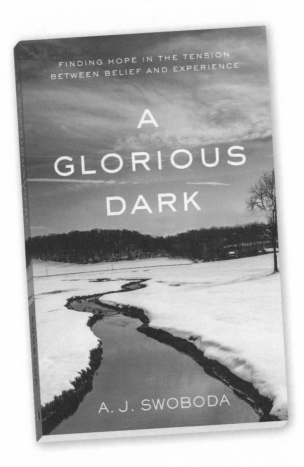

FINDING HOPE IN THE TENSION
BETWEEN BELIEF AND EXPERIENCE

A
GLORIOUS
DARK

A. J. SWOBODA

"*A Glorious Dark* touches a nerve by bravely wrestling with all the things that go bump in the night. But more importantly, it leads us into the presence of the One who once told a shadow-soaked prophet, 'I form the light and the dark.'"

—**Jonathan Merritt**, author of *Jesus Is Better Than You Imagined*; senior columnist for *Religion News Service*

BakerBooks
a division of Baker Publishing Group
www.BakerBooks.com

Available wherever books and ebooks are sold.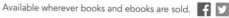

FOLLOW PASTOR, PROFESSOR,
AND AUTHOR

A. J. SWOBODA

BLOG: AJSWOBODA.COM

f : FACEBOOK.COM/THEAJSWOBODA

🐦 : MRAJSWOBODA

LIKE THIS
BOOK?
Consider sharing it with others!

- Share or mention the book on your social media platforms. Use the hashtag **#TheDustyOnes**.

- Write a book review on your blog or on a retailer site.

- Pick up a copy for friends, family, or strangers—anyone who you think would enjoy and be challenged by its message.

- Share this message on Twitter or Facebook. **"I loved #TheDustyOnes by @mrajswoboda. //@ReadBakerBooks"**

- Recommend this book for your church, workplace, book club, or class.

- Follow Baker Books on social media and tell us what you like.

 Facebook.com/ReadBakerBooks

 @ReadBakerBooks